MacBook Air®

Jason R. Rich

New York Chicago San Francisco Lisbon
London Madrid Mexico City Milan New Delhi
San Juan Seoul Singapore Sydney Toronto

The *McGraw·Hill* Companies

Cataloging-in-Publication Data is on file with the Library of Congress

McGraw-Hill books are available at special quantity discounts to use as premiums and sales promotions, or for use in corporate training programs. To contact a representative, please e-mail us at bulksales@mcgraw-hill.com.

How to Do Everything™: MacBook Air®

1234567890   QFR QFR   1098765432

ISBN   978-0-07-180249-9
MHID   0-07-180249-5

Sponsoring Editor Megg Morin	**Technical Editor** Guy Hart-Davis	**Production Supervisor** George Anderson
Editorial Supervisor Patty Mon	**Copy Editor** Lunaea Hougland	**Composition** Cenveo Publisher Services
Project Manager Harleen Chopra, Cenveo Publisher Services	**Proofreader** Bev Weiler	**Illustration** Cenveo Publisher Services
Acquisitions Coordinator Stephanie Evans	**Indexer** Jack Lewis	**Art Director, Cover** Jeff Weeks

This book is dedicated to my niece Natalie Shay Emsley Skehan, and to the late Steve Jobs, without whom there would be no Apple or MacBook Air computers to write about.

About the Author

Jason R. Rich (www.JasonRich.com) is the bestselling author of more than 54 books, covering a wide range of topics. Some of his recently published books include: *How to Do Everything™:Digital Photography* (McGraw-Hill), *How to Do Everything™: iCloud* (McGraw-Hill), *How to Do Everything™: Kindle Fire* (McGraw-Hill), *Your iPad at Work* (Que), and *iPad and iPhone Tips and Tricks* (Que).

To read more than 90 feature-length how-to articles about the iPhone and iPad, visit www.iOSArticles.com. His work also appears in a wide range of national magazines, major daily newspapers, and popular websites. You can follow Jason R. Rich on Twitter (@JasonRich7).

About the Technical Editor

Guy Hart-Davis is the author of several books, including *iPhone Geekery*, *Kindle Fire Geekery*, and *Mac OS X Administration*.

Contents

Acknowledgments

Thanks to Megg Morin at McGraw-Hill for inviting me to work on this book. Thanks also to Stephanie Evans, Guy Hart-Davis, and everyone else who contributed their talents and publishing know-how as this book was being created. My gratitude goes out also to the friendly and knowledgeable Apple Geniuses at the Apple Store in Dedham, Massachusetts, especially Josh Fleetwood, who helped me overcome some technical issues with my MacBook Air as this book was being written. It's this type of in-person technical support that makes Apple computers such a pleasure to use.

Thanks also to my friends and family for their endless support and encouragement, and to you, the reader, for choosing this book as your guide as you discover the power and capabilities of your MacBook Air.

Introduction

For years, the Apple MacBook computers have set new standards for mobile computing, providing state-of-the-art technology with the intuitive functionality of Apple's OS X operating system. When Apple released the MacBook Air notebook computers, it again revolutionized how people can use a computer just about anywhere. In July 2012, Apple launched OS X Mountain Lion, the latest version of the Mac operating system. When used in conjunction with a MacBook Air, the computer's features and functionality now more closely resemble an iPad tablet, but with the full computing power of a Mac and a traditional keyboard and touchpad.

Whether you use your MacBook Air as your primary computer or as a second computer for when you travel, *How to Do Everything™: MacBook Air*® will help you get the most out of the computer itself, plus quickly get you up to speed using the latest features added to the OS X Mountain Lion operating system.

In this book, you'll also discover how to use the MacBook Air in conjunction with your Apple iPhone, iPad, or iPod touch, as well as Apple's iCloud online-based file sharing service to ensure your important data, files, and documents are always accessible when and where you need them.

The MacBook Air computers currently come in two sizes (with an 11-inch or 13-inch screen) and a handful of hardware system configurations. Regardless of which MacBook Air model you use, *How to Do Everything™: MacBook Air*® will show you how to fully utilize the notebook computer, plus take full advantage of the apps that come preinstalled with the OS X Mountain Lion operating system. These apps include: Contacts, Calendar, Reminders, Notification Center, Notes, Mail, Safari, Messages, FaceTime, iTunes, App Store, Game Center, Preview, Dashboard, System Preferences, iPhoto, iMovie, and GarageBand.

You'll also discover how to find, acquire, and install additional apps onto your MacBook Air, as well as connect optional peripherals and accessories to the computer so that you can further enhance and expand its capabilities and functionality.

If you haven't already, from *How to Do Everything™: MacBook Air*®, you'll discover how truly remarkable and powerful your MacBook Air notebook computer is, plus learn about all of the different ways you can utilize it in your personal and professional life.

What Does this Book Cover?

This book covers all you need to know in order to get the most out of your MacBook Air. The book contains 18 chapters broken up into 5 parts.

Part I, "Get to Know Your MacBook Air"

- Chapter 1, "Get Familiar with the MacBook Air," introduces you to your new computer and provides an overview of what it's capable of.
- Chapter 2, "Learn the Basics of the Mac OS X Operating System," focuses on the latest edition of the OS X Mountain Lion operating system (released in Summer 2012) which runs on your MacBook Air.
- Chapter 3, "Make the Switch from Windows to a Mac," shows you how to easily convert from being a PC user to a Mac user, and discusses the differences between Microsoft Windows and OS X.

Part II, "Discover the Mac OS X Mountain Lion Operating System"

- Chapter 4, "Set Up the Software that Comes with the MacBook Air," explains how to use many of the apps that come bundled with OS X Mountain Lion.
- Chapter 5, "Install New Software onto Your MacBook Air," shows you how to find, download, and install new software (apps) onto your computer from a wide range of sources, including Apple's own App Store.
- Chapter 6, "Transferring and Organizing Data, Files, and Folders," demonstrates some of the ways you can transfer information (data, documents, photos, music, video, and files) between computers and mobile devices, often wirelessly.
- Chapter 7, "Use Apple's iCloud to Sync All Your Devices," explains the basics of using Apple's iCloud file sharing service and how to use it to back up and sync your important data.
- Chapter 8, "Add Optional Peripherals and Accessories to Expand Performance," showcases just some of the optional peripherals and accessories you can use with your MacBook Air, including a printer, scanner, headphones, and external speakers.

Part III, "Use Your MacBook Air Anytime and Anywhere"

- Chapter 9, "Word Processing, Spreadsheets, and Digital Slide Show Presentations on Your MacBook Air" focuses on using Apple's iWork apps as well as Microsoft Office, plus introduces you to other options for handling common computer-related tasks.
- Chapter 10, "Surf the Web on Your MacBook Air," teaches you how to use the newest features of the Safari web browser to surf the Web more efficiently. You'll also learn about other web browser options available to you.
- Chapter 11, "Set Up Existing Email Accounts for MacBook Air," explains how to use the Mail app to manage one or more of your existing email accounts from your MacBook Air.

- Chapter 12, "Bring the iLife Apps into Your Life," introduces you to Apple's iLife suite of apps, including iPhoto, iMovie, and GarageBand.
- Chapter 13, "Get Organized with the Contacts and Calendar Apps," shows you how to use the newly revamped Contacts (formerly known as Address Book) and Calendar (formerly known as iCal) apps.

Part IV, "Entertain Yourself with iTunes Content, Games, and More"

- Chapter 14, "Find and Enjoy Music, Movies, TV Shows, and More with iTunes," explains how to find and acquire content from Apple's iTunes Store that you can experience on your MacBook Air.
- Chapter 15, "Play Games on Your MacBook Air," focuses on the different types of games you can play on your computer, plus introduces you to Apple's Game Center.

Part V, "Easily Handle All of Your Mobile Computing Needs"

- Chapter 16, "Travel with Your MacBook Air," explores some of the options you have for using a case, cover, skin, or protective shell when transporting your MacBook Air in order to keep it safe.
- Chapter 17, "Use FaceTime, Skype, or VoIP Software to Communicate and Video Conference," teaches you how to use your computer for video conferencing, or as an Internet-based telephone to make and receive calls.
- Chapter 18, "Run Microsoft Windows and Windows Software on Your MacBook Air," demonstrates your options for running Microsoft Windows, and explains how to get your favorite Windows-based programs running flawlessly on your Mac.
- Appendix, "What to Do if Something Goes Wrong," will help you troubleshoot common problems you may encounter when using your MacBook Air, and provides simple solutions to address or solve these problems.

Conventions Used in this Book

To help you better understand some of the more complex or technical aspects of using your MacBook Air, plus to help focus your attention on particularly useful features and functions offered by the computer, throughout this book, you'll discover Note, Tip, and Caution paragraphs that highlight specific tidbits of useful information.

Plus, throughout this book, you'll discover How To... and Did You Know? sidebars that provide additional topic-related information and advice that pertains to what's being covered within the chapter you're reading.

PART I

Get to Know Your MacBook Air

1

Get Familiar with Your MacBook Air

HOW TO...

- Choose the right MacBook Air system configuration
- Understand the difference between a MacBook Air and a Windows-based computer
- Navigate your way around your MacBook Air
- Begin using your new MacBook Air
- Powering off your computer or entering Power Nap or sleep mode

As you're about to discover, your new MacBook Air is an extremely unique, cutting-edge, yet user-friendly computer that offers the power of a desktop computer, the portability of a netbook, plus some of the functionality of an iPad—all wrapped up into one sleek package that weighs between 2.38 and 2.96 pounds, depending on the model.

For the first time in the history of computer technology, Apple offers a truly mobile computing device that does not force users to give up the features or functionality of a desktop computer (or even a more cumbersome notebook computer).

By implementing the most advanced and affordable technology available, and then custom-designing its OS X Mountain Lion operating system to fully utilize the capabilities and design of the MacBook Air hardware, today's MacBook Air computers (shown in Figure 1-1) can easily meet the needs of mobile business professionals, students, or anyone who wants a computer that's ideal for using at a desk, but that can be taken virtually anywhere when computing power on-the-go is required.

Camera   Screen

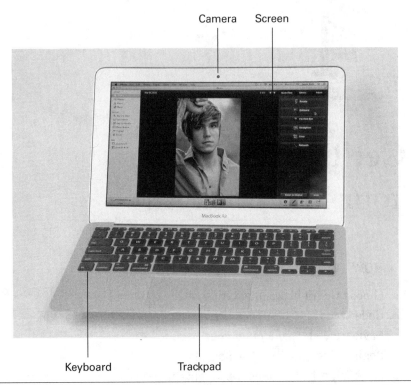

Keyboard   Trackpad

FIGURE 1-1   The 11-inch MacBook Air is affordable, lightweight, ultra-slim, and very powerful. The 13-inch model looks almost identical, but is slightly larger.

The Evolution of the MacBook Air

Since its founding in April 1976, Apple has always been a pioneer in the ongoing computer revolution. Not only has the company pushed the technological envelope each time it's released a newer and more powerful laptop or notebook computer model (known as MacBooks), it's also responsible for reinventing the tablet market.

By incorporating the computing power of a desktop computer, while trimming down the weight and bulk of a notebook computer, Apple introduced the first MacBook Air notebook computer in 2008. Since then, the MacBook Air computers have evolved...a lot.

In its most recent incarnation, today's MacBook Air computers are incredibly thin, extremely lightweight, and have a long-lasting battery when compared to other notebook or laptop computers. They also feature vibrant screens and contain powerful processors. The MacBook Airs are affordable and come in several sizes and hardware configurations, as you'll learn about shortly. They run using the latest version of the OS X Mountain Lion operating system—the same operating system used by Apple's iMac desktop computers and the MacBook Pro notebook computers.

One of the most innovative things about the latest MacBook Air models is their Multi-Touch trackpad (shown in Figure 1-2), which allows you to interact with the computer using a series of simple finger taps, swipes, and gestures, in much the same way as you'd use an iPad tablet.

FIGURE 1-2   The MacBook Air's Multi-Touch trackpad

Using the latest mobile computing technology, and adapting the OS X Mountain Lion operating system to it, not only is the MacBook Air easier to use, it also operates much more like an iPad or iPhone. If you use your MacBook Air in conjunction with an Apple iOS mobile device, such as an iPhone or iPad, you'll discover that many of the core software applications that come preinstalled on your MacBook Air are now extremely similar to apps running on your mobile device. And thanks to the Apple iCloud service, your data can sync automatically and wirelessly between your computers and mobile devices as long as they're connected to the Internet.

Today's MacBook Air computers have as much computing power as any mobile computer, and also offer similar software-based tools and functionality to what made Apple's iPad and iPhone so popular. The MacBook Air models available right now are truly versatile, powerful, and—most importantly—lightweight, ultra-thin, and extremely portable.

Did You Know?

The MacBook Air and MacBook Pro Models Are Different

There are a handful of important differences between the current MacBook Air and MacBook Pro models, although both are considered notebook computers. For starters, the MacBook Pro computers are larger, with your choice of a 13.3-, 15.4-, or 17-inch screen. The screen size impacts the entire computer's size and weight.

The MacBook Pro computers also have a built-in SuperDrive, which can read from or write to CDs or DVDs, and they offer a greater number of built-in ports, as well as other expansion and upgrade options not currently available in the MacBook Air models.

With the added technology that's built into the various MacBook Pro models, they are thicker and a bit heavier than a MacBook Air, and they offer functionality that's closer to an iMac desktop computer. To learn about the latest MacBook Pro computers available, visit www.apple.com/macbookpro.

Choose the Right MacBook Air Model

Let's take a closer look at what computer-related features are important, and then see what MacBook Air hardware configurations are currently available (as of June 2012).

The 11-inch MacBook Air comes in two primary system configurations. These system configurations are available from all Apple Stores, Apple.com, or authorized Apple resellers. It is possible to upgrade your MacBook Air's RAM (memory) and internal storage capacity using third-party products.

When choosing a MacBook Air model, some of the decisions you'll need to make relate to the following:

- **Screen Size**   You can currently choose between an 11.6-inch or 13.3-inch screen (measured diagonally). Which you choose is a matter of personal preference, but it directly impacts the size and weight of the entire computer.
- **Storage Capacity**   If you'll be storing a lot of large files on your MacBook Air, such as high-resolution photos, TV show episodes, movies, or other multimedia content, you'll definitely want 128GB or more of internal storage space. If most of the time your MacBook Air will be linked to an external storage system or sharing files and data with a network, 64GB capacity will probably be adequate.
- **RAM**   To get the best performance out of the MacBook Air, especially if you'll be working with large size files and documents, invest in at least 4GB of RAM, although you'll experience better performance if you upgrade to 8GB of RAM.

 If you need faster performance when using the computer for advanced calculations (when working with complex spreadsheets or editing photos, for example), or for handling multiple tasks simultaneously that require a lot of computing power, upgrading to the faster Intel Core i7 processor will be beneficial.

The 11-Inch MacBook Air System Configurations

As of June 2012, the basic MacBook Air model ($999) includes: 64GB of internal storage, a 1.7GHz dual-core Intel Core i5 processor (with 3MB shared L3 cache), and 4GB of RAM (memory).

 When ordering an 11-inch MacBook Air from Apple.com only, you can upgrade (for a fee) the basic system configuration to include 8GB of RAM. It's also possible to upgrade from the Intel Core i5 to the faster and more powerful Intel Core i7 processor.

The upgraded 11-inch MacBook Air system configuration ($1099) includes: 128GB of internal storage, a 1.7GHz duel-core Intel Core i5 processor (with 3MB shared L3 cache), and 4GB of RAM memory.

The 11-inch MacBook Air has an average battery life of up to five hours and can be placed in Sleep/Power Nap mode for up to 30 days. When closed, it measures a mere 0.68 inches high, 11.8 inches wide, and 7.56 inches deep. It weighs just 2.38 pounds.

See What the 13-Inch MacBook Air System Configurations Deliver

In addition to offering a larger and slightly higher-resolution display and an SD memory card reader port, the basic 13-inch MacBook Air model ($1199) includes: 128GB of internal storage, a 1.8GHz duel-core Intel Core i5 processor (with 3MB shared L3 cache), and 4GB of RAM.

 Available exclusively from Apple.com, you can upgrade the basic 13-inch MacBook Air system configuration (for an additional fee) to include a duel-core 2.0GHz Intel Core i7 processor (with 4MB shared L3 cache).

The upgraded 13-inch MacBook Air system configuration ($1499) includes: 256GB of internal storage, a 1.8GHz duel-core Intel Core i5 processor (with 3MB shared L3 cache), and 4GB of RAM.

The 13-inch MacBook Air has an average battery life of up to seven hours and can be placed in Sleep/Power Nap mode for up to 30 days. When closed, it measures a mere 0.68 inches high, 12.8 inches wide, and 8.94 inches deep. It weighs just 2.96 pounds.

 The $1099 11-inch and $1499 13-inch MacBook Air models can be upgraded to 256GB or 512GB of internal flash storage for an additional fee.

Additional MacBook Air Models Coming Soon

Every six to twelve months, Apple refreshes its major product lines with new models and/or system configurations for its current computer models, including the MacBook Air computers. By the time you read this, Apple may have released additional MacBook Air models with larger screens and more memory, or may enhance the system configurations of existing models with a faster processor, more RAM, and/or higher internal storage capacities. In June 2012, for example, the USB ports on all MacBook Air models were upgraded to USB 3.0. The graphics chip within the computers were also enhanced, as was the speed of the microprocessor.

 To learn about the current lineup of MacBook Air models, visit www.apple.com/macbookair. You can also visit any Apple Store or an authorized Apple reseller (such as Best Buy).

Upgrade Your Existing MacBook Air

Apple has designed the MacBook Air computers so they are not easily upgradeable after the time of purchase. Thus, it's important to analyze and anticipate your needs when choosing a model and system configuration. That being said, if you're technologically savvy, you can find MacBook Air upgrade kits on the Internet that allow you to use third-party products to upgrade the computer's memory and/or internal storage capacity. If you're interested in doing this, using any Internet search engine, enter the search phrase "MacBook Air upgrade."

For example, Other World Computing offers Mercury Aura Pro Express memory and internal storage upgrade kits for some MacBook Air models (http://eshop .macsales.com/shop/SSD/OWC/Aura_Pro_Express).

 If you opt to manually upgrade your MacBook Air, this may violate your Apple and/ or AppleCare warranty. It is also essential that you order parts that are compatible with your MacBook Air model, based on when it was purchased. The 2010 and 2011 MacBook Air models are incompatible from an upgrade standpoint with older or newer models.

What Makes the MacBook Air Different from a Windows-Based Computer?

There are several things that make Apple's MacBook Air computers vastly different from (and in the opinion of many users, vastly superior to) competing notebook computers that run the latest version of Microsoft Windows.

First, all MacBook Air models run OS X Mountain Lion, Apple's proprietary operating system that runs only on a Mac computer. OS X is powerful, intuitive, and was specifically designed to fully utilize the hardware of the MacBook Air, including its unique Multi-Touch trackpad.

One great thing about OS X when compared to Microsoft Windows is that it is not as susceptible to computer viruses. So you can surf the Web worry-free and not be concerned about accidentally downloading a virus that could damage your computer or corrupt your data.

 The OS X operating system has many advantages over Microsoft Windows, as you'll discover in Chapters 4 through 8. However, using optional software, you can also easily install and run the Windows operating system on your MacBook Air, as well as any Windows-based software, and switch between operating systems and software in seconds. How to do this is the focus of Chapter 18.

OS X comes with a handful of applications preinstalled, including Apple's own iLife suite. The applications incorporated into iLife, including iPhoto, make it easy to transfer, organize, view, edit, print, and share digital photos. Or, if you're more interested in shooting home videos, the iMovie software allows you to create, edit, view, and share video content with incredible ease.

 If you're on a budget, you can download the Open Office software for free. This software is fully compatible with the Microsoft Office suite for both Macs and PCs, and is distributed legally, without charge. To download Open Office, visit www .openoffice.org/porting/mac.

Your MacBook Air and the OS X operating system also offer seamless integration with Apple's iCloud service, so you can back up and sync files, documents, data, and

How to...   **Use Business-Oriented Software on Your MacBook Air**

If your computing needs are business oriented, Apple offers its iWork suite of software, available from the App Store (accessible directly from your MacBook Air when connected to the Internet). iWork integrates perfectly with OS X and compatible iOS apps for the iPhone and iPad.

The iWork suite includes Pages, Numbers, and Keynote (sold separately for $19.99 each), which are used for word processing, spreadsheet management, and digital slide presentations, respectively. You also have the option to purchase and install the Mac edition of Microsoft Office, which gives you full access to Microsoft Word, Excel, and PowerPoint. The files and documents created using Microsoft Office on your Mac are fully compatible with the Windows edition of the software suite.

Also available from the App Store, you'll discover thousands of business software applications designed for use on all Mac computers, including the MacBook Air. This includes Mac versions of popular Windows-based software. You'll learn how to find, download, and install new software onto your MacBook Air in Chapter 5.

a wide range of content wirelessly and automatically between all of your Mac-based computers and iOS mobile devices.

A vast and ever-growing selection of multimedia content, including music, TV show episodes, movies, ebooks, audiobooks, and educational content (via iTunes U) are available directly from Apple's online-based iTunes Store, which you can access using the free iTunes software that's installed on your MacBook Air. How to transform your MacBook Air into a powerful and mobile entertainment system is the focus of Chapters 14 and 15.

By the way, you've probably noticed that your MacBook Air does not have a built-in CD-ROM or DVD drive. This saves a lot of space, and allows Apple to create smaller and thinner computers. So, instead of loading or installing software or data from CD-ROMs or DVDs, you can acquire, download, and install software directly from the Internet using Apple's App Store (shown in Figure 1-3). Or you can link your MacBook Air to your iMac, for example, to utilize its SuperDrive to install software.

   Another option for installing CD-based software is to connect the optional MacBook Air SuperDrive to the computer via a USB cable connection. You'll learn more about this option in Chapter 5.

If you're a first-time Mac user, there is a slight learning curve associated with discovering how to use any Mac, especially if you're already familiar with how to use a Windows-based computer. While your MacBook Air can do pretty much anything that a Windows-based computer can do, how you access various features, functions, and menus is different when using OS X on a Mac. You'll get up to speed on how to use OS X in Chapters 2 and 3.

FIGURE 1-3   You can purchase, download, and install thousands of Mac-compatible software applications directly from the App Store.

Did You Know?

Your MacBook Air Has Many Ports and Useful Peripherals Built In

When it comes to connecting your MacBook Air to optional accessories or peripherals, such as a printer, this can be done using cables (via the computer's built-in USB ports or Thunderbolt port), or you can establish a wireless Bluetooth or Wi-Fi connection between the computer and the peripheral.

As for built-in peripherals, the computer has built-in stereo speakers, a headphone jack, and a microphone. Plus, some MacBook Air models have a built-in SD memory card reader.

Several additional peripherals, such as a camera, that are optional on competing computers, come preinstalled on all MacBook Air models. Thus, almost right out of the box, you can use your MacBook Air to take photos, shoot video, or for video conferencing via the Web (using FaceTime or Skype, for example).

The 720p FaceTime HD camera built into the current MacBook Air models is not anywhere near the resolution quality of a typical point-and-shoot digital camera, but it works fine for video conferencing and for shooting lower-resolution photos or video clips.

Discover What's Included with Your MacBook Air

Whether you purchase your MacBook Air from an Apple Store, Apple.com, or from an Apple authorized reseller (such as Best Buy), what the salesperson will hand you is a relatively small and thin box that contains your new MacBook Air computer, as well as a MagSafe power adapter (with an AC wall plug and a power cord).

There are several MacBook Air models and system configurations currently available. Which model you choose will determine the physical size and weight of the computer itself, the size of the screen, the speed of the microprocessor, as well as how much internal storage space and RAM (memory) the computer has installed.

Regardless of which MacBook Air model or system configuration you choose, already installed on your new computer (if purchased after July 2012) will be the OS X Mountain Lion operating system, plus a selection of software applications, some of which include:

- **AirDrop**   While this is more of an OS X feature than a stand-alone app, if you have multiple Macs, including iMacs, MacBook Pros, or MacBook Airs, you can wirelessly transfer files and documents between computers using it. This feature only works with more recent Mac models that are connected to the same wireless network.
- **App Store**   Use this app to access the online-based App Store to find, purchase, and download new software for your MacBook Air. All purchases are billed to the credit card that's associated with your Apple ID account. If you're also an iOS mobile device user, the App Store for Macs is different from the App Store for the iPhone, iPad, and iPod touch.
- **Calendar**   Manage your personal and work schedule, as well as to-do lists from this customizable software, which is also fully compatible with iCloud and the Calendar app that comes preinstalled on the iPhone and iPad. (In older versions of the OS X operating system, Calendar was called iCal.)
- **Contacts**   This is a powerful contact management database app. It seamlessly integrates and exchanges data with other software running on your computer and is fully compatible with iCloud and the Contacts app that comes preinstalled on the iPhone and iPad. (In older versions of the OS X operating system, Contacts was called Address Book.)
- **FaceTime**   Participate in real-time video conferences, for free, with any other Mac, iPhone, or iPad users who have a FaceTime account set up. An Internet connection is required. The software takes full advantage of the MacBook Air's built-in camera, microphone, speakers, and headphones jack.
- **Game Center**   This is an app that offers free access to Apple's online-based gaming service. Through Game Center, amongst other things, you can experience multiplayer games and be matched up with people to play against.

- **iLife (iPhoto, iMovie, and GarageBand)**   Using these software packages, you can create, edit, view, print, share, and organize digital photos, home videos, and music you record from scratch.
- **iTunes**   This software has several functions. It's used to manage and experience your multimedia content (music, TV show episodes, movies, etc.), and also to access the iTunes Store to find, purchase, and download new content. The iTunes software can also be used to sync and back up data, files, apps, and content between your MacBook Air and iOS mobile devices.
- **Mail**   This is an email management application that allows you to manage multiple email accounts simultaneously. It's very similar to the Mail app offered on all iPhones and iPads.
- **Messages**   This app is used for sending/receiving free and unlimited text messages or instant messages with other Mac, iPhone, iPad, and iPod touch users.
- **Mission Control and Launchpad**   Built into OS X Mountain Lion, both Mission Control and Launchpad allow you to easily navigate your way around your computer, launch apps, and then switch between software applications with ease. You'll learn more about Mission Control and Launchpad in Chapter 2.
- **Notes**   This is a basic text editing app that allows you to create notes on a virtual notepad and then organize, view, print, and share those notes via your MacBook Air. The app is also fully iCloud compatible and can automatically sync your notes with the other computers that are linked to your iCloud account.
- **Notification Center**   This app works constantly in the background and displays all alerts, alarms, and notifications generated by your MacBook Air in one convenient place. This app is customizable so it will display only the alerts, alarms, and notifications that are important to you. To access the Notification Center window, click on the icon that's constantly displayed near the upper-right corner of the screen along the menu bar. Notification Center can be customized using System Preferences.
- **OS X Mountain Lion Recovery**   If you ever need to reinstall the OS X operating system from scratch, this recovery software will help you reset your MacBook Air to its initial factory specs.
- **Photo Booth**   Take photos that have a whimsical theme directly from the camera that's built into your MacBook Air, and then edit and share the photos.
- **Reminders**   This is a versatile to-do list management app that allows you to create and manage multiple lists simultaneously, assign alerts and alarms to each item on each list, and then sync your lists with other Mac and iOS mobile devices that are linked to your iCloud account.
- **Safari**   When it comes to surfing the Internet, Safari is Apple's feature-packed web browser software. Its basic functionality is equivalent to what's offered by other popular web browsers, such as Microsoft Internet Explorer, Google Chrome, or Firefox.
- **Time Machine**   By connecting an external hard drive to your MacBook Air (either via a cable or through a Wi-Fi connection), your computer can maintain a complete backup of its primary flash drive, including all software (apps), data, files, documents, and multimedia content. Once it's set up and activated, Time Machine works automatically and in the background.

How to... **Upgrade from OS X Lion to OS X Mountain Lion**

If you purchased your MacBook Air before June 11, 2012, it came with the OS X Lion operating system installed. Thus, you'll need to pay an upgrade fee of $19.99 in order to purchase, download, and install the latest version of OS X Mountain Lion.

This latest operating system offers a large selection of new features, including better integration with the MacBook Air's Multi-Touch trackpad and Apple's iCloud service. You'll also discover apps and functionality that make the MacBook Air operate more like an iPad, and that allow for easier wireless data syncing between your iOS mobile devices and your computer.

To upgrade from OS X Lion to OS X Mountain Lion, launch the App Store and use the Search field to find the software update. Click on the Price icon to make your purchase, and then follow the onscreen prompts to enter your Apple ID, confirm the purchase, download the upgrade, and then install it.

When upgrading from OS X Lion to OS X Mountain Lion, be sure your computer is plugged into an AC outlet and perform a Time Machine backup before performing the upgrade. The upgrade process will take about 30 minutes.

All MacBook Airs purchased after July 2012 come with OS X Mountain Lion already installed. The majority of information covered within *How to Do Everything: MacBook Air* assumes you're using OS X Mountain Lion on your computer.

Get to Know Your MacBook Air

As of July 2012, there are two core MacBook Air models, one with an 11-inch screen and the other with a 13-inch screen. Both models are available in several different hardware configurations (which determine the internal storage capacity of the computer and the amount of preinstalled RAM, for example). The 13-inch MacBook Air models also have a built-in SD memory card reader that's not found in the smaller and lighter 11-inch models.

When closed, the MacBook Air is ultra-thin and ready for easy transport. On either side of the computer, you'll discover its built-in ports. Let's start with the 11-inch model. On the left side of the computer (shown in Figure 1-4), you'll find the MagSafe port for the power adapter, one of two USB 3.0 ports, the headphone jack, and the built-in microphone (which is slightly larger than the size of a pinhole). On the right side of the 11-inch MacBook Air is a second USB 3.0 port and a Thunderbolt port.

 Note   The 13-inch MacBook Air also has a built-in SD memory card reader on the right side.

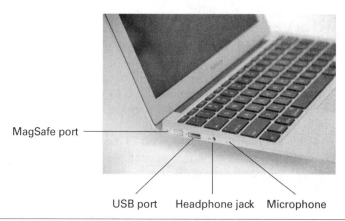

MagSafe port ——

USB port   Headphone jack   Microphone

FIGURE 1-4   The left side of an 11-inch MacBook Air

When you open the top of the MacBook Air, the top-flap of the computer contains the high-resolution LED screen. It's a backlit, glossy, widescreen display, measuring either 11.6 inches or 13.3 inches diagonally. Located just above the top-center of the screen is the built-in 720p FaceTime HD camera (refer back to Figure 1-1).

Below the screen of an open MacBook Air, you'll discover a full-size, backlit keyboard. This keyboard looks pretty much like any computer keyboard. The top row of keys, however, are used for special functions, which we'll discuss shortly. Below the keyboard is the MacBook Air's proprietary Multi-Touch trackpad. It's used instead of a mouse and responds to a variety of finger taps, swipes, and gestures.

Get Started with Your MacBook Air's Keyboard

While most of the QWERTY computer keyboard that's built into the MacBook Air will be familiar, each key in the top row of keys has a special function. To the immediate right of the ESC (Escape) key, located in the upper-left corner of the keyboard, are the F1 through F12 keys.

Did You Know?

Your MacBook Air Can Connect to a Monitor

Simply by purchasing an optional adapter and cable, you can connect your MacBook Air to an external computer monitor, high-definition television set, or LCD projector. This allows you to share information that's displayed on the computer's screen with groups of people when presenting a PowerPoint or Keynote presentation, for example.

The required optional adapter plugs into the Thunderbolt port on the right side of the MacBook Air, and connects to a cable that plugs into the monitor, television set, or projector. The Apple Mini DisplayPort to VGA Adapter ($29), for example, is available from the Apple Store or Apple.com, and is used to connect the MacBook Air to a VGA monitor or LCD projector.

Using OS X's AirPlay feature, you can stream content from your MacBook Air's screen wirelessly to your HD television set or monitor using the Apple TV device ($99) as a conduit.

The key located to the right on the keyboard (next to the F12 key) is the power button. It's used to turn on the MacBook Air when it's powered down. In addition to being turned on or off, the MacBook Air can be placed into Power Nap mode. When the computer is completely turned off, press the power button to turn it back on. To power down the MacBook Air, select the Apple icon from the upper-left corner of the screen and choose the Shut Down option. Then click on the Shut Down icon that appears in the center of the screen.

Using the Keyboard's Function Keys (F1 Through F12)

Here's a quick rundown of what each of the function keys on the keyboard (F1 through F12) are used for when using the OS X operating system. Keep in mind, some software applications use these keys for different, software-specific purposes.

- **F1 and F2**   Your MacBook Air computer has a light sensor built in and will automatically adjust the screen's brightness based on the available surrounding light. The F1 and F2 keys will temporarily override the automatic brightness setting. Press F1 to dim the brightness of the screen. Each time you press this key, the screen gets slightly dimmer. A screen brightness icon appears in the center of the screen. Press F2 to increase the screen's brightness.
- **F3**   Press this key to access OS X's Mission Control feature, view all software (apps) currently running on the computer, and then switch between apps. You can also view all open windows on the desktop. Another way to access Mission Control is to use three fingers on the trackpad and swipe them upwards.
- **F4**   The Dashboard can be used within OS X to display a user-selectable collection of widgets. If this feature is turned on, press F4 to access the Dashboard. You'll learn more about the Dashboard and how to use it in Chapter 2.
- **F5 and F6**   When working in a dimly lit area, the MacBook Air's computer keyboard automatically illuminates. Press the F5 key to dim the backlighting of the keyboard, or press F6 to increase the brightness of the keyboard's backlight.
- **F7 and F9**   When using iTunes or playing multimedia content, based on whether you press and release or hold down the FN-F7 key combination, it serves as a rewind or track back button. The FN-F9 key combination serves as a fast forward or track forward button.
- **F8**   When using iTunes or playing multimedia content, this key serves as a play/pause button to start and stop the music or video that's playing.
- **F10**   When audio is played by your computer, it can be heard using the built-in stereo speakers or through headphones (if you have headphones connected via the headphone jack or using a Bluetooth connection). The F10 key serves as a mute button and turns off any audio or sound being played or generated by your MacBook Air.
- **F11 and F12**   Use the F11 key to turn down the volume of the built-in speakers or headphones, or use F12 to increase the volume. Each time you press either button, the volume goes down or up by one notch, and a volume display temporarily appears in the center of the screen.

Start Using Your New MacBook Air

Once you've purchased your new MacBook Air, the battery should come at least partially charged. However, it's a good idea to plug in the computer and fully charge the battery right away. After taking the computer out of the box and turning it on, you'll discover the OS X Mountain Lion operating system is already installed.

Turn on the MacBook Air by pressing the power button located in the upper-right corner of the keyboard. You will be guided through a short setup and activation process. This will include allowing you to link your MacBook Air to your existing Apple iCloud account (or to establish a new and free account), as well as to create and/or link your Apple ID to the computer.

 If you already own any Apple computer or iOS mobile device, chances are you've already set up an Apple ID account. To manage your account, set up a new account, or look up a preexisting username or password, visit https://appleid .apple.com.

During the setup process, your computer will also check for updates to the OS X operating system and related software (including iTunes and the preinstalled iLife apps). It's important you have the latest version of the OS X running on your computer.

By linking your MacBook Air to your existing iCloud account, it will automatically load and sync data from your other Mac and iOS mobile devices. Within a few minutes, all of your Contacts, Calendar, Reminders, and Notes data, as well as your Safari bookmarks will be automatically loaded and accessible from your MacBook Air. By linking your computer to your existing Apple ID account, you'll immediately be able to make online purchases from the iTunes Store or the App Store. You'll also be able to quickly configure FaceTime and Messages to work with your existing account.

 You'll learn more about using iCloud with your MacBook Air in Chapter 7.

Navigate Your Way Around the Desktop Screen

Displayed along the top of the MacBook Air's desktop screen is a series of pull-down menus (near the top-left corner of the screen), starting with the Apple icon (shown in Figure 1-5). Over near the top-right corner of the screen is a series of icons that allow you to monitor and control various computer functions, like Time Machine, Bluetooth, Wi-Fi, and the volume of the computer's speakers, and the battery life monitor. The current time and date are also displayed, along with the current user's name and the Spotlight search icon. Tap the Spotlight search icon (which looks like a magnifying glass) to quickly find a file, document, or specific data stored on your computer.

Also displayed near the upper-right corner of the screen is the new Notification Center icon. Click on this icon to access the Notification Center window, which is a feature adapted from the iPhone and iPad. It allows you to view all alerts, alarms, and

FIGURE 1-5   The top of the OS X desktop screen displays a handful of pull-down menus and icons.

notifications generated by the computer (or software running on the computer) in one convenient place. You'll learn more about Notification Center and how to use it in Chapter 2.

The main area of your MacBook's desktop screen is where apps or Finder windows are displayed, and where information from software you're running is showcased and viewed. You'll learn more about the Finder feature later in this chapter.

Running along the bottom of the display is the Dock (shown in Figure 1-6). This includes a customizable collection of software icons. Each icon represents one software application or app that's installed on your computer. To launch an app from the Dock, simply click on it.

 Your computer can run multiple apps or software applications simultaneously, and you can quickly switch between active apps in several ways, such as using Mission Control or the Launchpad.

FIGURE 1-6   The Dock displays icons representing apps or folders stored on the MacBook Air.

If you're already familiar with how to use a Mac and the OS X operating system, you'll discover using your new MacBook Air is almost identical to using an iMac or MacBook Pro. While the operating system is identical, how you interact with the operating system on your MacBook Air will be slightly different, because the MacBook Air utilizes both a keyboard and the Multi-Touch trackpad (instead of a mouse). In Chapter 2, you'll learn the basics of using the OS X Mountain Lion operating system with your MacBook Air, in conjunction with the various finger taps, swipes, and gestures you'll need to know.

If you've never used a Mac before, but you're proficient using a Windows-based computer, Chapter 3 will help you quickly adapt to the OS X operating system, and explain the key differences between a PC and a Mac.

Connect Your MacBook Air to a Wi-Fi Internet Connection

The ability to surf the Web, manage your Facebook page and email accounts, and utilize the Internet in countless other ways while on the go is one of the features that many people love about their MacBook Air.

You can easily connect your MacBook Air to a Wi-Fi Internet connection by clicking on the Wi-Fi icon displayed in the upper-right corner of the desktop screen. Select the Turn Wi-Fi On option, and then choose the Wi-Fi network you want to connect to (shown in Figure 1-7).

If you're trying to connect to a password-protected (locked) Wi-Fi network, a small lock-shaped icon will appear to the right of the network's name next to the signal strength icon. When selecting a locked network, you will be required to enter the correct password in order to access it.

Once you're connected to the Internet via a Wi-Fi connection, the Wi-Fi icon displayed near the top-right corner of the screen will become a real-time signal

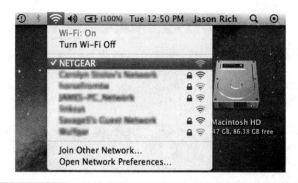

FIGURE 1-7 You can select an available Wi-Fi network to connect to from the Wi-Fi icon displayed near the top-right corner of the screen.

strength indicator. As long as you stay within the radius of the Wi-Fi hotspot's signal radius, your MacBook Air will be able to wirelessly connect to the Internet.

 If your Internet connection requires connecting your computer to a modem or Internet router using an Ethernet cable, you'll need to purchase an optional Apple USB Ethernet adapter ($29). It connects to the USB port of the computer. The MacBook Air does not have an Ethernet port built in. This adapter is available from Apple.com, the Apple Store, or from authorized Apple resellers.

Three other options for connecting your MacBook Air to the Internet include using a mobile Wi-Fi hotspot, tapping into the wireless Internet tethering capabilities offered by some smartphones, or investing in a wireless data modem offered by a wireless Internet service provider (such as AT&T Wireless, Sprint PCS, Verizon Wireless, or T-Mobile).

A wireless Internet modem is small and plugs into the USB port of your computer. It allows you to connect to a 3G or 4G wireless data network anywhere a compatible signal is available. A monthly service fee that includes a predetermined monthly wireless data usage allocation is required.

 The benefit to using a wireless data modem with your MacBook Air is that you can travel almost anywhere and connect wirelessly to the Internet, even if a Wi-Fi hotspot is not available. (The signal radius of a Wi-Fi hotspot signal is typically less than 200 feet. If you go beyond the Wi-Fi network's signal radius, the Internet connection is lost.)

Manually Check for OS X and Software Updates

With an Internet connection established, have your MacBook Air periodically check for OS X and software updates. To do this, click on the Apple icon located near the upper-left corner of the screen, and select the Software Update option. The App Store software will launch and the Updates icon (displayed near the top-center of the screen) will be preselected. A message saying "Checking for new software..." will be displayed.

If updates to the OS X operating system or related software are available, you'll be notified and prompted to download and install those updates. Otherwise, the message "All apps are up to date" will be displayed near the center of the screen.

Now that you have the latest version of the OS X Mountain Lion operating system running on your MacBook Air, and you've linked the computer with your preexisting iCloud and Apple ID accounts, you're ready to begin using your new computer for all of your computing and web surfing needs.

Powering Off vs. Power Nap/Sleep Mode

Whenever you're done using your MacBook Air, you can turn it off altogether by clicking on the Apple icon (displayed in the upper-left corner of the screen), and then choosing the Shut Down option. The message "Are you sure you want to shut down your computer now?" will be displayed. Click on the Shut Down icon.

When powered off, your computer uses no battery power and no software continues to function. Upon turning the MacBook Air back on (which requires that you press the power button), it will take a minute or two for your computer to boot up and for the operating system to load.

At anytime, regardless of what you're doing on your computer, you can place it into Power Nap mode (also referred to as Sleep mode). When you do this, the screen is turned off and battery consumption is greatly reduced. However, the computer and whatever software you're using remain held in the computer's memory.

To place your computer in Power Nap mode takes just a few seconds. Simply close your MacBook Air, or click on the Apple icon and select the Sleep option. To save battery life, you can also custom configure your computer to automatically place itself in Power Nap mode if it goes unused for a predetermined amount of time.

Once your computer is in Sleep mode, to wake it up, either open the MacBook Air, or if it's already open, tap any key on the keyboard. Instead of having to boot up from scratch, the computer will be ready to use within a few seconds. Whatever software was running before the computer was placed in Power Nap mode will automatically resume exactly where you left off.

Tip If you're working with important documents or files, before placing your MacBook Air into Power Nap mode, it's a good idea to manually save your work. How to do this will vary, depending on what software you're using.

How to... Configure Your Computer to Automatically Enter Power Nap Mode

To manually configure when and if your MacBook Air will automatically place itself into Power Nap mode after a predetermined period of non-use, launch the System Preferences option from the MacBook Air's Dock. Next, select the Energy Saver option.

When the Energy Saver window appears, click on the Battery or Power Adapter tab near the top-center of the window. This allows you to set up separate options based on whether the MacBook Air is using battery or AC power.

Using the sliders that are displayed, move the Computer Sleep slider to the time interval after which you want the computer to automatically enter into Power Nap mode. By moving the slider to the extreme left, the time interval is one minute of non-use. Move the slider to the right to select any time interval up to three hours, or choose Never (which means the computer will always remain on, until you manually power it down).

From this Energy Saver screen you'll discover other customizable options that can help you extend the battery life of your MacBook Air and/or manage when and how it turns itself off or places itself into Power Nap mode.

2

Learn the Basics of the Mac OS X Operating System

HOW TO...

- Master the finger gestures needed to interact with your MacBook Air
- Discover what's new in OS X Mountain Lion
- Navigate your way around the OS X operating system

Thanks to OS X Mountain Lion, the latest MacBook Air computers offer a vast collection of new features and functions, many of which were inspired by the iPad tablet. As a result, a handful of the apps that come preinstalled with OS X, including Contacts, Calendar, Reminders, Mail, Safari, Game Center, and Notification Center, function almost identically to their iPad counterparts.

In addition, OS X Mountain Lion seamlessly integrates with iCloud, making it easy to share and sync data, files, and documents between computers and iOS mobile devices that are linked to the Internet and the same iCloud account.

Using the MacBook Air's Multi-Touch Trackpad

On the MacBook Pro or older MacBook Air notebook computers, the touch pad was a convenient replacement for the mouse. When you look at the Multi-Touch trackpad that's built into the most recent MacBook Air models, however, you'll discover two things. First, the size of the trackpad is larger. Second, there are no buttons.

To fully utilize the Multi-Touch trackpad, you'll need to learn a few finger motions and gestures, including single and multi-finger taps, double-taps, swipes, and pinches, that allow you to interact with OS X and any software running on your computer. With a bit of practice, you'll find that using the trackpad is more efficient than working with a traditional mouse.

How to... **Customize the Finger Gesture Options Available on Your MacBook Air**

OS X Mountain Lion can utilize many different finger gestures to handle a variety of tasks. To customize which finger gestures will work and learn more about how to use each of them, from the desktop, launch System Preferences, and then click on the Trackpad option.

Displayed near the top-center of the Trackpad window are three command tabs, labeled Point & Click, Scroll & Zoom, and More Gestures. One at a time, click on any of these command tabs. Doing so will reveal a selection of default finger gestures and alternative gestures that OS X understands. Place a checkmark in the checkbox associated with each gesture that you want to activate and make accessible as you use your MacBook Air.

On the right side of the Trackpad window, you will see a short animated sequence that demonstrates how each gesture is used when you place the pointer over a particular option, such as Tap To Click, Look Up, or Smart Zoom.

When you're done customizing the trackpad options, exit out of System Preferences by clicking on the red dot in the upper-left corner of the window, or click on the System Preferences pull-down menu near the top-left corner of the screen, and then select the Quit System Preferences option.

Mastering the Multi-Touch Trackpad Finger Gestures

Here's a summary of the key finger gestures you'll need to know as you interact with your MacBook Air's Multi-Touch trackpad. The trackpad is extremely sensitive and accurate, so there is never a need to press down too hard. Always keep your finger motions smooth and light.

Move the Pointer

Place your index finger lightly on the trackpad and move it around freely. The pointer will mirror your movements on the MacBook Air's screen. Do this to position the pointer over icons, hyperlinks, or other clickable items on the screen.

Scroll Up/Down

Place your index and middle fingers together on the trackpad and drag them in an upward or downward direction along the trackpad's surface to scroll up or down on the screen you're looking at.

 Note To scroll up or down faster, use the same fingers, but perform a quick swipe in an upward or downward direction.

Scroll Left/Right

Place your index and middle fingers together on the trackpad and drag them from left to right, or from right to left, along the trackpad's surface to scroll left or right on the screen you're looking at. If you use a faster swipe motion, you will be able to switch between multiple screens.

 When using Safari or Preview (and some other compatible apps), a left/right scroll is equivalent to clicking on the Forward or Back icons to progress through multiple screens or pages.

Single Click

When a single click is necessary, use your index finger to position the pointer at the location on the screen, and then press your finger down on the trackpad once. You will hear a click sound.

In some situations, such as to select or highlight something on the screen, a single tap is required instead of a single click. A tap requires much less pressure on the trackpad than a click.

 To perform what would be compatible to a right mouse button click, hold down the CONTROL key on the keyboard while simultaneously performing a single finger click on the trackpad. When applicable, a pop-up window with options will appear.

Double Click

When a double click is necessary, use your index finger to position the pointer at the location on the screen, and then quickly press on the trackpad twice with your finger. You will hear a double-click sound.

In some situations, such as to select or highlight something on the screen, a double tap will be required instead of a double click.

Smart Zoom In/Out

To zoom in on a particular area of the screen (when using software that's compatible with this feature, or while interacting with OS X), use one finger to position the pointer in the location where you want to zoom, and then use your index finger and middle finger together to double-tap on the trackpad. To then zoom out, use your index and middle fingers to double-tap again.

Pinch Zoom In/Out

To zoom in on the area of the screen that's displayed, you can also use a reverse-pinch motion with your index and middle fingers, or use a pinch motion with your fingers to zoom out.

Launch Mission Control

Regardless of what you're doing on your computer, to launch Mission Control and quickly switch between apps that are running, place your index, middle, and ring fingers next to each other. Starting at the bottom of the trackpad, drag them in an upward direction.

While looking at the Mission Control screen, use your three fingers together to scroll left or right in order to switch between the Dashboard and desktop views.

When the Mission Control window appears, use one finger to move the pointer over the window for the app you want to access, and then use a single tap on the trackpad to open that app.

Regardless of what software is running, if you use a three-finger swipe from left to right, you'll switch from viewing the desktop or program window to the Dashboard screen.

Activate the Launchpad

Regardless of what you're doing on your MacBook Air, to launch the Launchpad (shown in Figure 2-1) at any time, use your thumb, index finger, middle finger, and ring finger simultaneously to perform a pinch motion on the trackpad. (Start with your fingers extended and then bring them together.)

Did You Know?

You Can Run Multiple Widgets on the Dashboard

The Dashboard screen of OS X (shown in Figure 2-2) allows you to display multiple widgets on the screen simultaneously. Accessing the Dashboard is easy, and it can be done while running any software or app on your MacBook Air. To launch the Dashboard, either click on the Dashboard icon on the Dock, or use a three-finger swipe motion (from left to right) on the trackpad.

A widget is a mini-app with a very specific purpose. When placed on the Dashboard, it looks like a functional sticky note or pop-up window. From the Apple website (www.apple.com/downloads/dashboard), you can browse through, download, and install hundreds of free widgets which you can freely place on your Dashboard to customize its appearance and function.

Sixteen widgets come preinstalled with OS X, including Address Book, Calculator, Calendar, Dictionary, Flight Track, Movies, Stickies, Weather and World Clock. The Address Book and Calendar widgets, for example, allow you to quickly look up specific information stored in your Contacts or Calendar databases. The Weather widget displays a six-day weather forecast for the city of your choice, and the Calculator widget allows you to perform basic mathematical calculations.

Using the Stickies widget, you can create and place virtual sticky notes on the Dashboard that display whatever text you add to them. Widgets give you quick and convenient access to specific tasks or information while using your MacBook Air.

FIGURE 2-1   The Launchpad displays app icons for all core (preinstalled) apps on your computer. Click on an icon to launch an app.

FIGURE 2-2   The Dashboard Screen of OS X. Each object on the screen represents a different widget.

The Launchpad replaces whatever you're doing with a collection of app icons on the screen, each of which represents a core application that's installed on your computer. Launchpad utilizes the entire screen, so it can simultaneously display more app icons than the Dock.

Once the Launchpad is displayed, use a single finger to position the pointer over the app icon you want to launch, and then click once on the trackpad.

Dictionary Lookup

To quickly look up the definition of any word that's displayed on the screen (within a compatible app), position the pointer over that word, and then use your index, middle, and ring fingers simultaneously to perform a quick double-tap motion on the trackpad. A pop-up window with the definition of the selected word will be displayed. Single tap anywhere on the screen to make the pop-up window disappear and continue working.

Drag Objects or Icons

When viewing the desktop or a Finder window, you can move app, folder, or file icons around on the screen by dragging them from one location to another. To drag an icon, use one finger to position the pointer over the icon or item you want to drag. Then press and hold down your thumb on the trackpad, while simultaneously using your index finger to move the icon to the desired location.

Dragging and dropping app icons or file icons between Finder windows is an easy way to move items between folders, or from the desktop into a folder (or vice versa).

Rotate

If there's an onscreen object you want to rotate when running a compatible app such as iPhoto, use one finger to highlight and select that object, and then move your thumb and index finger in a circular motion on the trackpad to rotate the selected object or item.

Launch Expose

To launch Expose, hold your index, middle, and ring fingers together and drag them in a downward direction, starting at the top of the trackpad.

Launch and Use Mission Control to Switch Between Open Windows or Running Apps

When you have multiple windows open simultaneously on your screen (a common occurrence), using Mission Control allows you to sort out the windows and view thumbnails of them in an orderly way. You can then switch between windows quickly, without first having to close or manually move any of them around.

Discover What's New in OS X Mountain Lion

Apple's OS X operating system, which powers all iMac and MacBook models, has always been powerful. However, in July 2012, Apple reinvented the operating system and incorporated a bunch of awesome new features. Throughout *How to Do Everything: MacBook Air*, as you read about how to use your computer, you'll also learn about some of the useful features available with the OS X Mountain Lion operating system.

For now, let's take a closer look at some of the new features that you'll probably want to take advantage of as you begin using your MacBook Air.

Sync Important Information with iCloud Integration

Your MacBook Air might be your primary computer, or perhaps you also have an iMac sitting on your desk at your home or office. Or you may also use some type of iOS mobile device, such as an iPhone, iPad, or iPod touch. Thanks to iCloud, app-specific data, documents, files, and photos can remain synchronized in real time when all of your Mac computers and iOS mobile devices are connected to the Internet. (iCloud can also sync some types of data with Windows-based PCs.)

After setting up a free iCloud account, from the desktop of your MacBook Air, launch System Preferences, and then click on the iCloud icon. When the iCloud pane appears (shown in Figure 2-3), select which app-specific data you want your MacBook Air to keep synchronized. Your options include Mail (relating to your free iCloud email account), Contacts, Calendars & Reminders, Bookmarks, Notes, Photo Stream, Documents & Data, Back To My Mac, and Find My Mac.

FIGURE 2-3   The iCloud pane in System Preferences allows you to turn on app-specific iCloud functionality.

You'll learn more about how to fully utilize iCloud with your MacBook Air in Chapter 7.

When you add a checkmark next to the checkbox associated with Contacts, for example, your Contacts database will automatically sync with iCloud. As a result, any time you add or modify a contact entry, those changes will upload almost instantly to iCloud, as long as your MacBook Air is connected to the Internet.

Once your app-specific data is stored in your iCloud account, it can automatically sync with your other Macs or iOS mobile devices that are also linked to that iCloud account and that have the same iCloud features turned on.

Thus, the additions or changes you make to a Contacts entry, for example, will almost instantly be reflected on your other computers and iOS mobile devices. Plus, using any device that's connected to the Internet, you can visit www.icloud.com and access an online-based Contacts, Calendar, Reminders, Notes, or Mail app, and use the Find My iPhone feature as well as the iWork feature to access your Pages, Numbers, or Keynote documents and files remotely.

Did You Know?

Photo Stream Gives You Access to 1,000 of Your Most Recent Digital Photos

When you activate iCloud's Photo Stream feature in conjunction with iPhoto on your MacBook Air, any time you import new digital images into iPhoto or snap photos using the computer's built-in camera, up to 1,000 of your most recent images can be automatically uploaded to your Photo Stream and become accessible from any of your Mac or iOS devices that are linked to your iCloud account.

Also, if you snap a photo on your iPhone, within seconds it will be uploaded to your iCloud Photo Stream and become viewable on your MacBook Air, iMac, iPad, or iPhone. Once photos are stored in your Photo Stream, they remain there for 30 days, or until you've reached 1,000 images, at which time older images are automatically replaced by newer ones.

As you view your Photo Stream on any computer or device that's linked to the Internet via a Wi-Fi connection, you can delete individual photos from the Photo Stream, or store individual images on the computer or device you're using.

If you're viewing photos shot using your iPhone that are displayed in your Photo Stream on your MacBook Air, you can save individual images on your notebook computer and then edit them using iPhoto, Photoshop Elements, Aperture, or another photo editing program, and then share them with ease.

Like the operating system itself, since the Photo Stream feature was released, it has undergone its own evolution. New features include the ability to manually add and delete photos from your Photo Stream and also share photos from the Photo Stream.

After you turn on iCloud functionality on your MacBook Air and other Mac or iOS devices, the data synchronization process happens automatically and in the background. As a result, your most current data, files, and documents are accessible to you anytime, regardless of which computer or device you're using.

Unlike other online-based file sharing services, such as Dropbox, iCloud is fully integrated with OS X, as well as many of the apps that come preinstalled with the operating system. This makes it very easy to sync app-specific data across multiple computers and devices, plus ensures an online backup of important data, documents, and files is available to you.

Send/Receive Text Messages and Instant Messages Using Messages

If you have a cell phone, you're probably already familiar with the concept of text messaging. Or, on the computer, you may use instant messaging to communicate with friends, family, or coworkers.

The new Messages app (shown in Figure 2-4) allows you to easily communicate in real-time via instant messaging with users of AIM, Yahoo! Instant Messenger, Jabber, and Google Talk. In addition, the Messages app that comes preinstalled with OS X Mountain Lion is fully compatible with Apple's own iMessage service, so you can send unlimited text messages to other Mac, iPhone, iPad, and iPod touch users.

FIGURE 2-4   Send and receive instant messages and text messages using the Messages app.

Unlike using the text messaging service available through cellular service providers, sending and receiving an unlimited number of text messages using the Messages app to connect to the iMessage service is always free.

Don't Forget Anything: Use Reminders

The Contacts app that comes preinstalled with OS X Mountain Lion is used to create and maintain a personalized contacts database, while the Calendar app is used for managing your schedule. The new Reminders app (shown in Figure 2-5) is a powerful to-do list manager that is nicely integrated with OS X and works seamlessly with iCloud.

Using Reminders, you can create one or more to-do lists, and then assign alarms and a priority to each item on each list. As to-do items are completed, they are moved

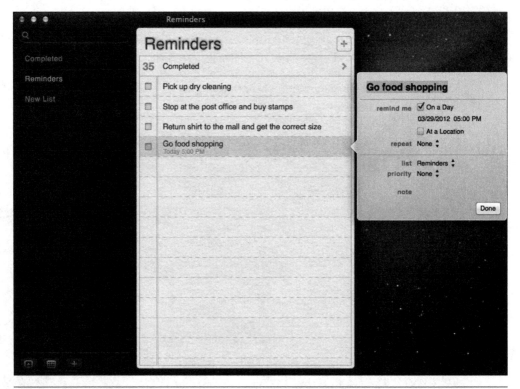

FIGURE 2-5   Reminders is a powerful to-do list manager that syncs data with your other Macs and iOS mobile devices via iCloud.

to a master Completed listing. What's great about Reminders is that when the iCloud sync feature is activated, all of your to-do lists and items are automatically synced to all of your Macs and iOS mobile devices.

As a result, you can create a grocery list on your MacBook Air, for example, and access it when you're at the supermarket using your iPhone. The Reminders app that runs on your MacBook Air is virtually identical to the iPhone and iPad version.

On the right side of the screen, you can create and manage specific to-do lists, and add or view items on a list. The left side of the screen is used to organize each of your separate to-do lists. When you first start using the app, a generic Reminders list is pre-created and ready to use. Simply click on the plus sign icon in the upper-right corner of the screen to begin adding individual to-do list items to that Reminders list.

If you want to create a to-do list from scratch, tap on the plus sign icon near the lower-left corner of the Reminders screen. Then create a title for your new list. Once it's created, add items to the list, one at a time.

In addition to having your to-do lists and items readily available to you regardless of which computer or device you access the information from, the ability to manage multiple lists simultaneously and set individual alerts or alarms for each listing gives you a lot of flexibility in terms of how you use this powerful app.

Tip   When you associate an alert or alarm with a to-do list or to-do list item, when that alert or alarm is actually generated, a listing for it will automatically appear in the Notification Center window of your MacBook Air, which is another powerful new feature offered by OS X Mountain Lion that will be explained shortly.

How to...   **Add a New To-Do List Item to Any of Your Lists Within Reminders**

Each time you create a new to-do list item by tapping on the plus sign icon displayed near the upper-right corner of the screen, you can then click on the 'i' icon next to the item to customize the listing.

A pop-up window will appear allowing you to edit the item's title or set up an alert associated with the to-do listing. An alert can be based on time/date and/or a location. You can also move a to-do listing from one list to another by clicking on the List option. Or you can click on the Priority option to set a Low, Medium, or High urgency to that specific item.

From within the pop-up window that appears when you click on the 'i' icon for a particular item, you can also click on the Note option, and then manually enter text-based notes of any length that you want to associate with that specific item.

Jot Down Important Memos with Notes

When it comes to word processing on your MacBook Air, you can purchase Apple's own Pages word processor, use the Mac edition of Microsoft Office (which includes Microsoft Word), or from the Mac App Store, you can purchase, download, and install a handful of other feature-packed word processors. Plus, there's always Open Office, which is a free Microsoft Office alternative (www.openoffice.org/porting/mac/download).

The Notes app that comes preinstalled with OS X is not a full-featured word processor. It is, however, a handy text editor that allow you to create text-based notes or documents of any length that can be organized within a virtual notebook with custom titles, and easily synced with your other computers or iOS devices via iCloud.

The Notes app resembles a notepad that's displayed on your screen. On the right side of the screen is a virtual yellow lined notepad. Click on the plus sign icon near the lower-left corner of the Notes window to create a new note and begin typing. As you're creating or editing a note, you can change fonts, typestyles, and font colors, and format your text using right, left, or centered justification. It's also possible to include numbered or bulleted lists in your notes, so creating an outline format is easy. When you're done creating or editing your text, the document will automatically be saved and synced with iCloud.

To delete a note, highlight its title on the left side of the screen, so that the individual note opens and is displayed on the right side of the screen. Then click on the trash can icon that's displayed near the bottom-right corner of the screen.

You can share a note using the Share icon that's displayed to the right of the trash can icon. Click on the Share icon, and then choose Email or Message. From within the Notes app, you can send a note to one or more recipients.

 Click on the Edit pull-down menu within the Notes app, and then select the Speech option followed by the Start Speaking command, to have your MacBook Air read the text in the note to you aloud.

The Notes app is ideal for notetaking, creating outlines, or jotting down ideas that you want to keep organized on your MacBook Air, sync with your other Mac and iOS mobile devices, or share with other people. It's very easy to use, with few commands and menu options to learn about.

 Like most apps that run on the MacBook Air, Notes is fully compatible with the OS X's Select, Select All, Copy, Cut, and Paste commands, which makes moving text or content around within a document, or between documents, an easy process.

Stay Informed with Notification Center

Many programs or apps you'll be running on your MacBook Air are capable of generating alerts, alarms, or notifications that will require your attention. For example, the Mail app will alert you of new incoming emails. The Calendar app will alert you of an upcoming appointment, obligation, or deadline. The Reminders app will alert you when a to-do list item's deadline is approaching. FaceTime will inform you if

You Can Send Tweets from Within the Notification Center Window

By clicking on the Notification Center icon that's displayed in the upper-right corner of the screen (along the menu bar), the Notification Center window will appear. Displayed near the top of this window, just below the Show Alerts and Banners option, is the Twitter option. Click on the Twitter button to make an outgoing tweet window appear. Type your tweet message (up to 140 characters) and click on the Send button to send the tweet to your Twitter followers, without having to launch the Twitter app. From this Twitter window you can send a text-based tweet that includes your current location (if you have Location Services activated on your computer).

you missed an incoming video conferencing call, and Messages will notify you when someone has sent you a text message or instant message.

With so many apps generating alerts, alarms, or notifications, keeping track of them all can be a bothersome task. That's where the Notification Center comes in handy. Built into OS X Mountain Lion is the new Notification Center app. It continuously monitors all of the compatible apps running on your computer and displays the alerts, alarms, and notifications generated by them in one convenient place.

At any time, click on the Notification Center icon in the extreme-right corner of the MacBook Air's screen. The Notification Center window will appear (shown in Figure 2-6) along the right margin of the screen. Within the Notification Center

Notification Center icon

Notification Center window

FIGURE 2-6 The Notification Center window displays all app-specific alerts, alarms, and notifications in a single window for easy reference.

How to...

Use the "Do Not Disturb" Feature of Notification Center

To temporarily turn off the alerts, banners, and notifications being displayed by Notification Center, as well as the audible alarms, click on the Notification Center icon that's displayed in the upper-right corner of the screen (along the menu bar), scroll to the top of the Notification Center window, and then click on the virtual on/off switch that's associated with Show Alerts And Banners.

When this switch is turned off, Notification Center will continue to collect alerts, alarms, and notifications generated by your computer and the apps it's monitoring and display them in the Notification Center window, but you will not be distributed with separate banners or onscreen alerts, nor will you hear audible alarms until the virtual on/off switch that's associated with Show Alerts And Banners is turned back on.

This feature is ideal for use while you're concentrating on important work and don't want to be disturbed.

window are sections. Each section represents one app that Notification Center is monitoring, such as Calendar or Mail.

Below each section heading will be a predetermined number of alerts, alarms, or notifications related to that app. By clicking on an individual listing, the relevant app will automatically launch and the information pertaining to the selected alert, alarm, or notification will be promptly displayed.

Because many apps are compatible with Notification Center, during a typical day, you could theoretically get bombarded with many alerts, alarms, and notifications. However, some of them may be deemed by you as unimportant. To ensure that only the alerts, alarms, and notifications from your most essential apps are displayed in Notification Center, invest a few minutes to customize the app.

How to...

Customize the Notification Center App

To customize the information that's displayed in your MacBook Air's Notification Center window, launch System Preferences from the Dock. When the System Preferences window appears, click on the Notifications icon.

On the left side of the Notification Center window (shown in Figure 2-7) is a listing of all apps that are compatible with Notification Center and that are currently and continuously being monitored. Highlight one app at a time. Once highlighted, look on the right side of the Notification Center window for the option that says Show In Notification Center: __ Recent Items.

(continued)

If you want Notification Center to monitor that particular app and display alerts, alarms, or notifications from that app in the Notification Center window, add a checkmark to the checkbox next to the Show In Notification Center: __ Recent Items option. Next, click on the pull-down menu associated with the __ Recent Items option, and choose how many alerts, alarms, or notifications from that particular app you want displayed in the Notification Center window at any given time. (Your options are 1, 5, 10, or 20.)

Ultimately, if you have Notification Center monitoring 10 apps, and each is allowed to display 10 alerts, alarms, or notifications in the Notification Center window, at any given time up to 100 items could be displayed. However, you can be selective in terms of which apps Notification Center monitors, and then limit how many alerts, alarms, or notifications each app displays. Doing this allows you to keep your personalized Notification Center window manageable.

Displayed below the listing of Notification Center compatible apps being monitored is a heading labeled Not In Notification Center. These are compatible apps that you have elected to keep the Notification Center app from monitoring. At any time, you can change this customization by adding a checkmark to the Show In Notification Center option that's associated with the app on the right side of the screen.

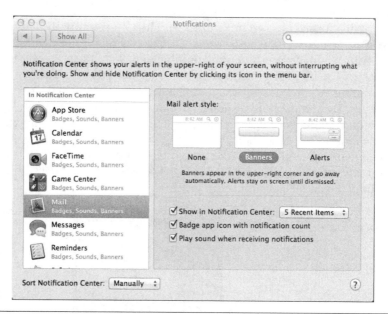

FIGURE 2-7   From within System Preferences, be sure to customize the settings for the Notification Center app.

Share In-App Content Using Share Sheets

Displayed within a handful of OS X preinstalled apps, as well as optional software you ultimately install and run on your MacBook Air, are new Share Sheets. When an app offers this feature, a Share icon is displayed. Click on the Share icon to quickly and easily share content from that app with others via email, Messages, Twitter, or another compatible service.

Figure 2-8 shows the Share icon that's prominently displayed in the Safari app while you're surfing the Web. Click on it to share the website URL that you're looking at with others via Email, Message, Facebook, or Twitter, for example.

Twitter Integration Allows You to Tweet from Within Apps

From the Share icons that are now built into a growing number of apps, you can access your preexisting Twitter account and send app-related tweets without exiting the app you're using. To do this, click on the Share icon and select the Twitter option.

Before you can take full advantage of Twitter integration as you use your MacBook Air, you first need to set up the feature and enter your Twitter account information. To do this, from the desktop, launch System Preferences, and then click on the Mail, Contacts & Calendars option. In the lower-left corner of the Mail, Contacts & Calendars window, click on the plus sign icon to set up an account.

On the right side of the Mail, Contacts & Calendars window, click on the Twitter option. When prompted, enter your preexisting Twitter username using the @ Username format (shown in Figure 2-9). Then, in the appropriate field, enter your existing Twitter account's password. Click on the Sign In option to continue.

After your account is verified, on the left side of the screen, your Twitter account name will be listed and highlighted. On the right side of the screen will be additional customizations you can make relating to how your MacBook Air will treat your Twitter account. For example, if you add a checkmark next to the Include My Location When Tweeting option, your exact location will be included in your outgoing tweets when you compose and send them.

If you have multiple Twitter accounts, click on the plus sign icon in the lower-left corner of the Mail, Contacts & Calendar window, and then click on the Twitter option again to repeat the account setup process.

FIGURE 2-8 A sample of the Share icon that's displayed in Safari and many other apps

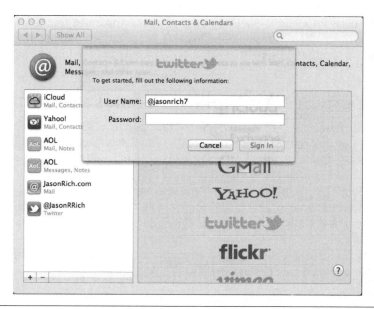

FIGURE 2-9   Once you set up Twitter integration, you can compose and send tweets from within a handful of compatible apps.

Tip   If you have multiple Twitter accounts stored on your MacBook Air, when you click on the Share icon and select Twitter, be sure to click on the From field to determine which account the tweet should be sent from.

In addition to the Twitter integration that's built into OS X, you can manage one or more active Twitter accounts using Safari. Point your web browser to www.twitter .com, and sign in as usual using your username and password.

You can also download and install one of many specialized apps designed for managing Twitter accounts. The official Twitter app is free, but you'll also discover free third-party apps, like TweetDeck, Echofone Lite for Twitter, Twitterific for Twitter,

Did You Know?

Facebook Functionality Is Now Integrated with OS X

One of the enhancements Apple made to OS X Mountain Lion is Facebook integration. Now you can update your Facebook page from within many of the MacBook Air's core apps, plus upload photos to Facebook, for example, by clicking on the Share icon that's now part of many apps. Plus, from within Contacts, it's now possible to access information about your Facebook friends without having to manually enter their contact-related data. In addition, the Notification Center window will display your Facebook-related notifications.

and Social for Twitter, available from the Mac App Store. See Chapter 5 for more information about finding, downloading, installing, and using optional software (or apps) on your MacBook Air.

Experience Multiplayer Games via Game Center

Playing games on a computer is a popular pastime. To make experiencing multiplayer games more exciting, Apple has created the Game Center, which is an online-based service that allows you to interact with other players, track your scores, and learn about new multiplayer games.

Signing up to participate in Game Center is free, though a charge may apply to purchase, download, and install some Game Center compatible games. To set up a free account, use your Apple ID when you launch the Game Center app for the first time.

 Game Center allows you to interact with other Mac users, as well as iPhone, iPad, and iPod touch users.

 To find, download, and install single-player or multiplayer games, visit the Mac App Store. You'll learn more about playing games on the MacBook Air in Chapter 15.

Share What's on Your Screen Using AirPlay Mirroring

When used in conjunction with an optional Apple TV device ($99, www.apple.com/appletv) and a wireless network, the AirPlay Mirroring feature of OS X allows you

How to...   Use Your MacBook Air's Dictation Feature

Using the new Dictation feature that's built into OS Mountain Lion, instead of typing text into certain apps, you can click on the Dictation icon or press the FN (Function) key twice, and then speak directly into your computer. The MacBook will translate your spoken words into text and place them into the app you're using.

To initially turn on this feature, launch System Preferences and click on the Dictation And Speech option. Next, turn on the Dictation feature, and then click on the Enable Dictation button. Now, almost anytime you can manually type text, you can press the FN (Function) key twice to begin dictation, or click on the microphone icon that's displayed within compatible apps.

When Dictation mode is activated, a large and animated microphone icon will appear. Click on the Done button below it when you're done with dictation and ready for the computer to translate what you've said into text.

to wirelessly display whatever is on your MacBook Air's screen on a separate HD television set or monitor. This makes it easy to share photos, videos, and presentations with a group, without having to connect your computer to an HD television or monitor using special (optional) adapters and cables.

Note AirPlay Mirroring does not allow you to share some copyrighted video material.

Take Control over Your Computer's Security with Gatekeeper

Surfing the Web and utilizing the Internet can be a fun and informative activity. However, it can also be a way that dishonest people hack into your computer, obtain confidential information about you, or potentially steal your identity.

In addition, if multiple people will be using your MacBook Air, you don't want them downloading apps, data, or other content that you don't approve of. In order to give you maximum control over who can access your MacBook Air, and what content you or anyone else can access with it via the Web, Apple has incorporated the Gatekeeper functionality into the OS X operating system.

Tip If you know multiple people will be using your MacBook Air, you can set up separate accounts for each person, and make yourself the system administrator. When you do this, each user's personalized settings for the computer are stored and then applied only when they sign into the computer. To set up multiple user accounts on your MacBook Air, launch System Preferences and then select the Users & Groups option.

As you get started using your MacBook Air, take a few minutes to customize the preferences offered by the Security & Privacy options in System Preferences. To access them, from the Dock, launch System Preferences. Then click on the Security & Privacy option. When the Security & Privacy window appears, four command tabs, labeled General, FileVault, Firewall, and Privacy, will be displayed near the top-center of the window. Click on one tab at a time and adjust the various menu options based on your needs and security preferences.

By clicking on the General tab, it's possible to change the master login password for the user. This is the password that's required when you first log into the computer or attempt to install new software, for example. By clicking on Require Password For Sleep And Screen Saver, this same password will be required when you wake the computer from Sleep mode or switch out of Screen Saver mode.

By clicking on the FileVault tab, you can have your MacBook Air automatically encrypt all data and files stored on the computer's primary hard drive.

When you turn on the Firewall option by clicking on the Firewall tab, you can control who can access your computer and its files or data when the MacBook Air is connected to a wireless network.

Turn on the Password Feature to Access Your MacBook

One of the Security & Privacy options in System Preferences is the ability to require a password every time someone tries to turn on or wake up your MacBook Air. To turn on this feature, from within System Preferences, select the Security & Privacy option. Next, click on the General command tab, followed by the Require Password For Sleep And Screen Saver option.

When you set up your MacBook Air for the first time, you created a master password for the computer (that's related to your user account). This password must be entered each time new software is to be installed, for example. By activating the Require Password For Sleep And Screen Saver option, that same password will now be required each time the MacBook Air is awakened from Sleep mode or taken out of Screen Saver mode.

Once this feature is turned on, you can further customize when and how the password feature will be utilized by adjusting the other options displayed in the Security & Privacy window of System Preferences.

If you click on the Privacy tab, you can control whether or not your MacBook Air will share certain types of data, such as your current location when the Location Services feature is being utilized.

Navigate Your Way Around the OS X Operating System

Now that you have previewed just some of the new features offered by the OS X Mountain Lion operating system, let's take a quick look at how you can begin navigating your way around your new MacBook Air.

Just about everything you do on your MacBook Air will begin from the desktop (shown in Figure 2-10). As you're viewing the desktop, you'll discover a handful of pull-down menus displayed near the upper-left corner of the screen, as well as command icons for controlling specific features of your computer that are displayed near the upper-right corner of the screen.

Displayed along the bottom of your MacBook Air's desktop is the Dock (shown in Figure 2-11). This is a customizable lineup of icons that represent apps you can launch by clicking on them. All of the apps installed on your MacBook Air are listed in the Applications window and Launchpad. You can drag and drop individual app icons from the Applications window to your Dock for easy access.

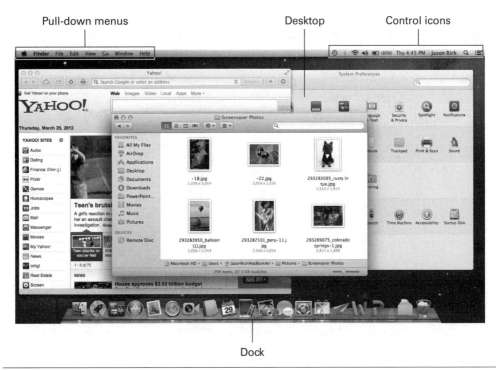

Pull-down menus   Desktop   Control icons

Dock

FIGURE 2-10   Your MacBook Air's desktop is customizable.

 Note   When you move an app icon from the Dock to the trash can, this does not delete the app from your computer. To delete an app altogether, open the Applications folder (using the Finder), and drag the app icon for the app from the Applications folder to the Trash Can. In some cases, the app or software will have a special Uninstall app icon or feature. If so, use it.

Find Apps, Documents, or Files Using the Finder

To locate and utilize any app, file, photo, document, or item that's stored on your MacBook Air, you can find and access it using the Finder. To open a Finder window,

Finder   Trash can

FIGURE 2-11   The Dock can appear at the bottom, left, or right side of your desktop, based on how you set it up in System Preferences.

How to... **Delete an App Icon from the Dock**

To remove an app icon from your Dock, drag it off of the Dock toward the main desktop. It will disappear in a virtual puff of smoke (but the app itself will not be deleted from your computer). If you want to delete files, photos, and documents from a Finder window, for example, one way to do this is to drag them into the trash can icon displayed on the Dock.

Once an item is placed in your trash can, it will not be deleted (erased) from your computer until you click on the Finder pull-down menu that's displayed at the top of the desktop screen and select the Empty Trash option. Until this is done, you can recover an item placed in the trash simply by dragging it back out and placing it into another folder or on your desktop. Or you can select and highlight the item in the Trash folder and select the Put Back option in the File pull-down menu on the menu bar.

click on the Finder icon to the extreme left of your Dock. Upon clicking on the Finder icon, the All My Files window is displayed.

On the left side of the All My Files window (shown in Figure 2-12) is a list of key folders, including Applications, Desktop, Documents, Downloads, Movies, Music, and

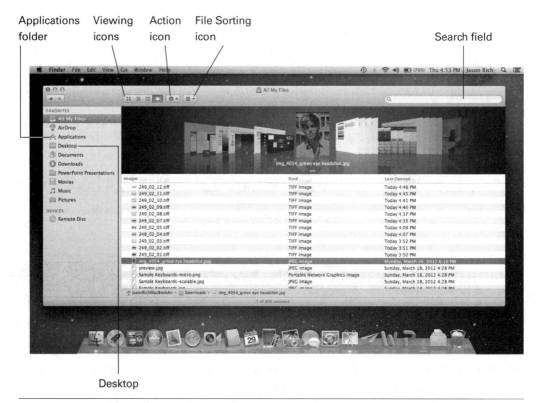

FIGURE 2-12   The All My Files window appears when you open a Finder window.

Pictures. Click on any of these folders to display their contents within the All My Files window. Or click on any other folder icon to view the contents of that folder within the All My Files window.

For example, to view all of the apps installed on your MacBook Air, click on the Applications folder option that's displayed on the left side of the All My Files window. You can then move your pointer over any app icon and double-click on it to launch that app.

 Located near the upper-right corner of the Finder window is a Search field. Enter any keyword, filename, or search phrase in this field to quickly find relevant content stored on your computer.

Displayed near the upper-left corner of the Finder window are a handful of command buttons. The View buttons allow you to determine the view offered in the Finder window. You can view app icons with filenames; view a listing of filenames, along with their descriptions and file sizes; view a listing of just filenames in a directory or folder; or view files using an animated carousel. With one or more files highlighted in Finder, click on the gear-shaped Action button to change its settings or make customizations to it. You can also click on the Arrange button to the right of the gear-shaped icon to sort filenames or icons by name, kind, application, date, size, or label.

In Finder, items can be copies, moved, renamed, or dragged to the trash can. Or you can open two Finder windows on the desktop, and then drag and drop files between folders.

Use Launchpad to Run Apps

As you become acquainted with OS X, you'll discover there are often multiple ways to perform the same tasks. You can use pull-down menu commands, keyboard shortcuts, or finger gestures on the trackpad, for example.

When it comes to launching apps, you can click on an app icon that's displayed on the Dock, open the Applications folder and double-click on an app icon, or use the Launchpad. To launch the Launchpad, click on the Launchpad icon on the Dock, or use your thumb, index, middle, and ring fingers on the trackpad to perform a grab motion. Once the Launchpad screen is displayed on the desktop, click on any app icon that you want to launch.

 When multiple apps are running simultaneously, you can switch between apps using a finger gesture or by launching Mission Control. This will display thumbnails of all active apps on the screen and allow you to quickly switch between them. Another way to switch between apps is to hold down the COMMAND (⌘) and TAB keys on the keyboard. Click the TAB key repeatedly (with the COMMAND (⌘) key held down) to highlight and select an app, and then release the keys to reopen that app.

How to Quit Any App

Once an app is running on your MacBook Air and is active (the one you're currently using), to quit that app, click on the pull-down menu in the upper-left corner of the screen that's labeled with the app's name, and then choose the Quit command from the pull-down menu.

 Only the app that's currently in use will have its menu options displayed on the menu bar.

For example, if you're running Safari, to exit out of Safari and close the app altogether, click on the Safari pull-down menu, and then click on the Quit Safari option (shown in Figure 2-13).

Keep in mind, if you click on the red dot that's displayed in the upper-left corner of a program window, in most cases, this will close the window so it's no longer displayed on the desktop, but the app will continue running in the background.

 Any time you quit an app, it stops running altogether. However, using OS X, you can keep multiple apps running simultaneously.

 All of the apps that are currently running display app icons on the Dock, and below their app icons is a small white dot indicating they are active.

Customize the Look of Your Desktop

There are many ways to customize the appearance and functionality of your MacBook Air. For example, you can change the wallpaper that's displayed behind the icons on your desktop. You can also select and then personalize your screen saver.

Quit Safari command

FIGURE 2-13   To quit any app, use the Quit command that's found under the app name's pull-down menu at the top of the screen.

To personalize the desktop, launch System Preferences, and click on the Desktop & Screen Saver option (shown in Figure 2-14). Displayed near the top-center of the Desktop & Screen Saver window are two command tabs, labeled Desktop and Screen Saver. Click on the Desktop tab to customize the look of your computer's desktop.

You'll be able to select from a handful of preinstalled wallpaper graphics, or choose a photo that's stored in iPhoto or in a folder. Using the commands displayed at the bottom of the window, you can keep the wallpaper graphic the same or opt for it to automatically change at predetermined time intervals.

By clicking on the Screen Saver tab, you can select and then personalize the screen saver that is displayed after a predetermined period of inactivity. One popular screen saver allows you to create an animated slide show using your favorite digital images (photos), and then customize that slide show by choosing a theme and image transition effect.

 Using a screen saver is an option, but not required. You can always opt to turn off the Screen Saver option by launching System Preferences, selecting Desktop & Screen Saver, and then from the Start Screen Saver pull-down menu, choose the Never option. (The default option is 5 minutes.)

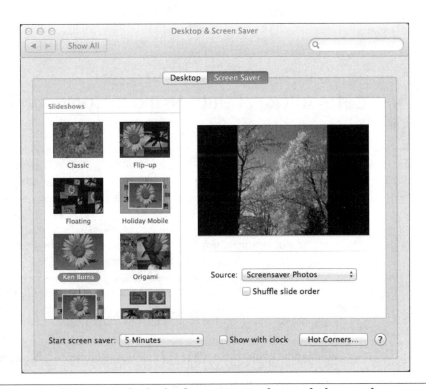

FIGURE 2-14   Customize the look of your MacBook Air's desktop and screen saver.

By default, the Dock is always displayed at the bottom of your computer's desktop. However, from within System Preferences, you can change this setting, so the Dock only appears when you drag the mouse toward the bottom of the screen, or when a particular app icon (such as the trash can) is needed.

To make this customization, from within System Preferences, click on the Dock option. In addition to choosing the size of the app icons, and the position of the Dock itself (on the bottom, left, or right side of the screen), you can place a checkmark next to Automatically Hide And Show The Dock if you want it to disappear (and conserve screen space) when it's not needed.

Many Customizations Can Be Made from Within System Preferences

From within System Preferences, you can adjust and customize a wide range of settings that relate to specific apps, the functionality of your MacBook Air, as well as various features and functions of the OS X operating system.

Some of the options available within System Preferences have already been explained, and others will be touched upon in future chapters. As you become more comfortable using your MacBook Air, spend some time looking at the various options offered within System Preferences to discover firsthand how adjusting some of the settings can make using your computer more efficient, secure, and enjoyable.

How to...   Get Additional Help Using OS X Mountain Lion

To learn more about how to use OS X's many other features and functions, visit Apple's website, access the Support section, and then choose MacBook Air or OS X Mountain Lion. You'll discover hundreds of free how-to articles, video tutorials, and other online-based reference materials.

Within the first 90 days of owning a new MacBook Air, you can also make unlimited calls to AppleCare for toll-free support to get your questions answered, or you can meet with an Apple Genius in-person at an Apple Store by making an appointment. Apple's 90-day support period extends to two years if you purchase AppleCare for your MacBook Air ($249).

For more in-depth, one-on-one private lessons using your new MacBook Air, available at any Apple Store, you can also purchase an Apple One To One membership ($99, http://store.apple.com/us/browse/campaigns/onetoone), which lasts for one year. Apple also offers an ongoing selection of free group workshops that you can register for and participate in at any Apple Store. To learn more about these workshops, visit www.apple.com/retail/workshops.

3

Make the Switch from Windows to a Mac

HOW TO...

- Adapt to the differences between OS X and Microsoft Windows
- Find Mac versions of your favorite software
- Transfer your important data to your MacBook Air

If you are a Windows user, making the switch from a PC to a Mac will take some adjustment. This chapter will help you plan for that learning curve, and discover what to expect in order to make a smooth and quick transition from a PC to a MacBook Air.

 Your MacBook Air is capable of running the latest version of the Windows operating system and your favorite Windows-based software. Apple offers its free Boot Camp software that allows you to run Windows and Windows-based software on a Mac, while third-party companies, such as Parallels (www.parallels.com), offer inexpensive solutions that allow you to switch back and forth between operating systems (and software running under those operating systems), without having to reboot your computer. You'll learn more about these solutions in Chapter 18.

Discover the Differences Between Microsoft Windows and OS X

Microsoft Windows 7 is a powerful and versatile operating system. However, many computer users find that Apple's OS X Mountain Lion operating system (which powers all Macs, including the MacBook Air computers) is more powerful, more secure, and easier to use. Plus, OS X integrates with Apple's iCloud file sharing service, and it comes bundled with a handful of apps that greatly enhance the capabilities of the computer it's running on, without you first having to purchase, download, and install additional software.

As a Windows user, you're probably already familiar with Windows Explorer. Instead of using Windows Explorer to manage your files, OS X Mountain Lion offers Finder. Windows Explore and Finder have many similarities.

Once you boot up your MacBook Air for the first time, you'll discover that OS X displays a central and customizable desktop screen. The desktop displays information or runs software within separate windows, just like a PC. Figure 3-1 shows several apps running on the MacBook Air simultaneously in different windows.

The desktop features pull-down menus and can utilize a wide selection of keyboard shortcuts that allow you to quickly handle many common computing tasks. Plus, your MacBook Air features the Multi-Touch trackpad. It allows you to interact with the OS X operating system, and the software or apps you're running, using a series of finger motions and gestures. Because it was inspired by Apple's iPad, this level of interaction using finger motions and gestures is unique to the MacBook Air and iPad, and not found on Windows-based computers.

Onscreen Differences Between Windows and OS X

Let's take a look at the MacBook Air's desktop and compare some of its components to what you'd find on a computer running the latest version of Microsoft Windows.

FIGURE 3-1   From the MacBook Air's main desktop, you can run software or apps, access your data, documents, and files, and work with many different types of multimedia content.

FIGURE 3-2   The Apple logo icon reveals a pull-down menu that has some features you'd find using the Start button in Windows.

The Apple Icon

Look to the upper-left corner of the MacBook Air's desktop screen. Here, you'll see an Apple logo. This icon reveals a pull-down menu that has some features you'd find using the Start button in Windows (shown in Figure 3-2). Use it to access Software Updates (to update software, similar to Windows Update), System Preferences (similar to Control Panel), Sleep (places your MacBook Air in Standby mode), Log Out (used to switch between MacBook Air users), and Shut Down (to power down your MacBook Air).

The Menu Bar

The row of pull-down menu options on which you find the Apple icon is the OS X's menu bar. It's a series of pull-down menus and command icons that are almost always visible and accessible, regardless of what software you're running. Except for the Apple icon, the rest of the pull-down menu options along the menu bar will change based on what app is currently active. When using Finder, for example, the menu bar options (shown in Figure 3-3) include the Finder menu, which gives you access to features like Empty Trash. If you're running Microsoft Word, as you can see in Figure 3-4, the menu options are different.

The command icons displayed on the right side of the menu bar are pretty consistent, unless you manually opt for a compatible app to display a command icon within this portion of the menu bar.

FIGURE 3-3   The menu bar when Finder is active

FIGURE 3-4 The menu bar when Microsoft Word is the active app running on the MacBook Air (other apps could be running in the background)

Red, Yellow, and Green Dot Window Icons

When a Finder window or program window is open on the desktop, displayed in the upper-left corner of each window are three colored dots (shown in Figure 3-5). The red dot is used to close a window, the yellow dot is used to minimize the window, and the green dot is used to zoom the window. As a Microsoft Windows user, you're probably accustomed to seeing similar icons in the upper-right corner of a window.

One key difference between OS X and Windows is that when you click on the red dot window icon, the window will close, but in most cases, the software or app will continue running in the background on your MacBook Air. To quit an app, you'll need to use the Quit command that's found under the application's pull-down menu. You can also use the COMMAND (⌘)-Q keyboard shortcut. You'll know what apps are running on your MacBook Air by looking at the app icons along the Dock. App icons with a white dot displayed below them are currently running.

Finder Window Item View Buttons

When a Finder window is open in OS X, displayed near the top-left corner of the window will be the item view buttons (shown in Figure 3-6). These are similar to the item view options available in Windows.

Click on one of these four buttons to determine how program or file items will be displayed within the window. When icon view is selected on your MacBook Air, for example, a thumbnail of each document, photo, or app-specific file will be seen as

FIGURE 3-5 The red, yellow, and green dot window icons can be found in the upper-left corner of a Finder or program window. When running Microsoft Windows on a PC, similar icons are located in the upper-right corner of windows.

Four View icons

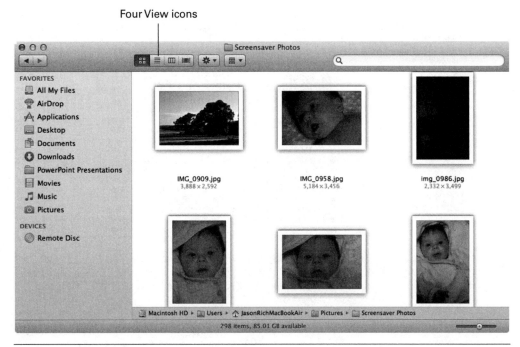

FIGURE 3-6   Click on one of the item view buttons, such as the icon view (seen here) to determine the appearance of items within the Finder window.

an icon. Figure 3-7 shows items as a filename listing, without icons displayed. As you can see, more information about each item, including its kind and when it was last opened, is displayed.

Finder's Action Menu

You'll notice that your MacBook Air's trackpad does not have any separate buttons. To use what would be equivalent to a left-mouse click, simply press down on the trackpad gently until you hear a click sound.

To simulate a right-mouse click, either click on the Action button (which is the gear-shaped icon displayed within a Finder window), shown in Figure 3-8, or press the control key at the same time you click on the trackpad.

Finder's Arrange Button

Located to the right of the Action button, typically near the top-left corner of a Finder window, is the Arrange button. It's used to manage filenames and icons, and sort them by name, kind, application, etc. Click on this button to access a pull-down menu that lists available options (shown in Figure 3-9).

Some of the commands available from the Item Arrangement pull-down menu are similar to what's possible using the Group By or Stack By command in Windows.

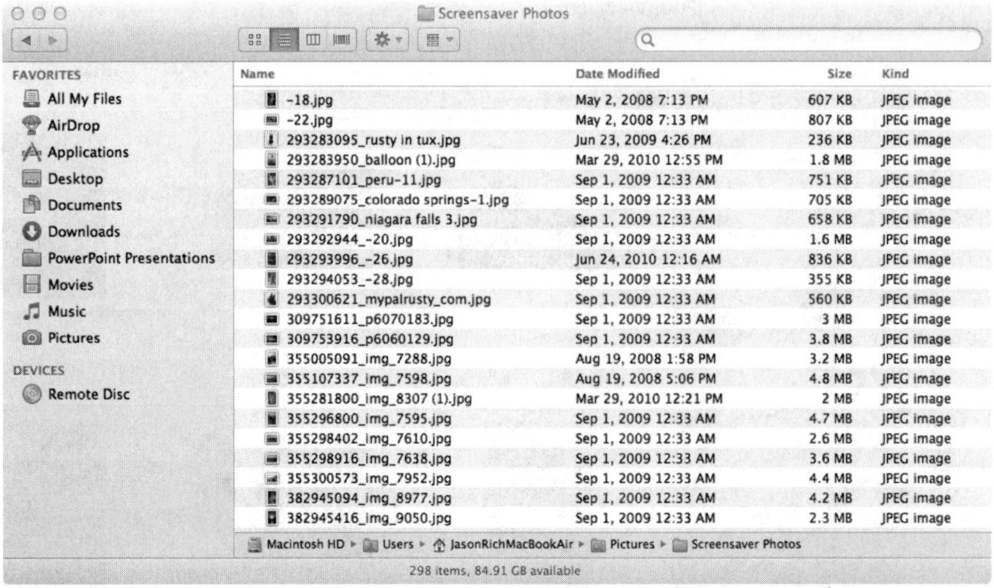

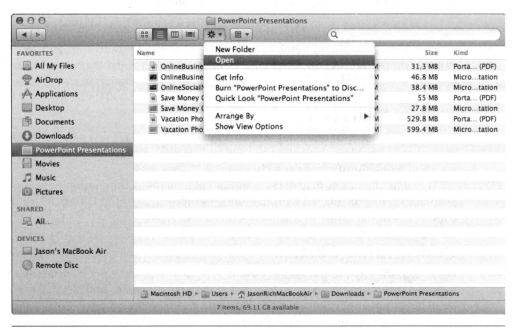

FIGURE 3-7 Shown here is the filename listing view within a Finder window.

FIGURE 3-8 The Action button within the Finder window offers many of the same options as a right-mouse click on a Windows-based PC.

Sort icon

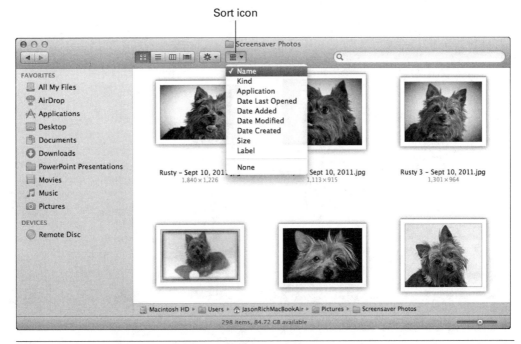

FIGURE 3-9   Sort items by name, kind, application, size, label, or one of several date-related options (last opened, added, modified, or created).

Finder's Search Field

While Windows has the Search command, your MacBook Air has a Search field that's located near the upper-right corner of any Finder window. Enter any keyword or phrase, and the Search feature built into OS X will find it in any related files stored on your MacBook Air and display the results.

Finder's Back/Forward Icons

The left and right arrow icons near the upper-left corner of a Finder window work just as they do in Microsoft Windows on a PC. When moving around within the directory or folder hierarchy, these arrow icons allow you to move back or forward, from a main folder to a subfolder or vice versa.

The Finder Window's Sidebar

Displayed on the left side of a Finder window (shown in Figure 3-10), this feature is similar to the task pane in Windows Explorer. On your MacBook Air, the sidebar has various headings, and under each heading are listings used to access specific folders or storage devices connected to your computer, including its own hard drive.

Sidebar

FIGURE 3-10   Access the contents of specific folders, hard drive, or other storage devices linked to your MacBook Air.

The Dock

By default, the Dock is displayed at the bottom of the desktop on your MacBook Air. However, from within System Preferences, you can move it to the left or right margin of the screen. It's a customizable display of icons that represent your most frequently used software or apps, as well as the apps or programs that are currently running on your MacBook Air. The Dock is similar to the Windows taskbar.

 Similar to using the Start command on a Windows PC, on your MacBook Air you can launch apps or software from the Dock; from app icons copied onto your desktop; by accessing the Applications folder using Finder, and then clicking on an app icon; or by using the Launchpad feature of OS X.

The Finder Application Icon

To open a Finder window, click on the Finder icon that's always displayed on the extreme-left side of the Dock (shown in Figure 3-11). A Finder window will open, regardless of what other apps or software are running. If multiple Finder windows are open, clicking on the Finder icon on the Dock will reopen the most recently used Finder window.

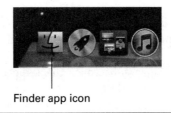

Finder app icon

FIGURE 3-11   The Finder app icon is always displayed to the extreme left on the Dock.

If a Finder window is already open, but tucked behind other windows, clicking on the Finder icon will bring the most recently active Finder window to the front. This is similar to accessing Windows Explorer on a PC.

OS X's Spotlight Search Feature

Another way to quickly find anything stored on your MacBook Air is to use the Spotlight search feature that's always displayed near the upper-right corner of the screen, along the menu bar. It too works very much like the Windows Search command. Click on the magnifying glass icon to access the Spotlight search feature on the MacBook Air.

Within the blank Search field, enter the filename, file extension, keyword, or a search phrase that's related to what you're looking for. The results from your search will appear in the main area of the Finder window. They'll be sorted by category, based on their type. Click on any of the search results to open or access that file, directory, photo, or app.

If you enter into Full Screen mode of a particular app, such as iPhoto or Calendar, the menu bar pull-down menus and the command icons displayed along it (including the Spotlight search icon) will temporarily be unavailable. To access them, first exit out of Full Screen mode by pressing the ESC key on the keyboard.

Trash

Like so many features of OS X, the Trash icon (shown in Figure 3-12) is located in a different place than where you're accustomed to seeing it when running Microsoft Windows, but it serves the same functionality as Window's Recycle Bin.

Trash icon

FIGURE 3-12   The Trash icon is located on the MacBook Air's Dock, to the extreme right.

Learn Keyboard Differences on the MacBook Air

When using a Windows-based PC, the keyboard features an ALT key, Windows key, and backspace key. On the Mac, the ALT key has been replaced by the option key (located on the bottom row of the MacBook Air's keyboard). The Windows key has been replaced by the COMMAND (⌘) key (also located on the bottom row of the MacBook Air's keyboard), and the backspace key has been replaced by the delete key (located near the upper-right corner of the keyboard).

 For tasks that require pressing the CTRL key and another key on the keyboard when using a Windows-based PC, you'll either use the control or COMMAND (⌘) key on the MacBook Air, depending on the function.

The top row of the MacBook Air's keyboard also includes a dozen function keys, as well as the power button. See Chapter 1 for a recap of what the function keys are used for. While Windows-based PCs also utilize function keys, what they're used for on your MacBook Air is different.

Tip You can drag and drop items into the Trash, or they will automatically be moved to the Trash folder when you delete them using the Move To Trash menu command. To view the contents of the Trash, double-click on the Trash icon. To empty the Trash and permanently delete its contents, select the Empty Trash command from the Finder pull-down menu on the menu bar when Finder is being used.

Switch to Full Screen Mode

When an app or software is running within a program window, click on the red, yellow, or green dot icons to close, minimize, or zoom that window. However, if the app has a Full Screen mode option, look for the Full Screen icon that's displayed in the upper-right corner of the program window to switch that app into Full Screen mode.

The Full Screen icon looks like two arrows moving away from each other (shown in Figure 3-13). To exit out of Full Screen mode press the ESC button on the keyboard. iPhoto '11 is one example of a popular app that has a Full Screen mode.

Working with Keyboard Shortcuts

Many of the keyboard shortcuts that are possible within Windows are also available on your MacBook Air. However, the key combinations used to execute the various shortcuts are different.

On your MacBook Air, instead of pressing control plus one or more keys, you'll typically press the COMMAND (⌘) key, plus one or more keys. Or instead of CONTROL-ALT-another key, on the MacBook Air, you'll press COMMAND (⌘)-OPTION-another key.

Full Screen mode icon in the
upper-right corner of the screen.

FIGURE 3-13   The Full Screen mode icon is displayed in the upper-right corner of
compatible apps such as Calendar or iPhoto (shown here).

To view a complete list of default keyboard shortcuts and to customize your own,
launch System Preferences, select the Keyboard option (listed under the Hardware
heading), and then click on the Keyboard Shortcuts tab that's displayed near the top-
center of the Keyboard window on your MacBook Air.

For example, the popular Copy, Cut, and Paste commands can be executed using
COMMAND (⌘)-C, COMMAND (⌘)-X, or COMMAND (⌘)-V, respectively. COMMAND (⌘)-P is
used to execute the Print command, and COMMAND (⌘)-S executes the Save command
when using most apps.

System Preferences Replaces Windows Control Panel

When it comes to customizing how your computer and software perform in Microsoft
Windows, these customizations are often made from within the Control Panel. On the
MacBook Air, similar functionality is offered with System Preferences.

To access System Preferences, click on the System Preferences icon on the
Dock; or, launch the Finder, select the Applications folder, and then double-click on
the System Preferences icon. The System Preferences window will be displayed (as
shown in Figure 3-14).

Tip   Two other ways to access System Preferences are to click on the Apple icon on the
menu bar and then select the System Preferences option from the pull-down menu,
or launch System Preferences from the Launchpad.

FIGURE 3-14 System Preferences offers many options for customizing your MacBook Air, the OS X operating system, hardware connected to your computer, and specific apps installed on the computer.

Get Used to the Windows vs. Mac Differences

As you begin using your MacBook Air running OS X Mountain Lion, you'll discover it offers many of the same features as the latest version of Microsoft Windows, but how you access the features will be slightly different. Getting used to the different locations of icons and menu options, for example, will take some getting used to, so be patient.

After you get accustomed to the new layout and menu structure of OS X, using your MacBook Air will become second nature. You'll soon be able to focus exclusively on the computing task at hand, not how to accomplish it using your new computer.

Migrating Your Data from a PC to the MacBook Air

Once you decide to migrate from a PC to a Mac, you'll need to analyze the data and files currently stored on your PC and figure out three things:

- What data needs to be transferred to the MacBook Air (including your documents, files, app-specific data or databases, photos, music, movies, etc.)
- What software or apps on your MacBook Air will be used to access and work with your existing data
- How you'll transfer the files from your PC to your MacBook Air

For example, your Windows PC offers Microsoft Outlook for managing your contacts and calendar. Your MacBook Air uses Contacts and Calendar for these purposes, however, a Mac version of Microsoft Outlook is also available as part of Microsoft Office for Mac.

Once you determine which data and files need to be transferred to your MacBook Air, first determine if the apps built into OS X Mountain Lion and iLife, for example, can handle that data, such as your contacts database, calendar, email accounts, photos, music library, documents, and movie library. Then determine what additional Mac software is required (which you'll need to purchase, download, and install) on your MacBook Air to accommodate other types of data.

For example, if you have Microsoft Office (Word, Excel, and/or PowerPoint) files on your PC, you'll want to install Microsoft Office for Mac on your MacBook Air. Your other options for working with Microsoft Office files include utilizing the iWork suite (Pages, Numbers, and Keynote), downloading and installing LibreOffice (for free), or purchasing and installing other third-party, Office-compatible apps that will allow you to work with your existing Office documents and files.

 You'll discover that Microsoft Office for Windows works almost identically to Microsoft Office for Mac (www.microsoft.com/mac), and that files and documents are usually fully compatible and can easily be transferred between platforms. You might run into minor file compatibility issues when dealing with fonts or PowerPoint slide animations or transitions, but these are almost always automatically fixed by the version of Microsoft Office you're running.

To work with your existing data, you can either import it into a app or software package that's bundled with OS X, find a Mac version of the software you're already using on your PC, or find and install Mac software that's compatible with your data or content.

Did You Know?

Microsoft Office 2011 for Mac Comes in Several Versions

Available for purchase and download directly from the Microsoft website (www.microsoft.com/mac), Microsoft Office for Mac comes in several configurations. Microsoft Office for Mac Home & Student 2011 is available in a single-user ($119.99) or family pack ($149.99) edition. It includes Word, PowerPoint, and Excel.

Microsoft Office for Mac Home & Business 2011 for one user, one Mac is available for $199.99. The one user, two Macs edition is available for $279.99. The Home & Business edition includes Word, PowerPoint, Excel, and Outlook, all of which are fully compatible with the PC versions of these Microsoft Office applications.

Determine if Mac Versions of Your Favorite Software Are Available

To determine if a Mac version of your favorite PC software is available, the first place to look is the App Store. From the Dock on your MacBook Air that's connected to the Internet, click on the App Store icon. Once the App Store launches, use the Search field to enter the name of the software you're looking for, such as Photoshop Elements or Quicken. If the App Store doesn't list the specific software you need, you can either visit the Windows software developer's website to see if a Mac version is available, or determine what other Mac software is compatible with the software you're currently using on your PC.

 See Chapter 5 for more information on finding, purchasing, downloading, and installing software on the MacBook Air.

Use Apple's Migration Assistant to Easily Transfer Your Files and Data

Built into OS X is a feature called Migration Assistant. It allows you to easily transfer your important Windows data, files, and system preferences to your MacBook Air.

For example, if you're transferring Microsoft Office files from your PC to Mac, your MacBook Air will need to have Microsoft Office installed to utilize those files. The same is true for Photoshop, Photoshop Elements, Quicken, FileMaker Pro, QuickBooks, Portrait Professional, and data or files from many other popular software applications that offer both Windows and Mac versions.

Using Migration Assistant, all of your photos, videos, and audio files, including your iTunes purchased content that is stored on your PC, can be transferred from a PC to a MacBook Air, and then accessed using compatible software on the Mac.

Migration Assistant analyzes what's stored on your PC, including your system preferences and customizations, web browser bookmarks, contacts database, scheduling information, documents, photos, and other data, and then helps you transfer those files, and place them in the appropriate folders on your MacBook Air.

For Migration Assistant to work, your PC and Mac need to be linked together through the same wireless network or directly connected using a USB cable. One of the easiest ways to link a PC and MacBook Air together in order to transfer files is to use the optional j5 Create Wormhole cable ($40.00, www.j5create.com/mobile/product.php?id=10). This cable plugs into the USB ports of both computers and allows you to literally drag-and-drop files, documents, and data between computers using auto-installing software that runs on both computers when the Wormhole cable is connected.

The Migration Assistant software comes preinstalled with OS X on the MacBook Air, but must also be downloaded (for free) onto your PC. To do this, from your PC, visit www.apple.com/migrate-to-mac.

Once the two computers are linked, launch the Migration Assistant software on both computers. To do this on the Mac, open the Finder and click on the Applications folder, then double-click on the Utilities folder. Double-click on the Migration Assistant app icon (shown in Figure 3-15) that's displayed within the Utilities folder.

When the Migration Assistant software launches on your MacBook Air, the Introduction screen is displayed. When asked, "How do you want to transfer your information?" select the From Another Mac, PC, Time Machine Backup, Or Other Disk option, and then click Continue (as shown in Figure 3-16).

It will then be necessary to enter your MacBook Air's master password. Enter this information when prompted and click OK. At this point, be sure to close all applications running on your MacBook Air and PC, except for the Migration Assistant software. Also, make sure your MacBook Air is plugged into an external power source (as opposed to running on battery) during this process.

Proceed through the various screens of the Migration Assistant software. From the MacBook Air, select the PC you want to transfer data and files from, and then wait for a passcode to be displayed. The same passcode should appear on your PC. Next, select

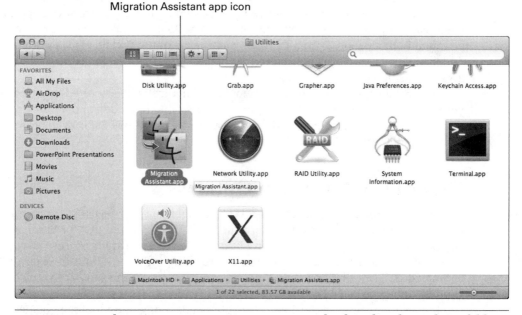

FIGURE 3-15   The Migration Assistant app icon can be found in the Utilities folder of your MacBook Air.

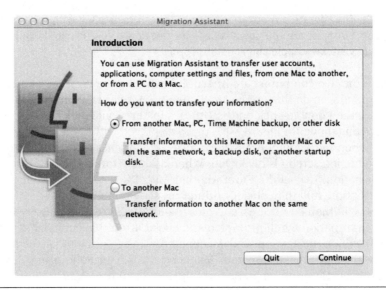

FIGURE 3-16 Migration Assistant not only transfers data and files from a PC to a Mac, it places everything in the proper location on your MacBook Air's hard drive.

the data and files you want to transfer. How long this process takes will be based on how much information needs to be copied from one computer to the other, so be patient.

When the process is complete, you'll see that document files from your PC have been placed in the Documents folder of your MacBook Air. Likewise, your photos will be found in the MacBook Air's Pictures folder, your music will be placed in the Music folder, and your Movies will be stored in the Movies folder (each of which can be accessed using Finder).

Meanwhile, your contacts database will automatically be imported into Contacts, your schedule data will be imported automatically into Calendar, and your Microsoft Explorer bookmarks and related data will be transferred to the Safari web browser on your MacBook Air.

Other Data Migration Options

Depending on the type of data you're transferring, it may be necessary to manually export data from software running on your PC so that it's saved in a format that's compatible with software running on your Mac. When this export process is necessary, chances are the PC software you're using will have a built-in Export command. Select a file format that will be compatible with the software you'll be running on your MacBook Air.

In some rare cases, a third-party or optional data migration tool may be necessary. This optional software will serve as a customizable conduit between two otherwise incompatible software packages.

Manually Transferring Data and Files from a PC to Your MacBook Air

Without using Migration Assistant, you can manually copy or transfer files from your PC to MacBook Air using a cloud-based file serving service, such as Dropbox. Or you can use a file transfer service, such as YouSendIt.com, via the Web. Yet another option is to copy your files or data from your PC onto a USB thumb drive, and then plug that thumb drive into your MacBook Air to transfer the necessary files or data.

Built into the OS X Mountain Lion operating system is a feature called AirDrop. It allows Macs connected to the same wireless network to easily exchange files using a drag-and-drop process which will be covered later in the book. AirDrop only works with more recently released Macs, but it's a handy tool for quickly transferring files between computers wirelessly.

 You also have the option to connect an external optical drive to your MacBook Air to load software, data, and files from a CD-ROM. The optional MacBook Air SuperDrive ($79) is available from Apple.com (http://store.apple.com/us/product/MC684ZM/A), Apple Stores, or through authorized Apple resellers. Use the supplied USB cable to connect the drive to your MacBook Air so you can directly access CDs, DVDs, CD-ROMs, and DVD-ROMs.

 A USB thumb drive is a portable storage device that plugs into the USB port of a computer. They are inexpensive and come in a wide range of storage capacities, ranging from 512KB to 256GB (or larger). They're available wherever computer products are sold, including office supply stores. USB thumb drives typically work with both PCs and Macs interchangeably (depending on how they're formatted).

Download Any of Your Past iTunes Purchases

Thanks to iCloud, all of your past iTunes-related purchases (movies, TV show episodes, music, etc.) will be readily available from within iTunes on your MacBook Air. To access this content, even if it was purchased on your PC, launch iTunes on the MacBook Air.

Once iTunes is running, click on the iTunes Store option, and then click on the Purchased option. It's displayed on the right side of the screen, under the Quick Links heading. When prompted, enter your Apple ID and password.

From the Purchased screen (shown in Figure 3-17), click on the Music, Movies, TV Shows, Apps, or Books tab to view your purchases, and then click on specific items that you want to download from iCloud to your MacBook Air. For each item that didn't already transfer using the Migration Assistant software, click on the iCloud icon. There is no need to repurchase any of the content you already own.

FIGURE 3-17 All of your past iTunes content purchases can be downloaded directly onto your MacBook Air, regardless of whether it was originally bought on a PC, Mac, or iOS mobile device.

Transfer Your Data and Go

Once all of your data, files, and content are successfully transferred from your PC to your MacBook Air, you're ready to take the computer and go...from your desk at work to your home, from your home office to your couch, on a business trip, to your next class, to the beach, or just about anywhere you want or need access to your files, data, or the Internet.

Starting in Part II, you'll learn all about how to use the software that comes preinstalled on your MacBook Air, plus discover how to find, purchase, download, and install new software onto the computer so you can fully access and utilize your data and files.

To help you adjust to the layout and differences that OS X offers compared to Microsoft Windows, don't forget that Apple Stores nationwide offer free group workshops, including several that focus on getting started using OS X. To learn more about these workshops, visit www.apple.com/retail/workshops.

PART II

Discover the Mac OS X Mountain Lion Operating System

4

Set Up the Software that Comes with the MacBook Air

HOW TO...

- Configure the apps and software that come bundled with OS X Mountain Lion
- Set specific apps to work with Notification Center and iCloud
- Expand your MacBook Air's font library

Apple's OS X Mountain Lion operating system comes bundled with a collection of powerful applications, such as Contacts, Calendar, Reminders, App Store, FaceTime, Safari, Notes, and Time Machine. Each is designed to work seamlessly with the operating system itself, exchange data with each other (when applicable), and potentially sync with iCloud.

Because many of the preinstalled apps are customizable, you'll want to invest a few minutes as you begin using your new MacBook Air to adjust its various settings, so that the computer will function in a way that's most beneficial to your work habits and needs. This chapter will help you customize some of the popular apps that come preinstalled on your MacBook Air.

Customizing the Settings in System Preferences

While System Preferences (shown in Figure 4-1) functions like a stand-alone app, think of it as a control center for your MacBook Air.

System Preferences window

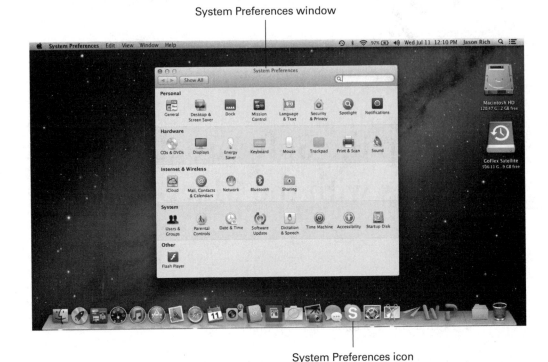

System Preferences icon

FIGURE 4-1   Launch System Preferences from the Dock, Launchpad, or from the Applications folder.

Options Available Under the Personal Heading of System Preferences

From the options listed under the Personal heading of System Preferences, you can adjust the appearance of various screens. Here's a quick rundown of what each of the options are used for:

- **General**   Adjust the general appearance of the desktop and various windows, including the color scheme used for buttons, icons, and windows. You can also control how large icons appear on the desktop, plus a handful of other appearance-related options.

From the General window in System Preferences, adding a checkmark to the Restore Windows When Quitting And Re-Opening Apps option, will cause OS X to remember what app or Finder windows were open anytime you shut down the computer or place it in Sleep mode. It will then automatically re-open those same windows when the computer is turned back on or when it's awakened from Sleep mode.

- **Desktop & Screen Saver**   Use this option to change the wallpaper graphic that's displayed on your desktop, as well as the animated screen saver that appears after a predetermined period of inactivity.
- **Dock**   Control the size of app icons displayed on the Dock, the location on the desktop where the Dock is displayed (the bottom of the screen, or along the right or left margin), as well as the visual effects used when the Dock is accessed. By adding a checkmark to the checkbox associated with the Automatically Hide And Show The Dock option (shown in Figure 4-2), you can save onscreen real estate by making the Dock disappear from the screen unless it's needed. To make it reappear, simply move the mouse cursor over the Dock's location.

To save space along the Dock when you minimize app or Finder windows, add a checkmark to Minimize Windows Into Application Icon. When an app-related window is minimized, it will then automatically be placed in the app icon on the Dock, as opposed to taking up its own space on the Dock.

- **Mission Control**   Customize settings related to the Mission Control feature of OS X, which allows you to quickly switch between windows, apps, or software that's running on your computer. Using Mission Control is one way to quickly switch between apps currently running on your MacBook Air.
- **Language & Text**   Choose the native language that your MacBook Air will utilize. The language is selected when you first set up your computer, but can be changed at any time. If you want to type in a foreign language using the MacBook Air's keyboard or an external keyboard, access the Language & Text option in System Preferences and click on the Input Sources tab. You can then choose the language and keyboard layout you want to use.

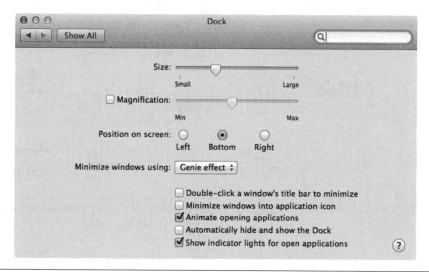

FIGURE 4-2   Control the location of the Dock, its appearance, as well as when it appears.

- **Security & Privacy** Determine when and if someone must enter a preselected password before accessing your MacBook Air. You can also adjust other security-related settings such as those related to your computer's firewall.
- **Spotlight** When performing a search using OS X's Spotlight search feature, determine which apps, databases, and files will be searched on your computer's hard drive. By default, all of the applications, files, documents, and folders are selected and searchable.
- **Notifications** Determine which apps and software the Notification Center will constantly monitor, and how many alerts, alarms, or notifications for each app will be displayed in the Notification Center window. For each app, you can also set up whether banners, alerts, or badges will be displayed in conjunction with alerts, alarms, and notifications generated (as shown in Figure 4-3).

 To learn more about Notification Center and the Notification Center window, see the section called "Stay Informed with Notification Center" in Chapter 2.

FIGURE 4-3 Highlight an app on the left side of the window, and then adjust its notifications-related settings on the right side of the window.

Did You Know?

What Banners, Alerts, and Badges Are and How to Use Them

Just like when using an iPad or iPhone, when an app running on your MacBook Air generates an alert, alarm, or notification that requires your attention, in addition to setting off an audible sound, you can set the app to display a banner, alert, and/or badge.

When an alert, alarm, or notification is generated by an app and you have it set up to display a banner, a small pop-up window will appear displaying text that's related to what needs your attention. The banner will only remain visible near the upper-right corner of the screen for a few seconds, and then it will automatically disappear.

If you have an app set up to display alerts, a small pop-up window will appear near the upper-right corner of the screen, but remain there until you manually dismiss it by clicking on an icon in the window.

In addition to or instead of a banner or alert, you can set up your MacBook Air to display a badge in the corner of the app icon when an alert, alarm, or notification is generated. Most apps will display a number in the tiny red badge icon, which indicates how many alerts have been generated (refer back to Figure 4-1 and look at the Mail app's icon on the Dock). However, a specific app may display a solid red dot or another symbol instead of a number.

If you set up badges to work with the Mail app, for example, whenever a new, unread incoming email is received, the badge will display the number of incoming messages in the Mail app icon that's displayed on the Dock.

From the Notifications window in System Preferences, it's possible to turn on or off banners, alerts, badges, and audio-based alarms for each compatible app that's installed on your computer.

Options Available Under the Hardware Heading of System Preferences

You can also make adjustments to MacBook Air–related hardware, such as the display, how the computer utilizes energy-saving features when operating on battery power, keyboard functionality, trackpad functionality, sound options, and the use of an optional printer or scanner. Here's a summary of the options available under the Hardware heading in System Preferences (refer back to Figure 4-1):

- **CDs & DVDs**   Unless you have an optional MacBook Air SuperDrive connected to your computer, these System Preferences settings are not relevant, and should be left at their default settings.

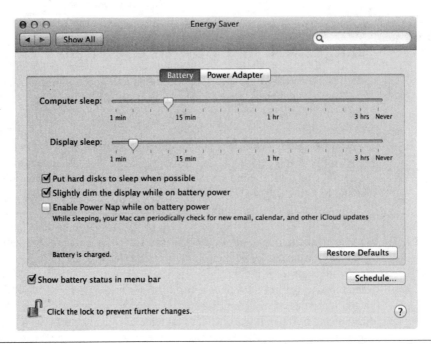

FIGURE 4-4   Determine when or if your MacBook Air will enter Sleep mode when it's running on battery or plugged into an electrical outlet.

- **Displays**   In addition to manually adjusting the screen brightness of the MacBook Air's built-in display, you can manually change the resolution. When applicable, you can also control the AirPlay Mirroring feature of OS X from this window. As long as you have the Automatically Adjust Brightness option selected (which is the default), you will rarely need to adjust the options found under this heading.
- **Energy Saver**   From the Energy Saver window (shown in Figure 4-4), you can determine how your MacBook Air behaves from a power management standpoint when it's running on battery, as well as when the power adapter is being used. You can change the settings for when the computer will automatically enter Sleep mode, and when the display will shut down due to inactivity in order to save battery power, and also decide whether or not the battery life indicator will be displayed on the right side of the menu bar.
- **Keyboard**   Adjust the options from this window to turn keyboard shortcuts on or off, plus manually adjust how the MacBook Air's keyboard behaves. Any customizations having to do with the keyboard's performance are done from this window.
- **Mouse**   Unless you connect a separate mouse to your MacBook Air, the options offered under this heading will not be used. If you do connect an optional mouse via a USB or Bluetooth connection, you can adjust its settings here.
- **Trackpad**   Learn how to use the finger gestures your Multi-Touch trackpad is capable of understanding, plus turn these gestures on or off. You can also set up an optional, external trackpad from this screen.

- **Print & Scan**   If you want to use a printer or scanner with your MacBook Air, you'll need to load the appropriate drivers from this window. However, if your printer or scanner offers downloadable setup software, chances are this software will automatically install the necessary drivers. Your MacBook Air can be set up to work with multiple printers and scanners simultaneously. From this window, you'll also need to select your default printer and paper size.
- **Sound**   Anything having to do with sound that's generated from your MacBook Air can be adjusted or controlled from this screen, including general output volume and alert volume. You can also opt to display a speaker icon on the right side of the menu bar, so you can manually adjust these options quicker. Or you can use the mute (F10), volume down (F11), or volume up (F12) function keys that are located along the top of the keyboard.

Options Available Under the Internet & Wireless Heading of System Preferences

Many of the apps and software you'll be using with your MacBook Air fully utilize the Internet. Plus, you can use your computer to surf the Web, manage emails, participate in web-based video conferences, and send and receive text messages.

The options under the Internet & Wireless heading of System Preferences are used to adjust settings related to your computer's Internet connection, as well as Bluetooth connectivity with various peripherals. Let's take a look at the options you can customize under this heading:

- **iCloud**   Manage how iCloud will function with your MacBook Air in general, as well as with specific preinstalled apps, such as Mail, Contacts, Calendars, Reminders, (Safari) Bookmarks, Notes, and Photo Stream (iPhoto). You'll learn more about using iCloud in Chapter 7.
- **Mail, Contacts & Calendars**   Use the options offered in this System Preferences window (shown in Figure 4-5) to create or delete email accounts that you want your MacBook Air to manage using the Mail app (and other compatible apps). You will need to enter details about each of your preexisting email accounts once, and then determine if you want the account to work with Messages and/or sync calendar and notes data (if applicable). You'll learn more about setting up email accounts to work with your MacBook Air in Chapter 11.
- **Network**   Your MacBook Air is capable of connecting to the Internet using a Wi-Fi connection. However, with an optional adapter, you can connect an Ethernet cable directly to the computer or plug in a wireless data modem via the USB port. The method you'll use to connect to the Internet can be set up from this window. If you're using a Wi-Fi connection, you should not have to make any changes to the default settings in this window.
- **Bluetooth**   If you plan to connect any Bluetooth devices to your MacBook Air, such as a wireless printer, headphones, headset, mouse, or external trackpad, you'll first need to turn on your computer's Bluetooth feature from this screen, and then "pair" each Bluetooth device to work with the computer.

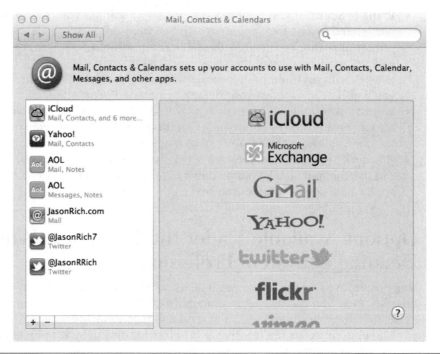

FIGURE 4-5 You'll need to set up each of your preexisting email accounts to work with your MacBook Air. This is done once from this Mail, Contacts & Calendars screen.

 If you're using a Bluetooth 4.0 compatible device, you will still need to turn on the Bluetooth feature of your MacBook Air, but pairing the device will not be necessary.

- **Sharing** On this screen you can decide what information from your computer will be accessible to others via the network should you opt to connect your MacBook Air to a wireless network. You can also set up remote access for specific users.

Options Available Under the System Heading of System Preferences

Under the System heading of System Preferences, you can customize various settings related to OS X operations and MacBook Air system maintenance. Here's a summary of what options you'll find:

- **Users & Groups** OS X allows you to set up your computer so that multiple users can utilize it. When each user signs in, all of the MacBook Air's settings will adjust to that user's saved preferences and settings. From this screen, it's possible to set up a Guest account, plus manage each user's unique password.

- **Parental Controls**   You can control what other users will be able to do when they use your MacBook Air, as well as limit certain abilities. For example, you can keep your children from making iTunes purchases or viewing TV show episodes or movies that contain inappropriate content. You can also block certain users from accessing the Internet.

Parental Controls is a password-regulated feature. As the primary computer user, it is essential that you do not forget your master password, or you too could get locked out from accessing features or content that you've blocked from your kids or other users.

- **Date & Time**   When connected to the Internet, your computer will automatically adjust the time and date. However, you can manually change this, as well as adjust the format used to display the time and date.
- **Software Update**   Using this feature, you can set up your MacBook Air to automatically check for OS X updates or new versions of software that's installed on your computer. Or you can manually check for updates by clicking on the Updates option in the Mac App Store, or by selecting the Software Update command from the Apple icon pull-down menu on the menu bar.
- **Dictation & Speech**   From this submenu in System Preferences (shown in Figure 4-6), you're able to customize settings related to the Mac's Dictation and Text To Speech features. Dictation allows you to speak to your computer and have what you say translated into text, and then inserted into the app you're using.

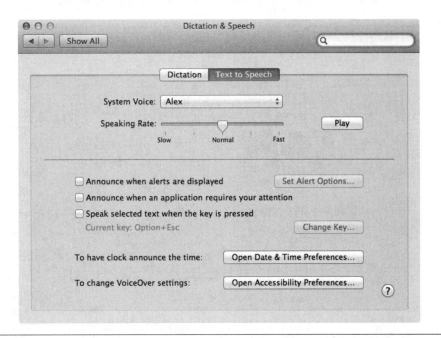

FIGURE 4-6   Customize the Dictation and Text To Speech features built into Mountain Lion from within System Preferences.

The Text To Speech feature allows your Mac to read aloud text that's displayed on the screen, using one of several computerized voices that you can select.

- **Time Machine**   Built into OS X is software that maintains a complete and automatic backup of your entire system, as long as it's connected to an external hard drive (via a USB or wireless connection). You are strongly advised to utilize this feature. It works with any external hard drive and can be customized by clicking on the Options icon (shown in Figure 4-7).

 Apple offers its own Time Capsule wireless hard drive ($299–$499, depending on capacity) that's designed to work with Time Machine. For more information, visit www.apple.com/timecapsule.

- **Accessibility**   The MacBook Air is designed to cater to the special needs of vision or hearing impaired people, as well as people with physical disabilities. Click on Accessibility to access and customize these features.
- **Startup Disk**   Select which drive or source your MacBook Air will initially boot from when turned on. The default is its internal hard drive. For most users, this option should not be changed.

 Displayed near the bottom of the System Preferences window is a heading labeled Other. Here, you'll find customization options for specific software that you install on your computer. Not all software, however, will have customizable options that are accessible from System Preferences. In most cases, you'll adjust the software-specific settings from within the program itself as necessary.

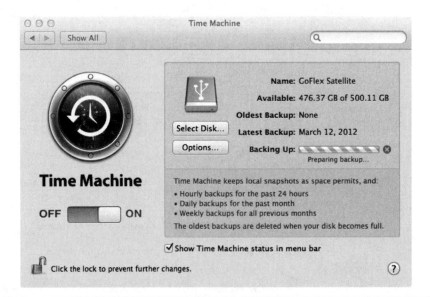

FIGURE 4-7   Set up Time Machine to maintain a complete backup of your MacBook Air. Files are saved to an external hard drive.

Customizing OS X's Preinstalled Apps

This section explains how to customize some of the more popular and frequently used apps that come preinstalled with OS X Mountain Lion.

For information about customizing and using the Mail app for managing one or more preexisting email accounts, see Chapter 11.

Customize Some Preinstalled Apps

Almost all of the apps that come preinstalled with OS X allow for some type of personalization or customization, which can be done from within the app itself while it's running. In some cases, even if iCloud functionality is turned on for your MacBook Air in general, you will still need to turn on iCloud functionality for specific apps, such as iPhoto, as well as the optional iWork apps (Pages, Numbers, and Keynote).

Typically, app-specific options that are customizable can be found by clicking on the Preferences option found under the pull-down menu on the menu bar that displays the app's name. For example, to access the Preferences options for Game Center, launch the Game Center app and then click on the Game Center pull-down menu. Likewise, after launching the Notes app, you can customize it from its Accounts menu.

From within System Preferences, click on the Dictation & Speech option to customize the Dictation and/or Text To Speech settings. Click on the Dictation button that's displayed near the top-center of the window (shown in Figure 4-8) to turn on Mountain Lion's Dictation feature, and then select the shortcut you'll use to access this feature, regardless of what app you're using.

The default keyboard shortcut to activate Dictation is to press the function (FN) key twice. You can also choose your native language and opt to use either the Mac's internal microphone or another microphone that's connected to your Mac.

The Dictation feature is used to speak directly into your computer, have the computer translate what you say into text, and then insert that text into the app you're using. To use the feature, click on the area within the app you're using where you want to input text. Press the function (FN) key twice to make the Dictation icon appear. When you hear the tone, start speaking for up to 30 seconds. Click the Done button when you're done speaking. As long as your Mac is connected to the Internet, the computer will translate what you said and insert the text into the appropriate location you selected.

(continued)

Click on the Text To Speech button within the Dictation & Speech window of System Preferences to set up how your computer can speak to you. Start by clicking on the pull-down menu that's associated with the System Voice option, and choose which computerized voice you want to use. Then, using the slider that's associated with the Speaking Rate option, make the necessary adjustments so you can understand what the computer is saying.

Now, on the bottom-half of the window, you can add checkmarks to various settings that allow the Mac to announce specific tidbits of information to you. For example, you can have the computer announce when alerts are displayed (as opposed to simply generating an audible tone). You can also have the computer speak to you when an app requires your attention.

Using a keyboard shortcut (that you select), you can also have the computer read aloud whatever text is displayed on the screen at any given time, regardless of what app you're using. Plus, you can have the Mac announce the time at predetermined intervals, such as every hour.

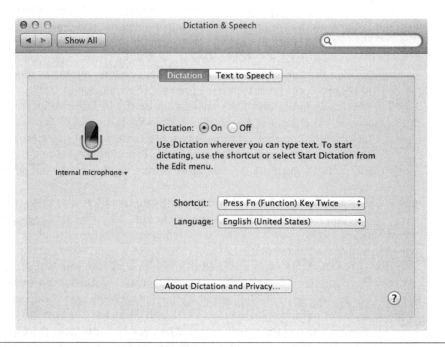

FIGURE 4-8 From System Preferences, you can customize the new Dictation feature that's built into Mountain Lion and that works with virtually all Mac apps.

FIGURE 4-9   Like many of the apps that come preinstalled with OS X, Contacts is customizable and can adapt to your personal needs.

Customizing the Contacts App

Once you launch the Contacts app, or most other apps for that matter, access the app pull-down menu to the immediate right of the Apple icon. It will display the name of the app itself. From this pull-down menu, select the Preferences option. This will grant you access to some of the app's customizable options (shown in Figure 4-9).

When you access the Preferences option in Contacts, you'll see four command tabs: General, Accounts, Template, and vCard.

Click on the General tab to determine how your contact entries will be sorted and what address format will be used globally throughout the app. By clicking on the Accounts tab, you can enable iCloud syncing or make the Contacts app sync with Google, Yahoo!, or another online-based contact management application you already use.

As you create new contact entries, the Contacts app will use a template that displays a handful of popular fields. You can customize these fields to better meet your own needs by clicking on the Template tab.

If you need to manually export one or more of your Contact entries, or the entire Contacts database, click on the vCard tab. From here, you can choose which export vCard file format to use, and determine whether or not photos and/or notes linked to entries will be exported as well.

 When actually using the Contacts app, you can adjust its onscreen appearance by selecting options on the View pull-down menu.

Customizing the Calendar App

Just like Contacts, you can adjust Calendar-related options once the app is running on your MacBook Air. Start by clicking on the Calendar pull-down menu from the menu bar, and then selecting the Preferences option. This time, you'll see four command tabs labeled General, Accounts, Advanced, and Alerts.

Click on the General tab to determine your default work week and what day the week will start on. You can also set your workday's start and end time, and determine if the app will display event times and birthdays (using data from the Contacts app).

In previous versions of the OS X operating system, the Calendar app was called iCal. The app's name was changed in OS X Mountain Lion, so that it more closely resembles the iPhone and iPad Calendar app (which this app can easily sync data with).

Click on the Accounts icon to set up iCloud functionality related to the Calendar app, as well as any other online-based accounts that may be applicable, such as Yahoo! or Google.

When you click on the Advanced icon, you can turn on or off Time Zone support, decide when and if events stored in your calendars will automatically delete themselves after a predetermined time period, and set up other features related to how information is displayed or imported into the app.

Time Zone Support is used to create Calendar events or appointments in a time zone other than the MacBook Air's default time zone, while still maintaining other events or appointments in your current time zone. This feature is useful if you're planning a schedule for a trip to a city or country in another time zone. For more information about Time Zone support, visit http://support.apple.com/kb/HT4504.

By clicking on the Alerts icon, you can set up when audible alerts will be used to notify you of specific types of events, such as birthdays.

When using the Calendar app, adjust the view of the onscreen calendars by clicking on the Day, Week, Month, or Year tab in the main Calendar app's window. You can also access the View pull-down menu from the menu bar to make adjustments.

Customizing the Dashboard

As you know from Chapter 2, the Dashboard allows you to display a handful of onscreen widgets, each of which handles specialized tasks. When looking at the Dashboard screen, you can manually move widgets around on the screen (shown in Figure 4-10) by placing the pointer on the widget, pressing and holding down the trackpad with your thumb, and simultaneously using your index finger to move the widget around.

To add new widgets, click on the plus sign icon that's displayed near the lower-left corner of the Dashboard screen. You can then choose from preinstalled widgets or access Apple's website (www.apple.com/downloads/dashboard) to download and install additional widgets.

To delete onscreen widgets, click on the minus sign icon that's also displayed near the lower-left corner of the screen. Upon doing this, small X icons will appear in the upper-left corner of each widget. Click on the X for each widget you want to remove from the Dashboard. Exit the Dashboard to save your changes.

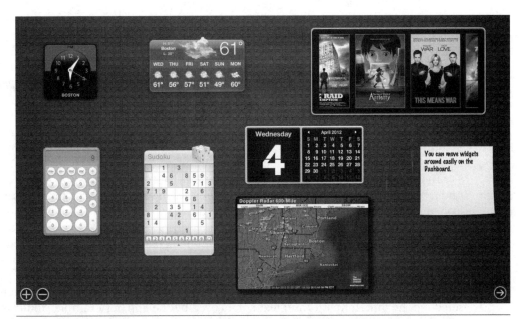

FIGURE 4-10   Customize the location of each widget on the screen, as well as which widgets are displayed.

Customizing the FaceTime App

Before you can begin participating in video conferences using Apple's FaceTime service and app, you'll need to initially set up the app. To do this, launch FaceTime, and when prompted, enter your Apple ID username and password.

By clicking on the FaceTime pull-down menu from the menu bar and selecting the Preferences option, you can add additional email addresses that people can use to contact you via FaceTime. Then, from the lower-right corner of the main FaceTime window, click on the Favorites icon to display and customize your Favorites list.

Favorites is a listing of people with whom you'll most often converse using FaceTime. It serves as a speed dial option for the app. To add people from your Contacts database to your Favorites list, click on the Favorites icon, and then click on the plus sign icon next to the Favorites heading. Choose a contact from your Contacts database (which is displayed in the FaceTime app), and then select the person's FaceTime ID or address.

See Chapter 17 for more information about using FaceTime to participate in online-based video conferences.

Customizing the Messages App

The Messages app is used to send and receive text messages with other Mac, iPhone, iPad, and iPod touch users. To use the app and Apple's free iMessage service, you'll first need to set up an account. To do this, launch the Messages app and supply your Apple ID and password.

The Messages app is also compatible with a handful of instant messaging services, including AIM, Yahoo! Instant Messenger, and Google Talk. If you already have accounts with any of these services, once you launch the Messages app, click on the Messages pull-down menu and select the Preferences option.

In the Preferences window, you'll see General, Accounts, Messages, Alerts, and Audio/Video icons. To add preexisting instant messaging accounts, click on the Accounts icon, and then click on the plus sign icon near the lower-left corner of the Accounts window.

By clicking on the General option, you can personalize what information will be displayed on the screen as you use the Messages app, as well as how your various instant messaging or text messaging accounts will behave.

Click on the Messages icon to customize the visual appearance of information by selecting the font, font size, and text colors used by the app, for example. You can also customize the audible alerts the app is able to generate by clicking on the Alerts icon.

If you'll be using the Messages app with an external microphone, speakers, or video camera, set up this optional equipment by clicking on the Audio/Video icon.

As you're using Messages, customize the photo and your own profile by selecting the Change My Picture or Change My Profile option from the Messages pull-down menu. From this menu, you can also personalize your current online status.

From the View pull-down menu, it's possible to manually adjust the size of text and what other applicable information is displayed in the Messages app, and/or switch the app into Full Screen mode (which can also be done by clicking on the Full Screen icon near the upper-right corner of the app's window).

 While Messages is running, access the other pull-down menus that are accessible from the menu bar to further customize the appearance and functionality of the app, as well as options related to the online-based services it's designed to be used with.

Customizing the Font Book

Built into OS X is a library of preinstalled fonts that are compatible with a wide range of apps and software you'll be using with your MacBook Air. The data files associated with each font are stored in the Font Book.

From System Preferences or from the Launchpad, you can directly access the Font Book in order to manage the fonts stored on your computer or to install additional fonts.

Once Font Book is launched (shown in Figure 4-11), click on the Preferences option (found under the Font Book pull-down menu) to adjust some of the app's customizable settings. For example, you can set up the app to automatically install new fonts that are downloaded to the MacBook Air. You can also have the app automatically delete duplicate fonts.

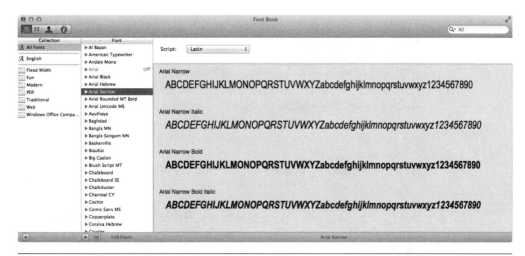

FIGURE 4-11 Manage the library of fonts that can be utilized by OS X and the software installed on your MacBook Air.

From the Preferences window in Font Book (select the Font Book pull-down menu from the menu bar), you can set the Default Install Location for your newly added fonts to be Computer or User. If you select Computer, the newly added fonts will be accessible from all user accounts of your MacBook Air. By selecting User, fonts added will be accessible only by the user who installed them.

From the main Font Book app window, click on any font name to preview what the font looks like in the right side of the window. You can also use this app to organize your fonts into collections or libraries, based on type or appearance, for example.

 Install New Fonts onto Your MacBook Air

During the installation process for new software, new fonts will sometimes automatically be installed onto your computer as well. These fonts are added for use by the software you're installing, but once they're added to your computer's Font Book, they also become accessible from other apps and software running on your computer.

To manually install new fonts, you can download them from a wide range of websites. Some companies charge for fonts. However, there are many websites that offer free downloadable fonts, such as www.1001fonts.com.

(continued)

When browsing for fonts to download, make sure you select Mac TrueType font files. When you download a new font file, it will most likely wind up in your Downloads folder.

To install the font on your MacBook Air and add it to your Font Book, double-click on the downloaded file. If it's a .SIT file, it will need to be decompressed. The Font Book app will launch, and if you have the auto-install feature turned on, the font you just downloaded will be installed and saved in the Font Book app. Otherwise, you will be prompted to install the font.

Now when you use any app or software that allows you to select a font, such as Microsoft Word, when you click on the font selection pull-down menu, the newly downloaded font will be listed and accessible (see Figure 4-12).

Using any Internet search engine, enter the search phrase "free Mac fonts," and you'll discover many websites that offer free, downloadable fonts, as well as individual specialized fonts or font collections that can be purchased. Fonts.com is an excellent resource for learning about free and purchasable fonts.

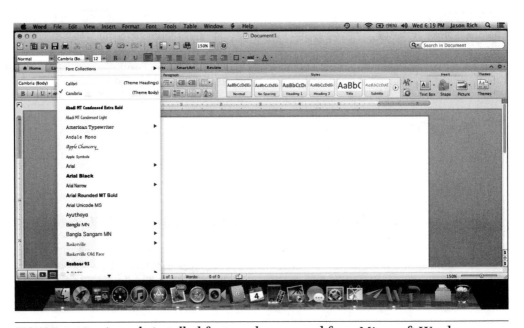

FIGURE 4-12 A newly installed font can be accessed from Microsoft Word or any software that allows you to pick and choose fonts.

Customizing Your MacBook Air's Apps Offers Many Benefits

There are many reasons why it's a good idea to spend some time customizing the various apps you'll be using with your MacBook Air. Not only will you have more personalized access to the information you need, it will be displayed in a format that's conducive to your work habits and personal preferences. You'll also be able to find and utilize information and apps faster.

When using the Contacts app, for example, by customizing the template settings, you can pick and choose which data fields will automatically be displayed for each contact entry. Thus, you'll be able to personalize how the contact-related information that's important to you is displayed. Of course, as you're creating a single new contact entry, you can always manually add or remove specific data fields, but adjusting the template allows you to focus on which data fields are most essential to you personally.

Likewise, by adjusting the Notification Center options, you can pick and choose which apps will be monitored, and then control what information will appear in the Notification Center window. This allows you to weed out unimportant information from apps that you don't deem as essential when it comes to being alerted by app-specific alarms or notifications.

Once you get the preinstalled apps working in a way that's best for you, you can easily figure out what additional software you want or need to install on your MacBook Air to give you all the functionality you desire. Finding, purchasing, downloading, and installing optional software are the focus of the next chapter.

5

Install New Software
onto Your MacBook Air

HOW TO...

- Find, download, and install software using the App Store
- Download and install software from the Web
- Install software from a MacBook Air SuperDrive or USB thumb drive
- Install software by sharing a SuperDrive with an iMac or MacBook Pro

In addition to the impressive collection of software that came preinstalled on your MacBook Air, you'll probably want to install and use some optional software. Thanks to the ongoing and increasing popularity of Macs, the selection of Mac software is constantly expanding. You'll find Mac versions of popular Windows-based software, as well as plenty of software that was designed exclusively for the Mac.

Six Options for Installing New Software onto Your MacBook Air

When it comes to installing new software onto your MacBook Air, you have six options:

- Launch the App Store from your MacBook Air that's connected to the Internet to find, purchase, download, and install software sold through Apple's online-based software store. (The App Store also offers a selection of free Mac software, as well as demo or trial versions of purchasable software.)
- Download and install software directly from a website. For example, you can visit a software developer's website to purchase and download software. The easiest way to acquire Microsoft Office for Mac and install it on your MacBook Air is to acquire it from the Microsoft website directly (www.microsoft.com/mac).

In addition to visiting a software developer's website to purchase, download, and install software, there are other online-based services, such as CNET's Download .com (www.download.com), that offer vast selections of Mac software, either for free or to purchase. You'll also find top-quality, open source Mac software (available for free) from websites like: www.freesmug.org, www.libreoffice.org, www.openoffice.org/porting/mac/download, and http://mac.appstorm.net/general/60-open-source-and-free-mac-apps.

- Purchase and connect the optional Apple SuperDrive to your MacBook Air ($79, http://store.apple.com/us/product/MC684ZM/A), and then load purchased software from a CD (or DVD).

Some Microsoft Windows-based software that's distributed on CD (or DVD) also includes a Mac version of that same software. So, if you're migrating from a PC to the MacBook Air, determine if you already own Mac versions of the software you're currently using on your PC.

- Transfer software from another Mac to a USB thumb drive, insert the thumb drive into the USB port of your MacBook Air, and then install the software from it.
- Link your MacBook Air to your iMac desktop computer or MacBook Pro, and then share that computer's SuperDrive to install CD- or DVD-based software on your MacBook Air.
- Connect your MacBook Air to a network and install apps from a network drive.

Whichever methods you use to install new software on your MacBook Air, once you find the software you want or need, you'll discover the installation process is straightforward. All software that you install onto your MacBook Air should be placed in the Applications folder, so you'll be able to find and launch it easily.

Once the software is installed and stored in the MacBook Air's Applications folder, double-click on the app icon to launch it. Or drag the software's app icon to the Dock if you plan to use the program often and want easy accessibility. Another option is to launch software from the Launchpad.

Shopping at Apple's Online-Based App Store

Without ever leaving your home or office, as long as your MacBook Air is connected to the Internet, you can access Apple's own App Store (shown in Figure 5-1) to find, purchase, download, and install software directly onto your MacBook Air.

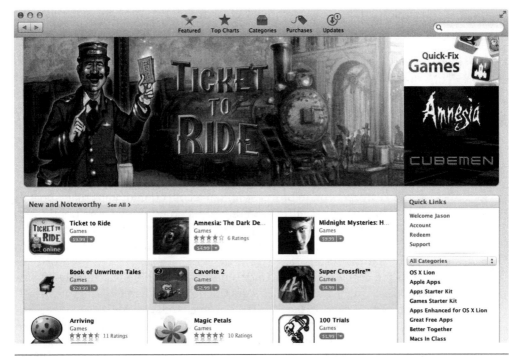

FIGURE 5-1   The App Store is a one-stop online shop for finding, buying, and installing Mac software.

   The benefit to buying software from the App Store is that the online-based store keeps track of your purchases, and allows you to download and automatically install future updates for these purchases from one centralized location. Plus, once you purchase software on one Mac from the App Store, you can download and install it on other Macs that are linked to the same Apple ID account so you don't need to repurchase the same application for multiple computers (such as your iMac and MacBook Air).

The App Store is accessible using the App Store app that comes preinstalled with OS X. Its selection of software is constantly expanding. With your MacBook Air connected to the Internet, from the Dock, click on the App Store icon to launch it. Keep in mind, if you're also an iPhone, iPad, or iPod touch user, the App Store for these devices is different from the App Store, which only sells Mac software.

Near the top of the App Store window, you'll see five command icons displayed (refer back to Figure 5-1): Featured, Top Charts, Categories, Purchases, and Updates. Use these command options to quickly navigate your way around the online store to find exactly the software you're looking for, or determine what your options are if you're looking for a certain type of software, but don't know the name of a specific software title.

The following is a quick summary of what the five App Store command icons are used for.

Tip   If you already know the title of the software you want to purchase and download, enter it into the Search field in the upper-right corner of the App Store window. You can also use this Search field to enter a keyword or phrase that describes the desired software; the type of software you're looking for, such as word processing or strategy games; or the name of a software developer, such as Adobe.

Learn About Featured Software

Click on the Featured icon to browse through a collection of apps that Apple deems worthy of attention. The Featured screen is divided into several sections, including New and Noteworthy, What's Hot, and Staff Favorites (shown in Figure 5-2). Browsing these sections is a great way to learn about new or popular Mac software from all of the different software categories.

Below each of the sections are a dozen software listings. Each listing focuses on one software package, and includes a graphic icon, the name of the software, the software's category, its average star-based rating, and its price.

To learn more about any specific software package, from its listing click on its graphic icon or title. A detailed product description will be displayed. The software showcased in the Featured section can be from any category. Figure 5-3 shows a sample software listing.

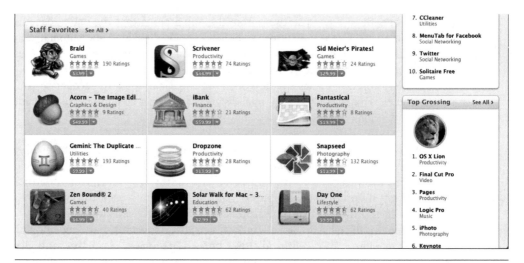

FIGURE 5-2   Click on the Featured icon, and then scroll down toward the bottom of the screen to view the current Staff Favorites.

FIGURE 5-3   A sample software listing in the App Store

When you initially look under the Featured heading, a dozen app software listings will be displayed. To view all of the software being featured by Apple, click on the See All option that's displayed to the immediate right of the New and Noteworthy, What's Hot, and Staff Favorites headings.

Displayed along the right margin of the Featured page are Quick Links, as well as popular software category headings. Scroll down to view a listing of Top Paid (shown in Figure 5-4), Top Free, and Top Grossing apps. These listings are based on current user popularity, sales, or downloads, and the lists change frequently.

For each chart, the top 10 software packages are listed along the right margin of the Featured page. To view the top 180 or so software packages from a particular list, click on the See All option next to the Top Paid, Top Free, and Top Grossing headings.

 The apps showcased on the Featured page change regularly.

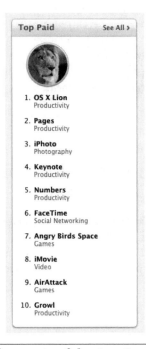

FIGURE 5-4   Look to the right margin of the App Store's window to quickly access the Top Paid, Top Free, and Top Grossing software.

How to...

Purchase and Download Software from the App Store

As you're looking at a software listing in the App Store, if you want to immediately purchase that software, click on its price icon. Upon doing this, the price icon will turn green and say Buy App.

You can also purchase software from the detailed Description page for a software application. Near the top-left corner of the Description screen will also be a price icon. When you click on it, it will turn green and say Buy App.

Click on this Buy App icon to initiate the purchase. When prompted, enter your Apple ID and password. The software will be purchased (using the credit or debit card that's linked to your Apple ID account), and automatically begin downloading onto your computer.

When the download process is complete, the software installation process will automatically begin. Follow the onscreen prompts to install the newly downloaded software. This will often require you to enter your computer's master password when prompted. This is the password you created when you first set up the MacBook Air. It is different from your Apple ID's password.

As you're looking at a software listing, immediately to the right of the listed price within the price icon will be a down-arrow icon. Click on it to reveal two options: Copy Link and Tell A Friend. The Copy Link option allows you to store the link for the specific page you're looking at, without making a purchase. The Tell A Friend option allows you to send an email to someone about the software you're currently looking at.

If software is offered for free from the App Store, instead of displaying a price within the price icon, the word Free will appear. The process for downloading free software is the same as downloading purchased software, but you will not have to pay for it.

See the Best-Selling Mac Software by Viewing the Top Charts

The Featured page of the App Store showcases software that Apple recommends. However, by clicking on the Top Charts icon in the App Store, you will see detailed listings for the Top Paid, Top Free, and Top Grossing apps available. These listings are compiled based on purchases and downloads from fellow Mac users, not Apple's recommendations.

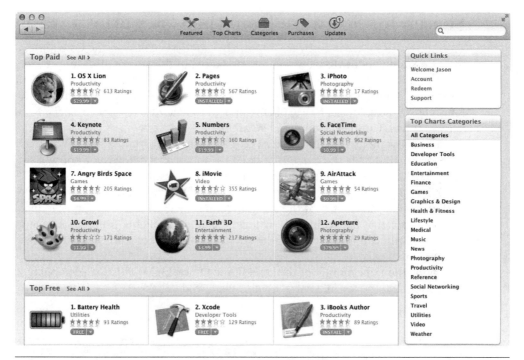

FIGURE 5-5   View a more comprehensive listing of Top Paid, Top Free, and Top Grossing apps by clicking on the Top Charts icon.

Shown in Figure 5-5, displayed in order of popularity, the Top Paid section shows the top 12 most purchased Mac software packages available from the App Store.

The Top Free section shows the top 12 most downloaded free Mac software packages (apps) available from the App Store. These free apps may be stand-alone programs, or they could be demo or trial versions of paid programs. It's important to read the descriptions to see what you're downloading.

The Top Grossing section lists the top 12 highest revenue generating software packages available from the App Store. To achieve a top ranking on this list, a software package will be extremely popular or extremely high priced. After all, a software package priced at $19.99 will need to sell many more copies than a software package priced at $199 or $899 to be included on this list. The Top Grossing section includes in-app purchases, as well as the actual purchase price of the software.

Click on the See All option next to the Top Paid, Top Free, or Top Grossing heading to view the top 180 listings for that category.

The apps featured in the Top Charts lists change constantly, as their rankings change based on sales and downloads.

Search for Software from the Categories Listings

The App Store sorts the software it offers by category. Click on the Categories icon in the App Store window to view a complete listing of the store's 21 different categories.

As shown in Figure 5-6, App Store categories include Business, Developer Tools, Education, Entertainment, Finance, Games, Graphics & Design, Health & Fitness, Lifestyle, Medical, Music, News, Photography, Productivity, Reference, Social Networking, Sports, Travel, Utilities, Video, and Weather.

The software listing displayed as part of each Category heading in the main Categories window is the current bestselling app in that category. Choose a software category that interests you, based on the type of software you're looking for.

When a specific category is selected, you'll discover listings for the top five apps in that category at the top of the screen. Below it will be a comprehensive listing of all other apps that fall within that category that are available from the App Store. Click on the See All icon to the right of the All [Category Name] Apps heading to see the comprehensive list.

Along the right margin of the screen, the Quick Links, a listing of popular software categories, and the top 10 charts are also displayed.

FIGURE 5-6   Choose one of 21 different categories to begin your search for the software you want or need for your MacBook Air.

Additional Software Categories Are Listed Along the Right Margin of the App Store

Located just below the Quick Links heading along the right margin of the App Store window is a menu that offers 10 additional software categories. These are categories created by Apple that change periodically.

The OS X Mountain Lion category brings you right to the Description page for upgrading your MacBook Air from OS X Lion to OS X Mountain Lion. The Apple Apps category showcases a collection of Mac software created and published by Apple, including the latest versions of iPhoto, iMovie, GarageBand, Pages, Numbers, Keynote, Aperture, Final Cut Pro, and iBooks Author.

The Apps Starter Kit category includes a list of app suggestions for new Mac users, while the Games Starter Kit category showcases a collection of popular games for first-time or novice gamers. You'll also discover category headings that group together popular apps used for a specific purpose, such as Macs In Class or Apps For Photographers.

For almost any task that your MacBook Air is capable of, chances are there are multiple software packages available from the App Store (or elsewhere) that can handle those tasks. Browsing the App Store by category allows you to learn about multiple apps that may serve similar purposes, or that will address your needs using a slightly different collection of features and functions.

Review and Access Your App Store Purchases

Just like the iTunes Store, the App Store keeps track of your past software purchases. This allows you to re-download past purchases anytime on any Mac that's linked to the same Apple ID account.

So, if you've already purchased several software packages for your iMac desktop computer, click on the Purchases icon in the App Store's window to view a listing of those purchases (shown in Figure 5-7), and then download the same apps, for free, to your MacBook Air (or vice versa).

Tip

Downloading and installing software is a two-step process. Once software is purchased, on the Purchases screen, you will see an icon that says Download. This means the software is available, but needs to be downloaded to your MacBook Air. Once downloaded, the icon will say Install. Click on it to actually install the newly downloaded software on your computer. After this process is done, the icon displayed to the right of an app's listing on the Purchases screen will say Installed, meaning it's already installed on the computer you're currently using.

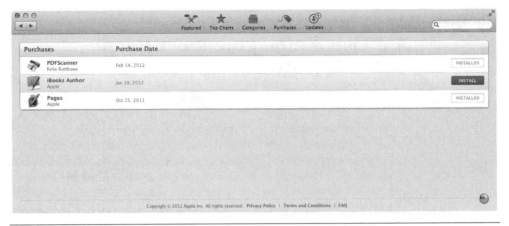

FIGURE 5-7 Access past purchases to re-download them or download and install them on another Mac that's linked to the same Apple ID account.

Keep Your Apps Up to Date Using the Updates Feature

One of the benefits of purchasing and downloading software from the App Store is that it keeps track of new updates that are available for the various software packages you've purchased or downloaded for free. By clicking on the Updates icon in the App Store window you can determine if any of the software you've purchased requires an update and, if so, download and install those updates from one central screen.

How to... ## Manage Your Apple ID Account from the App Store

Your Apple ID account is linked to a major credit card or debit card. All of your online purchases from the App Store, iTunes Store, and Apple's other online ventures are automatically billed to the credit or debit card on file. To manage your Apple ID account, under the Quick Links heading in the App Store, click on the Account option, which is displayed along the right margin of the App Store window.

If you have received a prepaid iTunes gift card, you can redeem it while shopping from the App Store. Click on the Redeem option that's also displayed under the Quick Links heading. To receive online support related to the App Store, click on the Support option. It too is displayed under the Quick Links heading.

If you've forgotten your Apple ID or its password, or you still need to set up a free Apple ID account, visit https://appleid.apple.com using the Safari web browser.

Download and Install Software Directly from the Web

Some software developers that sell or distribute Mac software have decided to make their offerings available directly from their own websites as opposed to the App Store. Thus, you can also download and install software directly from the Web.

To do this, you'll use the Safari web browser (or another Mac-compatible web browser, such as Firefox or Chrome). Visit the website where the software you want is being offered. Purchase the software online using a major credit or debit card, if applicable, and when prompted, download the software to your MacBook Air by clicking on the appropriate Download link.

The downloaded file will wind up in your Downloads folder (unless you direct it elsewhere). Once the file is downloaded, access your Downloads folder using Finder, and double-click on the downloaded file. If the file had been compressed into a .SIT or .ZIP file, you'll need to decompress it before installing it. You may need to download free decompression software such as StuffIt Expander for Mac (www.stuffit.com/mac-stuffit.html).

Once a downloaded application is ready to be installed, you'll see a file with the .dmg extension listed in your Downloads folder. Double-click on this file or icon. A Finder window will open and you can run the Installer for the application you've downloaded so that the installation process begins. Or you will be prompted to drag the app icon into your Applications folder. If prompted, enter the master password for your computer. You'll need to select the destination drive where the software will be installed. This should be the main hard drive of your MacBook Air.

Most Mac software will automatically install itself in the Applications folder on your computer. However, as you're installing some software, you may be required to manually drag the app icon into your Applications folder.

 When you purchase and download some Mac software, you'll be provided with an unlock or registration key. This can be a long chain of numbers and/or letters. The first time you run the newly installed software, you may be required to manually enter this key when prompted. When doing this, keep in mind that the letters are typically case-sensitive, so pay attention to capital letters versus lowercase letters, as well as any spaces or dashes between sets of numbers and/or letters. To save time, you can copy and paste this registration key or unlock code from one location (such as an incoming email) to the proper field in the app.

Installing Software Using the MacBook Air's Optional SuperDrive

Available from Apple Stores, Apple.com, and wherever Apple computers are sold, the MacBook Air SuperDrive ($79, http://store.apple.com/us/product/MC684ZM/A) is an optional CD/DVD drive that attaches to your computer via a supplied USB cable.

In addition to using this drive to watch DVD movies from your MacBook Air, it can be used to install software that's distributed on CD. Mac software purchased from retail stores, such as an Apple Store, Best Buy, OfficeMax, or Staples, is typically distributed on CD and will require the optional SuperDrive to install.

Once the SuperDrive is connected to your MacBook Air, insert the supplied software CD into the drive, and follow the onscreen prompts for installing the newly acquired software onto your MacBook Air.

Install Software from a USB Thumb Drive

If you also own another Mac, such as an iMac desktop computer, some software applications allow you to copy the .dmg file that's associated with an app from one location to another. In this case, you can plug a USB thumb drive into your iMac, and then copy the appropriate software to it.

 USB thumb drives are also called USB flash drives.

Next, eject the thumb drive from your iMac by highlighting the drive on your desktop and pressing the eject button on the keyboard, or by dragging the icon for the USB drive to the iMac's Trash on the Dock.

Once ejected, remove the thumb drive from your iMac's USB port and plug it into your MacBook Air's USB port. An icon for the thumb drive will appear on your MacBook Air's desktop. Double-click on this icon to display its contents in a Finder window.

Locate the .dmg file for the software you want to install and double-click on it. You can then click on the Install icon or drag the program icon into your Applications folder. The normal software installation process will begin.

 Some software is distributed in a way that cannot be easily copied from one drive to another. This includes many software packages available from Adobe (such as Photoshop), for example. In this case, you will need to either download the software from the developer's website, find another online source to download the software from, or install it from a CD.

 Yet another easy way to transfer many programs from one Mac to another is to use the optional j5 Create Wormhole cable (http://j5create.com/juc400.htm), which allows you to connect two Macs via a supplied USB cable, and then simply drag and drop program (.dmg) files, data files, photos, music, movies, and other content between computers.

Link Your MacBook Air to an iMac or MacBook Pro to Share a SuperDrive

To make the MacBook Air as thin and compact as it is, Apple had to forego incorporating a SuperDrive into the computer. However, if you want to install software onto your MacBook Air from a CD, one option is to link your MacBook Air to your iMac or MacBook Pro via a wireless network, and then wirelessly share that computer's SuperDrive.

In order to link your MacBook Air to your iMac or MacBook Pro that contains a SuperDrive or optical drive, you'll use the DVD/CD Sharing feature that's built into OS X. For this feature to work, both computers must be connected to the same wireless network, and both computers need to be running OS X Lion or OS X Mountain Lion.

Once the two computers are linked to the same wireless network, on your iMac (or MacBook Pro), launch System Preferences and select the Sharing option. On the left side of the Sharing window (shown in Figure 5-8), select the DVD Or CD Sharing option. Exit out of System Preferences.

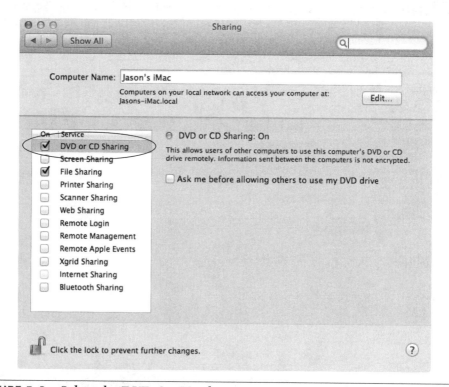

FIGURE 5-8   Select the DVD Or CD Sharing option from the Sharing window on your iMac or MacBook Pro that contains a SuperDrive.

Now, on the MacBook Air, launch System Preferences. On the left side of the Sharing window, select File Sharing. Exit out of System Preferences.

Next, insert a CD or DVD into the SuperDrive or optical drive installed in your iMac or MacBook Pro. Then, on your MacBook Air, launch Finder. In the sidebar of the Finder window, under the Devices heading, will be an option that says Remote Disc. Click on it. On the right side of the Finder window, a graphic icon and/or the name of the CD that's been inserted into the iMac or MacBook Pro's SuperDrive will be displayed (shown in Figure 5-9). Double-click on it.

At this point, a CD-shaped icon will appear on your desktop and the contents of the CD will be displayed in the Finder window that's open on your MacBook Air. When this occurs, your MacBook Air is "borrowing" or sharing the SuperDrive or optical drive that's installed in your iMac or MacBook Pro.

If the software on the CD doesn't begin auto-installing, click on the Install icon for the software that's on the CD, and follow the onscreen prompts. From this point forward, your MacBook Air will act as if a SuperDrive is connected directly to it.

 In addition to DVD and CD sharing, you can also activate file sharing, printer sharing, scanner sharing, Bluetooth sharing, and a handful of other options that allow you to easily share hardware between an iMac, MacBook Pro, a Windows-based PC, and your MacBook Air. All of these settings can be adjusted in the Sharing window of System Preferences.

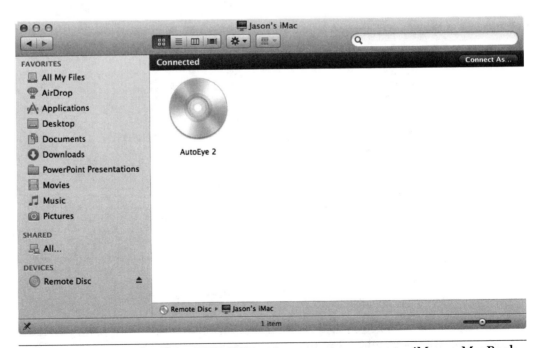

FIGURE 5-9 Using the Share DVD/CD option you can access your iMac or MacBook Pro's SuperDrive or optical drive to install software on your MacBook Air.

How to Learn About New Mac Software

In addition to keeping an eye on the New & Noteworthy section of the App Store, you can learn all about new Mac software from a wide range of printed Mac-related computer magazines such as *Macworld* and *Mac|Life*, or access websites, blogs and other online resources that review Mac software.

The following are some additional online resources for finding, learning about, purchasing, and/or downloading Mac software:

- **Amazon.com: The Mac Software Store**   www.amazon.com/software (click on the Mac option)
- **Apple Insider**   www.appleinsider.com
- **CNet's Download.com**   http://download.cnet.com/mac
- **Mac Games Store**   www.macgamestore.com
- **Mac|Life**   www.maclife.com
- **MacMall**   www.macmall.com (click on the Mac software option)
- **Macworld**   www.macworld.com
- **Softpedia**   http://mac.softpedia.com

 Microsoft (www.microsoft.com) directly offers the Microsoft Office for Mac suite of software. Adobe (www.adobe.com) directly offers several photography, graphics, and publishing software solutions, such as Photoshop and Photoshop Elements for the Mac. Intuit (www.intuit.com) is the publisher of Quicken and QuickBooks, two popular bookkeeping and financial management software packages available for PCs and Macs. Electronic Arts (EA) is a popular computer game developer that offers Mac-based games (www.ea.com/mac).

6

Transferring and Organizing Data, Files, and Folders

HOW TO...

- Move data, files, and content between folders and elsewhere on your MacBook Air
- Use an external hard drive or storage device with the computer
- Transfer files, data, and content between computers

Just like any computer, your MacBook Air allows you to work with your personal data, databases you create, and many types of other files. In some cases, files are kept by themselves. Others are grouped together into folders. To help differentiate between data types, files are given different extensions.

The Finder that's built into the OS X operating system is used to manage your computer's files and folders. From within Finder, you can view filenames and file-related icons, rename files, delete files, copy files, move files around, email files as attachments to others, label files with a highlighted color around the filename, and open files in appropriate applications. You can also create folders, organize them, and view their contents.

To use many of these features in Finder, launch Finder, highlight a file, folder name, or icon, and then click on the Action icon (the gear-shaped icon) in the Finder window (shown in Figure 6-1). You can also access this menu by launching Finder, highlighting a file, folder name, or icon, and then holding down the control key while simultaneously clicking on the trackpad.

Tip While the Finder allows you to view filenames and file-related icons, to actually view many types of text or graphic files (including digital photos), you'll use the Quick Look feature or Preview app that also comes preinstalled on your MacBook Air. You can also use software designed to handle that type of file. For example, if you have a .doc or .txt file, which is a text-based document, you can open it in Microsoft Word, Pages, or another compatible application, or view it with Preview of OS X's Quick Look feature.

Action icon

FIGURE 6-1   Manage files or folders by highlighting them in Finder, and then clicking on the gear-shaped Action icon or pressing the control key while clicking on the trackpad.

Regardless of what type of computer you're using, you'll definitely find it beneficial to keep your files and folders well organized. This is why Finder comes with several main folders, including Applications, Desktop, Documents, Downloads, Music, Movies, and Pictures, which have been precreated on your behalf.

Note   From within Finder, you have the option to create an unlimited number of additional main folders, as well as subfolders in main folders, in order to properly organize your data and files.

How to...   ## Create a New Folder or Subfolder

As you're working with Finder, to create a new folder from scratch, go to the location where you want to create the folder. Click on the File pull-down menu (from the menu bar) and select the New Folder option. A new folder will appear within the Finder and be placed in the folder or directory that is currently being viewed.

(continued)

The new folder will have the default name Untitled Folder, which will be highlighted in blue. While the folder name is highlighted, simply type the new, custom folder name you want, and then click the trackpad to save your update. The new folder, with your customized folder name, will now be displayed within Finder.

Double-click on the folder to open it. It's now possible to copy and paste or drag and drop existing files or other folders into this newly created folder, or as you're using various apps, save new files or data in the new folder using the Save or Save As command.

To quickly rename a folder within Finder, highlight it by moving the pointer over the folder name or icon and clicking once. When the folder name is highlighted in blue, press the return key or click the pointer again. Then type a new folder name. Click the trackpad again to save your changes.

To delete a folder from within Finder, drag and drop it into the Trash icon on the Dock. An alternative is to select and highlight the folder, click on the File pull-down menu from the menu bar, and select the Move To Trash option. Or select and highlight the folder within Finder, click on the gear-shaped icon (or press COMMAND [⌘] and at the same time click on the trackpad), and choose the Move To Trash option. To delete a highlighted folder (or file), you can also use the COMMAND (⌘)-DELETE keyboard shortcut.

Regardless of which method you use to manage your files and folders, it's important that you become familiar with and proficient using the Finder application that's built into OS X Mountain Lion.

Quick Tips for Using Finder

As you're using Finder, it's easy to customize some of its features by clicking on the Finder pull-down menu from the menu bar, and then selecting Preferences (shown in Figure 6-2). Click on the General icon, for example, and opt to display folders and devices on your desktop, as well as in the sidebar of the Finder window.

 When using Finder, you can control the appearance of folder and filename icons, and alter their arrangement, labels, and color scheme. To do this, access the View pull-down menu and select Show View Options. Or when a filename or folder is highlighted, use the COMMAND (⌘)-J keyboard shortcut.

Use the options under the Labels icon to customize the label that's associated with each color that you can later link with filenames and icons as a visual tool within Finder. For example, you can associate the color red with the label Urgent. Then you can later color-code specific files or folders in red and know they're important. There are seven different color-coding options available.

General command
icon

Finder Preferences
window

FIGURE 6-2 From Finder Preferences, you can customize various features of Finder and how it displays file- and folder-related information.

To associate a color with a file or folder, select and highlight it within Finder, and then either click on the gear-shaped icon in the Finder window, or press the control key while clicking the trackpad. From the menu that appears, click on a color icon that's displayed below the Label heading. As you drag the pointer over each color, the label you previously associated with that color in Finder Preferences will be displayed.

Click on the Sidebar icon (shown in Figure 6-3) to determine what favorites, shared devices, and devices will be displayed in the sidebar of the Finder window. Then click on the Advanced icon to determine if you want filename extensions displayed in the Finder window. These are just some of the customizable options available from the Finder Preferences menu option.

As you're becoming familiar with how to use Finder, it's easier to identify many types of files if you utilize the Show Icons option, which displays each file or folder in the Finder window as a graphic icon, as well as showing its file or folder name.

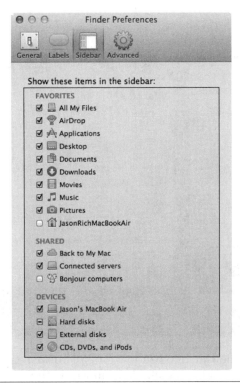

FIGURE 6-3   Determine what information Finder will display in the easily accessible sidebar of the window.

As you're viewing the Finder window, once you highlight and select any file, click on the gear-shaped Action icon or press the control key at the same time you click the trackpad, and then choose the Open With command to open that file in a specific application. The compatible apps that are stored on your MacBook Air will be displayed. If you use the Open command, the file will open in whatever the default app is for that type of file. Double-clicking on the icon is the same as using the Open command.

 By default, when you select the Open command in Finder, many types of document, photo, and graphic files will open in the Preview app.

To view more information about a file and edit certain details relating to it, click on the Get Info command in Finder. A separate pop-up window (shown in Figure 6-4) will appear that contains details about that particular file. While much of the information in this window is non-changeable, you can alter the Label, Name, and Extension of the file, as well as the default Open With app. If applicable, you can also adjust Sharing and Permission options related to that single file.

Get Info window   Finder window

FIGURE 6-4 The Get Info window for a file displays detailed information about that file, some of which is editable from within the window.

 To find the Get Info command, access the File pull-down menu from the menu bar and select the Get Info option, or use the COMMAND (⌘)-I keyboard shortcut when a folder or filename is highlighted.

To quickly find a file or content in a file or folder, use the Search field displayed near the upper-right corner of the Finder window, and type a keyword or search phrase relating to what you're looking for, such as a filename. If you're looking for all files with a particular extension, for example, simply enter that extension (such as .doc or .pdf) in the Search field. Your search results will be displayed in the Finder window.

 To learn more about the many features and functions offered in Finder, visit http://support.apple.com/kb/HT2470.

You Can Easily Remove Items from the Trash or Undo Mistakes When Using Finder

As you're learning to use Finder, you can always use the Undo command (available from the Edit pull-down menu on the menu bar) to undo your last action.

If you've accidently sent a file to the Trash, unless you've already used the Empty Trash command (found under the Finder pull-down menu on the menu bar), you can always double-click on the Trash icon on the Dock, and then drag and drop or copy and paste any files or folders out of the Trash folder and return them to their original locations.

While the Trash folder is open, you can also click on a file or folder to highlight and select it, and then click on the gear-shaped icon in the Finder window and select the Put Back option to remove it from the Trash and return that file or folder to its original location. This same Put Back command is available under the File pull-down menu on the menu bar, or you can use the COMMAND (⌘)-DELETE keyboard shortcut when the file or folder is highlighted in the Trash folder.

Once you execute the Empty Trash command, however, any files or data in the Trash folder will be permanently deleted.

If you opt for the icon view in the Finder window, you can further customize the appearance of the icons by accessing the View pull-down menu from the menu bar and selecting Show View Options. You can then set the default for how icons in the Finder window will be sorted, the size of the icons, the spacing between icons, the text size used to display the file or folder names, and other details related to the appearance of the Finder window and the icons displayed in it. It's also possible to customize any of the three other icon views in the Finder window.

How to Move Files or Folders Around on Your Computer

On your MacBook Air, moving files or subfolders between folders, or from the desktop to a folder (or vice versa), is easy and can be done in several ways. With the proper Finder window open that displays the file or folder you want to move, you can drag and drop a selected file or folder into another folder, or use OS X's Select, Select All, Copy, Cut, and Paste commands.

Drag and Drop Files from One Location to Another

Using the drag-and-drop feature in Finder allows you to quickly move individual files or entire folders from one location to another. To accomplish this, launch Finder and locate, select, and highlight the file or folder you want to move. This is done by clicking on it once.

If you'll be moving the file or folder to a master folder in the sidebar of the Finder window (such as Applications, Documents, Downloads, Movies, Music, or Pictures), first select and highlight the file or folder to be moved. Then hold down the trackpad with your thumb, and use your index finger to drag the file or folder name or icon from the right side of the Finder window to the folder name in the sidebar. The selected file or folder will be moved from one location to the other.

You can use the drag-and-drop or cut-and-paste method to move a single file or folder. From within Finder, you can also select and highlight multiple files or folders, and move them to the same location simultaneously. To highlight and select more than one file or folder, click on the first file or folder you want to move. Next, move the pointer to another file or folder. Press and hold down the command key on the keyboard, and at the same time click on the trackpad. Repeat this process for each file or folder you want to highlight and select.

To select all file or folder icons in a Finder window, use the Select All command found under the Edit pull-down menu on the menu bar (which selects and highlights all of the file and/or folder icons in the window). Or, to highlight and select just one file or folder icon, simply click on it. However, to highlight and select multiple file or folder icons in a window, select and highlight one, and then hold down the command key while selecting others.

To drag and drop files or folders between subfolders in Finder, you can open two separate Finder windows at the same time on the desktop (shown in Figure 6-5). To do this, launch Finder once and select the files or folders you want to move. Next, click on the File pull-down menu from the menu bar and select the New Finder Window option.

A second Finder window will be displayed on the desktop. In this second Finder window, access the location where you want to copy the selected files or folders to. Then drag and drop those files and folders from one Finder window to the other. To do this, after the files or folders are selected, hold down the trackpad with your thumb and use your index finger to drag the content from one location to the other. Release the trackpad when the files are hovering over the desired location.

To copy a file or folder directly to the desktop, drag it from within a Finder window to anywhere outside of the window onto the main desktop. You can also drag and drop or copy and paste a file or folder from the desktop into a folder by moving it into a Finder window with its intended destination open.

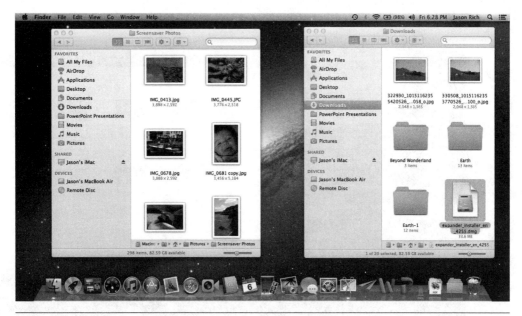

FIGURE 6-5   You can open two or more separate Finder windows on your MacBook Air's desktop.

Move Files or Folders Around Using the Select, Select All, Copy, and Paste Commands

Microsoft Windows and Apple's OS X have some similarities, including compatibility with the popular Select, Select All, Copy, and Paste commands, which can be used to move files or folders around on your computer. This is an alternative to using the drag-and-drop method.

The concept behind using these commands is simple. You select one or more files, copy them to OS X's virtual clipboard (where they are temporarily stored), and then paste them into the new desired location. When files or folders are pasted into a new location, they will also remain in their original location, but a duplicate will be created in the new location.

When using the Select, Select All, Copy, and Paste commands, you can access each command from the Edit pull-down menu on the menu bar (shown in Figure 6-6). Or you can use the keyboard shortcuts outlined in Table 6-1.

To select one file or folder from within Finder, click on its name or icon to highlight and select it. The Select All command will automatically highlight and select all of the files and folders stored in the folder you're viewing in Finder. When using Select All, Cut, Copy, and Paste, only those commands that are applicable will be displayed at any given time. You must select one or more items before you can cut, copy, or paste them.

Edit pull-down menu

FIGURE 6-6 Access the Select All, Copy, and Paste commands from the Edit pull-down menu in Finder and many other apps.

Just like when using the drag-and-drop method to move files or folders around, you can use the Select, Select All, Copy, Cut, and Paste commands to move files or folders between folders on your MacBook Air. You can also use these commands to move selected content in applications around within that application or between applications.

For example, if you're using Microsoft Word or Notes to create a text-based document, you can select some or all of that text, copy it to the virtual clipboard, and then paste it elsewhere in the document or into another document or file altogether (such as an outgoing email being composed from the Mail app).

TABLE 6-1 Select All, Copy, and Paste Command Keyboard Shortcuts

Command	Keyboard Shortcut
Select All	COMMAND (⌘)-A
Copy	COMMAND (⌘)-C
Paste	COMMAND (⌘)-V

Many Apps Now Have a Share Icon

Many of the preinstalled apps that come with your MacBook Air, plus a growing number of other apps, now have a Share button. When you click on the Share button, you can share app-specific content with other people via email, the Messages app, Facebook, Twitter, or another supported service. In some cases, if a Share button is not featured within an app, a Share pull-down menu may be offered.

To share app-specific data, files, or items, click on the Share button to view a Share menu that offers options compatible with that particular app. Using the Share Via Email or Share Via Messages option, you can enter in one or more recipients.

Using an External Hard Drive or Storage Device with the MacBook Air

In addition to connecting an optional external hard drive to your MacBook Air to utilize the Time Machine backup feature, you can use it as a storage or archive device for files, documents, data, and content that you utilize day to day.

When you drag and drop files or folders between your MacBook Air's hard drive and an external drive, such as a USB thumb drive, this will move the files from one location to the other, not duplicate the folders or files. Thus, what you move will be deleted from the original location. Instead of using drag and drop, you can use the Select, Copy, and Paste commands to transfer files or folders between drives. This creates a duplicate of what's being transferred and will not remove the original files or folders.

Likewise, you can use a USB thumb drive as a portable storage device to save files and easily transfer them between computers. Any time you plug an external storage device into your computer directly (using the USB port) or you connect to an external storage device via a wireless network, that device will be listed in the sidebar of the Finder window under the Devices heading. An icon for it will also be displayed on your desktop (as shown in Figure 6-7).

Once an external storage device is connected to your MacBook Air, you can manually drag and drop or copy and paste data, files, or content to or from it. You can also save files and data directly to that storage device using the Save As command offered in most applications. Or you can set up software to use the external storage device as an app's primary storage location (which is typically done from within the Preferences window of an app), and then simply use the Save command to store your app-specific files and data there.

There are several reasons why using an external storage device with your MacBook Air is advantageous. For example, using an external storage device makes it

Thumb drive icon

FIGURE 6-7 On the right side of the desktop, you can see an icon for the MacBook Air's main hard drive, as well as a USB thumb drive that's connected to the computer. These storage devices are also listed in the sidebar of the open Finder window.

easy to transfer large amounts of data or files between computers. Using an external storage device also allows you to save storage space on your MacBook Air's internal hard drive.

If you're an avid photographer and take lots of photos using a high-resolution digital camera, each image file will take up between three and eight (or more) megabytes of storage space. Multiply this by hundreds or thousands of images, and the internal hard drive of your MacBook Air will fill up quickly.

 If you opt to store important data or files on an external hard drive, keep in mind that when you're on the go, you'll need to plug in that drive to access your data or files (anything that's not stored on the MacBook Air's internal hard drive). If portability is your goal, using anything but a tiny thumb drive will be counterproductive.

 If you opt to store your important data or files on a wireless external hard drive that's linked to the MacBook Air through a wireless network, once you move outside of the network's wireless signal radius (usually between 150 and 200 feet from the wireless router), you will lose the connection with the external hard drive and won't be able to access your data. As a general rule, store your important and most accessed data or files on your MacBook Air's internal hard drive.

Sharing Files and Data with Other Computers

When it comes to sharing files and data with other computers, you have a variety of options. Some of your easiest and more viable options include:

- Use email to send yourself files from one computer and retrieve them on another.
- Use a cloud-based file sharing service, such as iCloud or Dropbox. (You'll learn more about this option in Chapter 7.)
- Use an online-based file transfer service, such as YouSendIt.com, that allows you to send extremely large files, multiple files, or entire folders via email.
- Use a USB thumb drive to copy files from one computer, and then insert that same thumb drive into another computer to transfer the data or files.
- Connect two Macs together (including your MacBook Air) using the wireless AirDrop feature of OS X. No preexisting wireless network is required
- Link your MacBook Air with another Mac or PC computer using OS X's File Sharing option, if both computers are linked to the same wireless network.

Using Email to Transfer Files Between Computers

If you only have a few, smaller files to share with another computer (or a compatible mobile device), one easy way to make the transfer is to email yourself the files from one computer and retrieve them on another using your Mail app. Keep in mind, many email accounts have a 5MB maximum file size for email attachments.

Using a Cloud-Based File Sharing Service

Depending on what app you're using, your data, files, photos, and/or documents can be synced with your iCloud account, and then automatically become available to all of your other computers and iOS mobile devices that are linked to the same iCloud account. This makes transferring certain types of data a hassle-free process, because it happens in the background. Thus, your compatible data, photos, documents, and files are always accessible to you on each of your computers and iOS mobile devices.

When it comes to working with documents, spreadsheets, or digital slide presentations, your iCloud account automatically syncs Pages, Numbers, and Keynote files and documents.

If you're working with Microsoft Office, or other apps that utilize other types of files, you can use another cloud-based file sharing service such as Dropbox (www .dropbox.com). This service and others like it, including Google Docs (https://docs .google.com) and Microsoft SkyDrive (http://windows.microsoft.com/en-US/skydrive/ why-SkyDrive), allow you to manually upload files to the cloud and then retrieve them from other computers or devices. These services work with any type of file, regardless of file size, and also allow you to share files with other people, not just your own computers.

A basic Dropbox account includes 2GB of online storage space and is available for free. You can pay an annual fee for premium services and additional storage space.

In addition to sharing files between computers or using a cloud-based file sharing service to collaborate with others, these services provide a viable solution for maintaining a secure, remote backup of your important files and data. So, if your MacBook Air gets lost, stolen, or damaged, you can still retrieve and utilize your files and data from another computer at any time, and know you have the most recent versions of that data safely and remotely stored.

Using Online-Based File Sharing Services

A cloud-based file sharing service allows you to store files or data in the cloud (a server that's located somewhere in cyberspace), and then retrieve those files from another device. It works like a wireless hard drive that's located virtually on the Web.

Another option for transferring one or more large files (or entire folders) is to use an online-based file sharing service, such as YouSendIt.com. This service allows you to email a vast amount of information either to yourself or to other people, and not be limited by the 5MB file size limitation offered by traditional email.

Using the basic YouSendIt.com service is free. However, the service has three premium service plans (a monthly fee applies), which have far fewer limitations and offer more features. The monthly fee starts at less than $5 per month.

Use YouSendIt.com directly from the Internet by visiting www.YouSendIt.com, or you can download and install the free YouSendIt desktop app or free YouSendIt Express app (shown in Figure 6-8) onto your MacBook Air, which makes using the file transfer service even easier and more efficient.

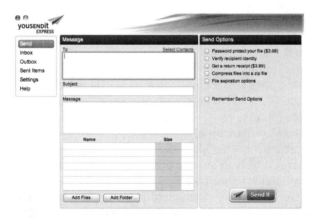

FIGURE 6-8   For paid users of YouSendIt.com, the YouSendIt Express app makes it easy to send large files, multiple files, or entire folders to other computers or other people via email.

Use OS X's AirDrop Feature to Share Files Wirelessly Between Mac Computers

OS X Mountain Lion offers a feature called AirDrop, which works in much the same way as file sharing, but it's a feature that's only available on newer iMac, MacBook Air, MacBook Pro, Mac Pro, and Mac mini computers.

If two compatible computers are within the same immediate radius and their Wi-Fi is turned on, the computers can create a secure peer-to-peer private network. AirDrop works whether or not a separate wireless network or Wi-Fi Internet connection is available. The great thing about this feature is that it just works, with no configuration or setup required.

To activate AirDrop, launch Finder, and click on the AirDrop option (found under the Favorites heading on the sidebar). Repeat this step on your other compatible Mac computer(s). If a connection can be made, icons representing each computer in the peer-to-peer network will be displayed in the AirDrop window (shown in Figure 6-9) within seconds.

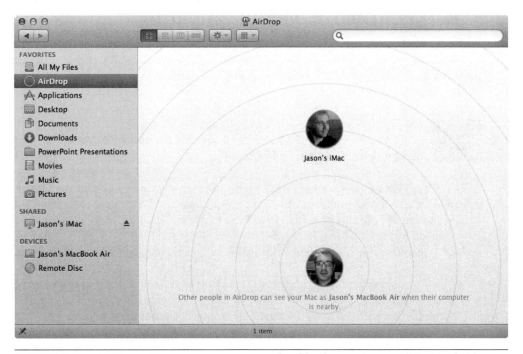

FIGURE 6-9 AirDrop is an easy way to transfer files between your MacBook Air and another compatible Mac that's located nearby.

You can now freely drag and drop files or folders between these computers from within Finder. Drag the file or folder over the icon that represents the other computer in the Finder window and the file will transfer. Files will wind up in the main Downloads folder of the computer they're sent to. The link created between the computers using the AirDrop feature is automatically encrypted.

 As an added layer of protection, you can set up AirDrop to only connect with Mac users who are already included in your Contacts database or who use a specific Apple ID to verify their identity. This can be set up in System Preferences under the Sharing option.

 All MacBook Air computers purchased in 2010 or later support AirDrop. To determine if your other Macs also support this feature, visit http://support.apple .com/kb/HT4783.

To close the peer-to-peer AirDrop connection between two or more computers, simply close the active Finder window in which the AirDrop feature was activated.

Use OS X's File Sharing Feature to Move Files Between Two or More Computers Wirelessly

Built into the OS X operating system is a file sharing feature which allows your MacBook Air to wirelessly share files with other computers. For this feature to work, your MacBook Air and the other Mac or PC both need to be connected to the same wireless network via Wi-Fi.

 The file sharing feature works with computers that are or are not AirDrop compatible, including PCs and older model Macs (running OS X Snow Leopard, Leopard, Lion, or Mountain Lion).

To activate this feature, launch System Preferences and click on the Sharing option that's found under the Internet & Wireless heading (shown in Figure 6-10). On the left side of the Sharing window that appears, click on the File Sharing option to select and activate it. Then, on the right side of the Sharing window, adjust the settings under the Shared Folders heading to determine who will be able to utilize this feature.

Once the green dot in the Sharing window appears and the message File Sharing On is displayed, exit out of System Preferences. Repeat this process on the other Macs on your wireless network that you want to transfer or share files with. For more information about this feature, visit http://support.apple.com/kb/HT1549. Only the Mac that's sharing the files or folders (not the Mac that's being shared with) needs to have the file sharing feature turned on.

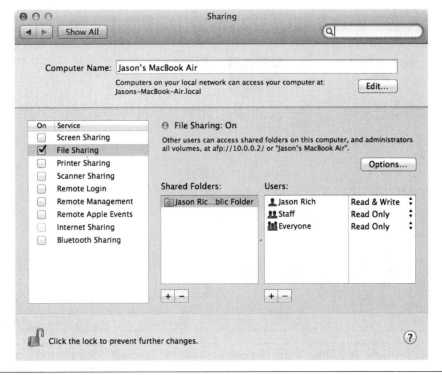

FIGURE 6-10 Turn on the file sharing feature in System Preferences.

If you want to freely share files back and forth between two Macs, make sure file sharing is turned on and active so you can access files and folders on the remote computer(s) by launching Finder. From the sidebar of the Finder window on your MacBook Air, click on the All option that's displayed under the Shared heading. On the right side of the Finder window, an icon representing each computer your MacBook Air can wirelessly share files with will be displayed (shown in Figure 6-11). Double-click on the icon.

By clicking on the Connect As icon that's displayed near the top-right corner of the Finder window (below the Search field), you can access the remote computer as a Guest or as a Registered User (with the proper password).

Files placed in the master Public folder on a computer can then be shared with other computers linked wirelessly using the file sharing feature. This folder is treated just like a folder on your MacBook Air's hard drive. Thus, you can copy and paste or drag and drop files or subfolders into or out of it to exchange information between computers, assuming you, the user, are set up with permission to do this from within the Sharing window of System Preferences.

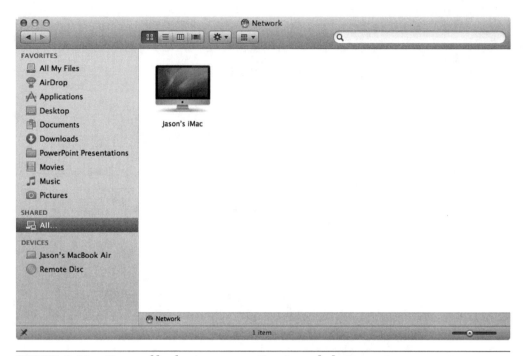

FIGURE 6-11 Once a file sharing connection is made between two computers, click on that computer from your MacBook Air to access files from it or transfer files to it.

If you're an iPad user, it's possible to control your MacBook Air remotely and access files and data from it. To do this, download the Splashtop app from the App Store (or visit www.splashtop.com/remote). This iPad app (when used in conjunction with the free Splashtop Streamer software for your MacBook Air) allows you to run software or access files stored on your MacBook Air from your iPad's screen, as long as both have an Internet connection. This is just one way to wirelessly share files between an iPad and your MacBook Air.

7

Use Apple's iCloud to Sync All Your Devices

HOW TO...

- Set up an iCloud account to work with your MacBook Air
- Set up popular apps to work with MacBook Air and sync with iOS mobile devices
- Use iCloud in conjunction with iTunes

Synchronicity is the word that best describes the improvements made to the OS X Mountain Lion operating system in terms of making the MacBook Air function more like an iPad. It is now easier than ever to sync app-specific data, documents, photos, and files between your MacBook Air and Apple's iCloud cloud-based service.

Unlike traditional cloud-based file sharing services like Dropbox, iCloud functionality is fully integrated into your MacBook Air's operating system. It is designed to automatically work with preinstalled apps such as Contacts, Calendar, Notes, Reminders, Safari, and iPhoto, as well as with Apple's iWork apps (including Pages, Numbers, and Keynote).

iCloud is also fully integrated with iTunes, allowing you to easily access all of your past, present, and future iTunes Store content purchases from all of your Macs and iOS mobile devices, regardless of which device purchased them.

Because of the integration of iCloud into the OS X operating system, once you turn it on, many of its features are designed to work automatically and in the background. So when you create, modify, or delete data, files, or documents in a particular app, your changes are almost instantly uploaded to iCloud (assuming your MacBook Air is connected to the Internet), and then automatically downloaded by your other Macs and iOS mobile devices (including your iPhone, iPad, or iPod touch) that are linked to the same iCloud account.

In other words, if you create a new contact entry in Contacts, for example, that new entry will automatically be uploaded to iCloud and then be added to your contacts database on your other computers and iOS mobile devices within seconds.

As a result, you're always working with the most current version of your data, files, or documents, regardless of how or where you access the information.

In addition to accessing your Contacts, Calender, Notes, or Reminders data and documents from your Macs and/or iOS mobile devices, you can visit www.icloud .com from any computer or device with a web browser, sign into the iCloud service using your Apple ID and password, and then use free online-based apps to access your data, documents, and files.

iCloud is already designed to serve many purposes, and Apple continues to enhance the service with new features. Plus, third-party software developers are beginning to add iCloud functionality or integration to their Mac software, so over time you'll probably see seamless and automatic file syncing between your favorite Mac software and iCloud.

Other cloud-based file sharing services are designed to serve as remote (online-based) hard drives that allow you to manually upload, download, and store data, files, or documents. While these services are extremely useful for a variety of purposes, they are not integrated with the computer's operating system or designed to work automatically and seamlessly with your computers and mobile devices.

Setting Up an iCloud Account

Creating an iCloud account is free of charge. It includes 5GB of online storage space for your personal data and files, plus as much additional online storage space as you need for your iTunes Store and other online purchases from Apple and its online ventures.

When you first set up your new MacBook Air—or any other new Mac, iPhone, iPad, or iPod touch—you are prompted to set up a free iCloud account in the process. This is done using your preexisting Apple ID and password.

An Apple ID is a free, password protected, online account that you set up with Apple. It's used for a variety of purposes, including utilizing iCloud, using FaceTime, iMessage, Find My iPhone/iPad/Mac, and making purchases from any Apple online store (such as the App Store, iTunes Store, or iBookstore). Your credit card or debit card gets linked to your Apple ID, so you can make payments with a simple click, and not have to reenter your payment information repeatedly. To learn more, visit: https://appleid.apple.com.

However, if you opted to skip this step during the computer's setup process and you don't yet have an iCloud account, you can set one up quickly. Having an Apple ID is a prerequisite. Launch System Preferences and click on the iCloud option. Follow the onscreen prompts for creating a new account, which includes entering your Apple ID and password. You only need to set up an iCloud account once.

How to... **Increase Your iCloud Online Storage Allocation**

If you require more than 5GB of online storage for your personal data, documents, and files, it can be purchased online for an annual fee. An additional 10GB of online storage (which gives you a total of 15GB) is $20 per year. For an additional 20GB of online storage (which gives you a total of 25GB), the annual fee is $40. Or you can upgrade your iCloud account with an additional 50GB of online storage (which gives you a total of 55GB) for $100 per year.

To purchase additional iCloud storage from your MacBook Air that's connected to the Internet, launch System Preferences, and then click on the iCloud icon. Click on the Manage button that's displayed near the lower-right corner of the iCloud window. Then, in the upper-right corner of the Manage Storage window, click on the Buy More Storage button.

From the Buy More Storage window, click on how much additional storage you want or need, followed by the Next button. You'll be prompted to enter your Apple ID's password. Within a few seconds, your newly purchased online storage space will become accessible.

You can upgrade your iCloud account with additional online storage at any time, so it's only necessary to purchase the storage space you'll need to utilize immediately. Don't forget that Apple provides as much additional online storage space as you need, for free, to accommodate your music, movie, TV show, eBook, app, and other content purchases, as well as your Photo Stream.

Tip For assistance setting up or using an iCloud account, visit www.apple.com/support/icloud.

Managing Your iCloud Account from Your MacBook Air

Even if you have iCloud set up and working properly on another Mac and/or your iOS mobile devices, you'll still need to turn on iCloud functionality on your MacBook Air, and then turn on the specific iCloud features you want to utilize with this particular computer.

Once iCloud functionality is turned on, you'll see your account name displayed directly under the iCloud logo on the left side of the iCloud window (shown in Figure 7-1). When you click on the Account Details button, you'll see your Apple ID, username, and the description given to your iCloud account.

FIGURE 7-1   From System Preferences, click on the iCloud option to manage your iCloud account as it relates to your MacBook Air.

To manage iCloud functionality on your MacBook Air, launch System Preferences and click on the iCloud option. On the right side of the iCloud preferences window, you'll see separate options for Mail, Contacts, Calendars & Reminders, Bookmarks, Notes, Photo Stream, Documents & Data, Back To My Mac, and Find My Mac. Each is accompanied by a checkbox.

Add a checkmark to the checkboxes that correspond with the iCloud features you want to utilize.

If you're familiar with using iCloud on your iPhone or iPad, there is one major difference when using iCloud with your MacBook Air: iCloud will not and cannot automatically back up your entire computer. While iCloud offers the iCloud Backup feature for iPhones and iPads, this feature does not apply to Macs. To maintain a backup of your Mac, you'll want to use Time Machine and/or an optional remote (online) backup service. In conjunction with your Mac, iCloud will back up and sync compatible app-specific data only, such as your Contacts, Calendars, or Reminders databases.

Here's a quick summary of what each option available from the iCloud preferences window is used for:

- **Mail**   Turn on automatic iCloud synchronization for the free email account that comes with your iCloud account. When you update the account by composing or deleting email messages, for example, those changes are reflected in almost real-time on all of your computers and mobile devices. This only applies to your iCloud email address, however.
- **Contacts**   When turned on, your MacBook Air will automatically sync your personal Contacts database with iCloud, and then sync this data with your other Macs and/or iOS devices. So any contacts you've created in your Contacts database on your other computers, iPhone, iPad, or iPod touch will automatically become accessible on your MacBook Air, and any Contact entries you add or modify on your MacBook Air using the Contacts app will be reflected on your other computers and iOS mobile devices.
- **Calendars & Reminders**   When turned on, your MacBook Air will automatically sync your Calendars and Reminders databases with iCloud, and then sync this data with your other Macs or iOS mobile devices. It works exactly the same as the Contacts feature, but related to your Calendars and Reminders app-specific data.
- **Bookmarks**   This feature will sync your Safari web browser bookmarks with your other computers and iOS mobile devices. It's also compatible with a handful of other popular web browsers that may be running on your other computers. Your personal bookmarks list, Bookmarks bar, and Reading List associated with Safari will remain synced, giving you access to your favorite websites (bookmarked websites) on all of your computers and iOS mobile devices that are linked to the same iCloud account.

 More information about surfing the Internet using Safari on your MacBook Air is covered in Chapter 10.

- **Notes**   When you turn on this feature, it works the same way as the Contacts, as well as the Calendars & Reminders iCloud options, but syncs data related specifically to the Notes app.
- **Photo Stream**   This is an iCloud service that allows you to access up to 1,000 of your most recently shot or imported digital photos on all of your computers and iOS mobile devices that are linked to the same iCloud account. It works slightly differently than the syncing process used for other apps.

Once turned on, your Photo Stream becomes accessible from within iPhoto (as shown in Figure 7-2). You'll notice that a new album has been created, called Photo Stream. Unless your MacBook Air is your primary computer, images in your Photo Stream become accessible from your MacBook Air for viewing and downloading, but are not automatically and permanently stored on the computer. Before you can edit images from your Photo Stream, you'll need to transfer them from Photo Stream to another album or event in iPhoto.

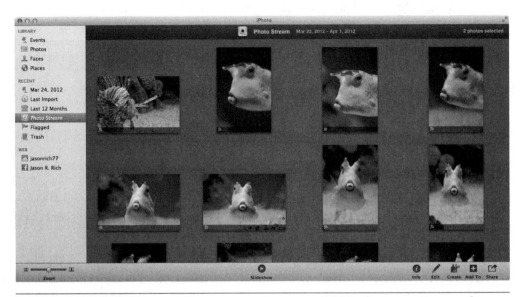

FIGURE 7-2 Photo Stream allows you to view up to 1,000 of your most recently shot or imported digital images.

When you use the Photo Stream feature, the online storage space required to store up to 1,000 of your high-resolution digital photos does not count against the 5GB of free online storage space provided by Apple for your iCloud account.

Note Images that automatically become part of your Photo Stream, remain there for up to 30 days, or until you reach the 1,000 image limit. After 30 days or upon reaching 1,000 images, the older photos are removed from the Photo Stream to make room for your most recently shot or added (imported) digital photos. This includes photos imported into iPhoto from your digital camera, or photos shot using the camera that is built into your computer or iOS mobile device.

Did You Know?

You Can Add and Delete Photos Manually from Your Photo Stream

Once turned on, the Photo Stream feature will automatically add photos to the Photo Stream as soon as they're shot on any computer or device that's linked to your iCloud account. If you import photos from your digital camera (or another source) into iPhoto, they too will be automatically added to your Photo Stream.

(continued)

From your MacBook Air, you can manually add photos to your Photo Stream simply by dragging them into the Photo Stream album in iPhoto. The images can be dragged from another Event, album, or the Places Or Faces section of iPhoto. When you manually add photos to your Photo Stream, they are displayed in the order in which they were shot, not the date they were added to the Photo Stream.

To manually delete photos from the Photo Stream as you're viewing them using iPhoto on your MacBook Air, launch iPhoto and click on the Photo Stream option (displayed on the left side of the screen). As you're looking at the image thumbnails in your Photo Stream, select and highlight the images you want to delete, and drag them to the Trash option that's displayed on the left side of the iPhoto window (not to the Trash icon on the Dock).

Alternative, once one or more images are selected, access the Photos pull-down menu from the menu bar, and select the Delete From Photo Stream option. The keyboard shortcut is COMMAND (⌘)-DELETE. Within seconds after deleting images from the Photo Stream, they will no longer appear in the Photo Stream listing on your MacBook Air, or on any of your other computers or iOS mobile devices that are linked to the same iCloud account.

As you're looking at the image thumbnails in the Photo Stream, select and highlight one image by clicking on its thumbnail. A yellow box will appear around it. To select and highlight additional images, move the pointer over those image thumbnails, one at a time, and press the command key on the keyboard simultaneously with a click on the trackpad.

Just like OS X Mountain Lion, the features and functionality of iCloud are constantly evolving and new options are frequently being added for managing a Photo Stream. For example, one new feature is the ability to share photos from within a Photo Stream.

- **Documents & Data**   This feature relates to documents and data created using the optional iWork apps (which are sold separately from the Mac App Store). They include Pages (a word processor), Numbers (a spreadsheet management application), and Keynote (for creating and showing digital slide presentations). Documents and files created using these apps are automatically stored on iCloud and synced with other computers and iOS= mobile devices that are linked to the same iCloud account. This was a feature previously offered by Apple's iWork.com service, but has since been incorporated directly into iCloud.

After turning on the Documents & Data feature from within the iCloud window of System Preferences, you must also turn on the iCloud syncing feature in Pages, Numbers, and Keynote separately.

To do this, launch one of the iWork apps, access the Share pull-down menu from the menu bar, and enter your Apple ID password when prompted. Click the Sign In button to continue.

The Documents & Data feature does not currently work with Microsoft Office documents or files, although Pages documents can be exported into Microsoft Word format, Numbers files can be exported into Microsoft Excel format, and Keynote files can be exported into Microsoft PowerPoint format from whichever computer or device they're being used on.

If you turn on document and file syncing for Pages, Numbers, or Keynote, when you manually delete a file or document from one computer, that same document or file will automatically and almost instantly be deleted from iCloud, and from the other computers or iOS devices it's synced with.

- **Back To My Mac**   With an active iCloud account, the Back To My Mac feature allows you to connect to your other Mac computers (also linked to the same iCloud account) over the Internet. This feature allows you to share files remotely with other Macs, as well as use the Screen Sharing feature to actually take control of another Mac remotely. To use this feature, both computers must have Internet access and have the Back To My Mac feature turned on. They must also be signed into the same iCloud account. This is yet another way to wirelessly share files and data between two computers.

Back To My Mac has fewer limitations than AirDrop and file sharing (which were discussed in Chapter 6), because the computers can be linked via the Internet, regardless of their geographic proximity. They do not need to be connected to the same wireless network.

- **Find My Mac**   When turned on, you can access the iCloud website (www .iCloud.com/#find) from any computer or mobile device with a web browser, and determine the exact location of your MacBook Air on a map, assuming that it's connected to the Internet (as shown in Figure 7-3).

When viewing a map, you can zoom in on a location to see extreme detail, by clicking on the plus sign located near the top-right corner of the map. You can also switch between the Standard, Satellite, and Hybrid map views by clicking on the appropriate button displayed near the bottom-right corner of the map screen.

Once the location of your computer is pinpointed and displayed (which takes just seconds), you're given several options, such as the ability to lock down the computer from unauthorized users. You can also locate your MacBook Air from your iOS mobile device using the free Find My iPhone app.

On the iPhone and iPad, iCloud also works with the free Find My Friends app, which allows you to keep tabs on the exact location of people you know (with their permission), and allows your friends to track your location in real-time as well. This feature does not yet work with Macs, but could become part of an OS X Mountain Lion update or be made available by downloading a free Mac app in the future.

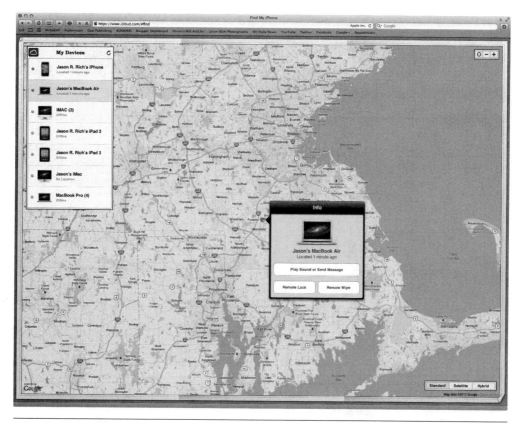

FIGURE 7-3   You can track the location of your MacBook Air from any Internet-enabled device with a web browser by visiting www.iCloud.com/#find.

Once you activate any of these app-specific iCloud-related features, they begin working immediately, automatically, and in the background. Thus, after activating the Contacts feature, for example, when you launch the Contacts app, your contacts entries from other computers or iOS mobile devices will be downloaded and displayed, and entries created on your MacBook Air will be uploaded and synced without any further action on your part.

Using iCloud with iTunes

The iTunes software that comes preinstalled on your Mac is the focus of Chapter 14. However, all of the content (music, TV shows, movies, music videos, eBooks, audiobooks, etc.) that you have purchased in the past on any of your Apple devices is now stored for free in your iCloud account.

This means those purchases are accessible from all of your compatible Apple devices, including your Mac computers, iPhone, iPad, iPod touch, and Apple TV, as long as those devices are linked to the same iCloud account. You can now enjoy the purchased content on all of your devices and computers without having to repurchase it multiple times.

 The iTunes software comes preinstalled on your MacBook Air and is used to manage your multimedia content, manually sync data with your iOS mobile devices (using the iTunes Sync process), or to access the iTunes Store (an online-based store that sells music, movies, TV shows, audiobooks, ringtones, music videos, ebooks, and other content). Free content (such as podcasts), as well as movie rentals, are also available from the iTunes Store.

Customizing How iTunes Works with iCloud

Upon activating iCloud to work with your MacBook Air, it will automatically work with iTunes. However, you can adjust iCloud-related settings in iTunes. To do this, launch the iTunes software, and from the iTunes pull-down menu on the menu bar, select the Preferences option.

When the iTunes Preferences window appears, click on the Store icon (shown in Figure 7-4). Under the Automatic Downloads heading, you can set it up so iTunes automatically downloads all new music, apps, or ebook purchases, regardless of which computer or device they were purchased on.

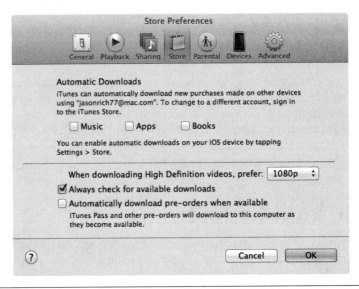

FIGURE 7-4 From iTunes Preferences, determine how iCloud will function with iTunes.

By checking the Music option under Automatic Downloads, for example, if you purchase a new song from iTunes on your iPhone, that same song will automatically download and be added to the music library of your MacBook Air immediately, or as soon as your MacBook Air is turned on and connected to the Internet. From this window, you can also customize the resolution that video content will be downloaded in (1080p should be selected to view the highest resolution possible).

 When you select 1080p as the preferred resolution for downloading video, as you're browsing the iTunes Store for TV show episodes or movies, the Buy or Rent icons will automatically default to the high definition (1080p) setting, which is slightly more expensive than purchasing (or renting when applicable) and downloading the same content in standard definition. The onscreen quality between 720p and 1080p is significant, especially when viewing it on your MacBook Air's screen.

Downloading Past iTunes Purchases on Your MacBook Air

To access any music, TV shows, movies, iOS device apps, or ebooks that you've purchased in the past on other Apple devices, launch iTunes on your MacBook Air and click on the iTunes Store option that's displayed on the left side of the screen.

If this is your first time trying to access previously purchased content from your MacBook Air, access the Store pull-down menu from the menu bar, and select the Authorize This Computer option. When prompted, enter your Apple ID password. Up to five different computers can be authorized per Apple ID account. This only needs to be done once.

 In the future, Apple plans to phase out Ping, which is an online community focusing on music that can be accessed from iTunes. Thus, in future editions of the iTunes software, the Ping tab will not be visible.

Then, under the Quick Links heading on the right side of the iTunes Store screen (shown in Figure 7-5), click on the Purchased option. At the top of the Purchased screen, select the type of content you're looking for. Based on what you've already purchased, your options may include music, movies, TV shows, apps, and books, but could also include audiobooks and/or ringtones, for example (shown in Figure 7-6).

If you select Music, a listing of recording artists will be displayed on the left side of the screen. Click on an artist listing to see the digital music you own from that artist. A listing of specific songs will appear in the main area of the screen if the default Songs tab is highlighted. Click on the Albums tab to display album titles (as opposed to individual songs).

Displayed to the right of each song list or next to the album listing will be an iCloud icon if you own that content but it has not yet been downloaded to your MacBook Air's hard drive. Click on the iCloud icon (shown in Figure 7-7) to download it for free.

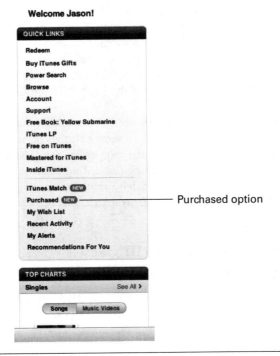

FIGURE 7-5 Click on the Purchased icon to access past iTunes purchases, regardless of which computer or device they were previously purchased on.

FIGURE 7-6 From the icons near the top of the Purchased screen, choose a type of content (music, movies, TV shows, etc.).

iCloud icons

FIGURE 7-7   Click on the iCloud icon that's associated with specific already purchased iTunes content to download it to your MacBook Air. The Albums view under Music is shown here.

Tip   Content that does not have an iCloud icon associated with it has already been downloaded and stored on the MacBook Air, and is accessible from the iTunes software. To view a listing of only content that is not stored on your MacBook Air from the Purchased screen, click on the Not On This Computer tab.

When prompted, enter your Apple ID password. The song or album will be downloaded to your MacBook Air's hard drive and become accessible in iTunes. The iCloud icon that was displayed will be replaced by the word Downloaded.

To listen to the song, click on the Music option under the Library heading on the left side of the iTunes screen. The newly downloaded, but previously purchased song will now be listed. Select and highlight the song, and click the Play button or double-click on the song title to play it. See Chapter 14 for more information about how to use the iTunes software that came preinstalled on your computer.

The process for accessing pre-purchased movies, TV shows, and other iTunes content is almost identical to the process just outlined for accessing pre-purchased music on your MacBook Air.

When you rent a movie from iTunes, the movie file will be downloaded to the computer or device it was rented from. It will remain stored there for up to 30 days. However, once you begin watching it, you can watch it as often as you'd like for a 24-hour period before the rented movie is automatically deleted. A rented movie file can only be stored on one computer, iOS device, or Apple TV device at a time. During your rental period, you can manually move it between devices, however. Or you can use the Home Sharing feature on your MacBook Air to stream the rented movie from your MacBook Air to your Apple TV in order to watch it on your HD television.

Using iTunes Match to Access Your Entire Digital Music Library Through iCloud

Your ability to access your digital music using iCloud includes only music purchased from Apple's iTunes Store. So if you have digital music acquired from other sources, such as Amazon MP3 Music Store, or if you've "ripped" your CDs and transferred that music into digital music files, or recorded your own music (using GarageBand), for example, those songs or tracks will not be synced to iCloud or become accessible from all of your computers and iOS mobile devices.

To learn more about the iTunes Match service, visit www.apple.com/itunes/itunes-match.

If you want access to your entire digital music library via iTunes, regardless of how the music was acquired, subscribe to Apple's premium iTunes Match service ($24.99 per year). Upon upgrading to iTunes Match (from within the iTunes Store), the iTunes software will analyze the content of each computer and iOS mobile device that's linked to your iCloud account, and then sync all of the music.

Once iTunes Match is activated on your various computers and iOS mobile devices, it works automatically and in the background. When you add a new song or music track to one computer or device, it becomes available on all of the computers and devices linked to your iCloud account. All of the additional online storage space that's needed to accommodate your entire digital music library is provided by Apple as part of the $24.99 annual subscription fee.

After subscribing to iTunes Match, you'll need to manually turn on the feature on each computer or device that's linked to your iCloud account. To do this, click on the iTunes Match option that's listed under the Store heading on the left side of the iTunes window (shown in Figure 7-8). Then click on Add This Computer. If you need to subscribe to iTunes Match, click on the icon for purchasing this premium service.

FIGURE 7-8   To access iTunes Match on your MacBook Air, click on the iTunes Match option that's displayed on the left side of the iTunes window.

Note The iTunes Match annual fee will be billed to the credit card that's linked to your Apple ID account. This is an auto-renewing service. To cancel it, click on your iTunes username that's displayed near the upper-right corner of the iTunes screen to access the Account Information screen. Enter your Apple ID password when prompted. Then scroll down to the iTunes In The Cloud heading, and click on the Turn Off Auto-Renew icon that's associated with the iTunes Match service.

8

Add Optional Peripherals and Accessories to Expand Performance

HOW TO...

- Understand the difference between the USB ports, the Thunderbolt port, Bluetooth, and Wi-Fi
- Connect Bluetooth devices to your MacBook Air
- Use a printer with your MacBook Air
- Use an external storage device with your MacBook Air

Even though the MacBook Air was designed to be ultra-thin and lightweight, Apple did not have to compromise too much in terms of providing useful ports so that external peripherals could easily be connected to the computer. In fact, you have easy access to two USB ports and one Thunderbolt port, as well as a headphone jack, Wi-Fi, and Bluetooth capabilities. Figure 8-1 shows the right side of an 11-inch MacBook Air with its Thunderbolt and USB ports.

 Tip To accommodate different-shaped devices being plugged into the USB port on the left side of the computer, you can plug the power cord for the computer so it faces in either direction in the MagSafe power port.

To expand the capabilities of either or both USB ports that are built into the computer, it's possible to connect an external USB hub to add more USB ports to the device. The Belkin Travel USB Hub ($14.99, www.belkin.com/IWCatProductPage. process?Product_Id = 469617), for example, is a tiny device that plugs into one USB port and makes four USB ports available.

Thunderbolt port

USB port

FIGURE 8-1   The 11-inch MacBook Air has Thunderbolt and USB ports on the right side. The 13-inch model also has an SD card reader on the right side.

Priced between $10 and $30, you'll find a vast selection of portable USB hubs from a wide range of companies available online, as well as from computer and consumer electronics retail stores. If you invest in an optional and external Apple Thunderbolt Display or some other third-party display, it will have a USB hub built in as well.

Using a USB hub allows you to simultaneously plug multiple USB devices into a single USB port on your computer. This takes away from the computer's portability, but while it's being used on a desk, a USB hub can expand the computer's capabilities.

Between the different ports that your MacBook Air offers, and its Wi-Fi and Bluetooth capabilities, you can easily connect a wide range of peripherals to your computer, including:

- One or more printers
- A scanner
- External speakers
- An external mouse and/or trackpad
- Headphones
- An external keyboard
- An external microphone
- One or more external hard drives
- USB thumb drives
- The USB iTunes Sync cable to connect an iPhone, iPad, or iPod touch to the computer
- A digital camera (to directly transfer photos or video clips to your MacBook Air)
- Apple's MacBook Air SuperDrive (http://store.apple.com/us/product/MC684ZM/A)

Any computer peripheral that's Mac compatible and that connects to a computer using a USB or Thunderbolt port, or using a wireless Bluetooth connection, will work with your MacBook Air. In some cases, you will have the option of establishing a wireless connection between a peripheral (such as a printer or hard drive) and your computer, as opposed to connecting the two devices with a cable.

You Can Transform Your MacBook Air into a Desktop Computer

When you're not on the go, you can easily connect an external and full-size keyboard, mouse, trackpad, and/or monitor to your MacBook Air so that it looks and functions more like an iMac desktop computer, and is more ergonomic when working from your desk at home or work.

Apple offers a selection of optional, full-size keyboards, which can connect to the MacBook Air via a USB cable or Bluetooth. The Apple wireless keyboards, which come in several configurations (with or without a numeric keypad) are priced at $69.

The traditional corded Apple mouse is priced at $49, while the wireless Apple Magic Mouse is priced at $69. Instead of or in addition to an external mouse, you can use Apple's Magic Trackpad ($69) with the MacBook Air, which offers a larger surface than the built-in Multi-Touch trackpad. Because it's a stand-alone device, the external Magic Trackpad can be positioned anywhere that's convenient for your hand. You can also connect an external and full-size monitor to the MacBook Air.

All of these Apple products are available from Apple Stores, Apple.com, and Apple authorized resellers. Compatible products from other manufacturers are also available. If you have a wireless keyboard, Magic Mouse, or Magic Trackpad that came with your iMac, for example, you can configure those devices to work with your MacBook Air as well by adjusting the settings in System Preferences select the Bluetooth option.

Understanding the Differences Between USB Ports, the Thunderbolt Port, Wi-Fi, and Bluetooth

Your MacBook Air can utilize one of several totally different technologies in order to successfully link an optional peripheral to the computer using a cable or potentially a wireless connection. Each of these connection methods has its advantages. Which you use will depend on what type of peripheral you're connecting to your MacBook Air, and what technology that peripheral is compatible with.

Using Your MacBook Air's USB Ports

There are two USB ports built into your MacBook Air—one on the right side and one on the left side of the computer. Either of these ports can be used to connect a USB-compatible peripheral to your computer using a USB cable or connector.

USB stands for Universal Serial Bus. It's an industry standard technology that was developed in the 1990s to allow peripherals to easily be connected to computers.

If you purchased your MacBook Air after June 11, 2012, the two USB ports that are built into your computer are USB 3.0 compatible. However, if you purchased your MacBook air prior to June 11, 2012, the two USB ports that are built into your computer are USB 2.0 compatible. Thus, if you have USB 3.0 ports built into your MacBook Air, seek out peripherals that support a USB 3.0 connection to experience significantly faster data transfer speeds.

On newer MacBook Air computers (purchased after June 11, 2012), the USB 3.0 ports will also work with USB 2.0 devices, but at a slower data transfer rate. USB 2.0 ports in older MacBook Air computers, however, will not work properly with USB 3.0–specific devices, unless those devices are also USB 2.0 compatible.

USB 3.0 is capable of data transfer speeds up to 5Gbits/second, which is approximate 625MB/per second. This is about 10 times faster than USB 2.0 capabilities, which transfer data at just 480Mbits/second or 60MB/second.

USB devices are typically plug-and-play. This means you simply plug it into your computer, the computer identifies what it is, loads the appropriate drivers automatically, and a connection between your computer and the USB device is established in a few seconds. A wide range of peripherals, such as printers, scanners, and external storage devices (hard drives and USB thumb drives), as well as the optional MacBook Air SuperDrive, are USB compatible.

When connecting a printer to the USB port of your computer, you will initially need to load drivers for that specific printer. How to do this is explained later in this chapter.

When connecting a peripheral to your MacBook Air, one end of the USB cable will offer a standard, Type A, USB connector. It plugs directly into the USB port of your computer (shown in Figure 8-2).

The opposite end of the cable might feature a USB Type B, USB Mini-A, USB Mini-B, USB Micro-A, or USB Micro-B connector or another proprietary connection (such as Apple's Dock Connector port), which plugs into the peripheral or that's connected permanently to the peripheral. In situations where the peripheral does not use a standard USB Type A to USB Type A cable, the required cable will typically come with the peripheral.

Standard USB cables, in a variety of lengths up to five meters (approximately 16.5 feet), are readily available wherever computers and computer accessories are sold, including office supply superstores, or even Wal-Mart and Target.

FIGURE 8-2   The MacBook Air has two standard Type A USB ports.

What the MacBook Air's Thunderbolt Port Offers

Instead of adopting the latest USB 3.0 technology (which is faster than USB 2.0) when designing the current MacBook Air models, Apple also incorporates a Thunderbolt port into the computer, which allows for high-speed data transfer via a cable connection. Thunderbolt technology was developed by Apple as part of a joint venture with Intel. It utilizes technology that allows for data transfer speeds up to 20 times faster than a standard USB 2.0 connection or 10 times faster than a USB 3.0 connection.

The Thunderbolt port of your MacBook Air is designed for connecting a high-definition monitor, external hard drive, or video capture card, for example, that requires a tremendous amount of data to quickly transfer between the computer and the peripheral.

If you'll be using an external hard drive in conjunction with your MacBook Air and Time Machine, or to manually back up a vast amount of data that includes very large files, such as high-resolution digital photos or HD video, connecting a Thunderbolt-compatible hard drive makes sense.

While you'll experience much faster data transfer speeds using a Thunderbolt-compatible external hard drive, from a price standpoint expect to pay more compared to a typical USB 2.0-compatible hard drive with the same storage capacity.

When working at your desk, use the Thunderbolt port to plug in an external full-size Thunderbolt-compatible HD display to your MacBook Air, so it will function much more like a desktop computer. The Apple Thunderbolt Display ($999, www.apple.com/displays), for example, is a 27-inch HD monitor that includes a built-in MacBook Air hub (which in turn offers a USB hub for connecting multiple peripherals). Plus, you can daisy-chain multiple Thunderbolt peripherals to the computer and use them simultaneously.

Note   To learn more about Thunderbolt technology, visit www.apple.com/thunderbolt.

Making a Wireless Connection via Wi-Fi

You already know that your MacBook Air has built-in Wi-Fi 802.11n capabilities for connecting to a wireless network or Wi-Fi Internet hotspot. When connected to a wireless network, your MacBook Air can also wirelessly connect to other computers (PCs or Macs), as well as printers, scanners, or hard drives that are also connected to that network.

As long as you're in the signal radius of the wireless Internet router, your MacBook Air can easily connect to a wireless network simply by turning on the Wi-Fi feature of the computer. How to do this was covered in Chapter 1.

There are two ways to connect a printer or another type of peripheral to a wireless network. First, you can connect that device directly to a computer that's already connected to the network, and then allow that computer to share the peripheral with others via the network. To set this up on a Mac, launch System Preferences and select the Sharing option. On the left side of the Sharing window, activate the Printer Sharing option.

When you do this, the printers that are currently directly connected to that computer (which in turn is connected to the wireless network) will be displayed on the right side of the Sharing window in System Preferences (as shown in Figure 8-3).

Add a checkmark to the checkbox that's associated with each printer that you want to share on the wireless network (so it becomes available to your MacBook Air,

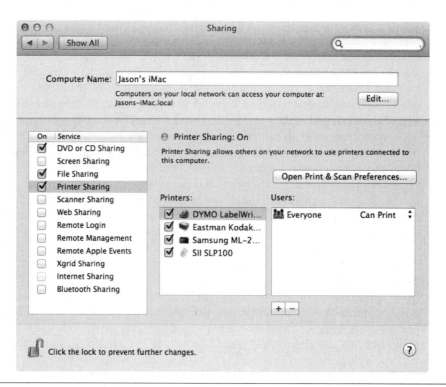

FIGURE 8-3   From whatever Mac a printer is connected to, if it's also connected to a wireless network, turn on Printer Sharing from System Preferences.

for example). As an added security measure, you can also determine exactly who will be able to access the shared printer or peripheral, or you can simply select Everyone (meaning anyone who is connected to the wireless network).

The second way to connect a printer or peripheral to a wireless network is to purchase a peripheral that has Wi-Fi capabilities and/or an Ethernet port built in, and that can connect directly (wirelessly or via an Ethernet cable) to your network's router, as opposed to another computer on the network. If you'll be moving your MacBook Air around within the signal radius of a wireless network, having printers connected wirelessly to your computer is beneficial.

When peripherals such as a printer or scanner, are connected directly to a wireless network, and you connect your MacBook Air to that same network it will have access to those peripherals.

Using the Bluetooth Capabilities of Your Computer

Yet another way to connect peripherals to your MacBook Air without using cables is to use Bluetooth. Your MacBook Air is compatible with the latest Bluetooth 4.0 technology. You'll discover a nice selection of optional Bluetooth-compatible peripherals that work with the MacBook Air, including external stereo speakers, headphones, and headsets.

Jawbone (www.jawbone.com), for example, offers several Bluetooth headsets that work well with Skype on your MacBook Air. The company also has an extremely portable, battery-powered, and powerful stereo speaker system, called the Jambox ($199.99, www .jawbone.com/speakers/jambox/overview), which works nicely with the MacBook Air.

As an alternative to listening to music using speakers or even wired stereo headphones (or ear buds) that plug into the standard headphone port that's built into the MacBook Air, a handful of companies offer wireless Bluetooth stereo headphones and/or ear buds. Altec Lansing, Bose, Creative Labs, Motorola, Sony, Plantronics, and Logitech are among the companies that offer these products.

In addition to the convenience of not being hindered by cables, one major benefit to Bluetooth is that multiple devices can be linked ("paired") to your MacBook Air simultaneously.

 Depending on the device, the radius of the Bluetooth signal between your MacBook Air and the Bluetooth peripheral can be up to 32.8 feet (10 meters), but this will vary greatly.

How to "Pair" a Bluetooth Device with Your MacBook Air

To utilize any Bluetooth devices with your MacBook Air, you first need to turn on the Bluetooth functionality of the computer. To do this, click on the Bluetooth icon that's displayed on the right side of the menu bar, and select the Turn Bluetooth On option. Or from System Preferences, click on the Bluetooth option (which is displayed below the Internet And Wireless heading).

The first time you use a Bluetooth device with your MacBook Air, you'll need to "pair" the device with the computer. Pairing a Bluetooth device only needs to be done once. To do this, turn on Bluetooth on your computer. Next, turn on the Bluetooth device and place it into pairing mode so that it becomes "discoverable." How to do this will be explained in the directions that came with the Bluetooth device.

On your MacBook Air, launch System Preferences, and select the Bluetooth option. When the Bluetooth window appears (shown in Figure 8-4), click on the Set Up New Device button. When the device name shows up in the Bluetooth Setup Assistant Window (shown in Figure 8-5), click Continue. The pairing process will commence automatically and will take several seconds. When the process is done, a Congratulations! message will be displayed (shown in Figure 8-6).

If you're setting up multiple Bluetooth devices, once the first one has been paired with your computer, place subsequent devices into pairing mode, access the Bluetooth Setup Assistant Window, and click on the plus sign that's displayed in the lower-left corner of the window. Then, one at a time, add the additional Bluetooth devices by pairing them with your MacBook Air.

Click Quit to continue. The Bluetooth device will now function properly with your MacBook Air. In the future, when that same device is turned on and placed in proximity of your computer, a connection will automatically be established, as long as the Bluetooth function of your MacBook Air is also turned on.

FIGURE 8-4   The Bluetooth window in System Preferences

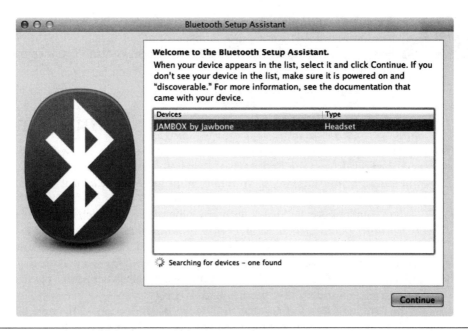

FIGURE 8-5 The Bluetooth device's name will appear when the wireless device is found ("discovered") by your MacBook Air.

FIGURE 8-6 Once paired, the Bluetooth device will work wirelessly with your MacBook Air.

If you're using a Bluetooth 4.0-compatible device, it is not necessary to manually pair the device. The pairing process happens automatically when the MacBook Air's Bluetooth feature is turned on, the Bluetooth device itself is turned on, and both are within range of each other.

Connecting a Printer to Your Computer

No matter how you connect a printer to your MacBook Air, you will need to install the proper printer drivers the first time you try to use the printer. This applies if you're connecting a printer directly to your computer using a cable, or if you're connecting to a printer that's connected to a wireless network.

Your MacBook Air will work with any type of printer, such as a laser printer, inkjet printer, photo printer, or label printer. Plus, you have the option of connecting multiple printers simultaneously, using one or several different connection methods.

Each printer, however, will most likely come with its own printer drivers that need to be installed in OS X. The operating system already has drivers for hundreds of printer makes and models preinstalled. If this is the case, when you plug the printer into the computer for the first time (or attempt a connection with a networked printer), the appropriate drivers will automatically load, and the printer will begin working.

If the appropriate and most up-to-date printer drivers for your printer make and model are not preinstalled in OS X Mountain Lion, you'll first need to download them (for free) from the printer manufacturer's website.

Some less popular printers do not have OS X–compatible drivers available for them, in which case you won't easily be able to get them to work with your MacBook Air, unless you connect them through a network using compatible drivers.

Set Up a New Printer or Scanner to Work with Your MacBook Air

To set up a new printer or scanner to work with your MacBook Air, plug the printer into the computer using a USB cable or connect it to the wireless network. Next, launch System Preferences and select the Print & Scan option from under the Hardware heading.

When the Print & Scan window appears, if the printer make and model do not appear as a listing in the window, click on the plus sign near the lower-left corner of the printer listing box (on the left side of the Print & Scan window). Select the Add Printer Or Scanner option.

If your MacBook Air is connected to a wireless network and printers are available on that network, they will be listed in a pop-up menu that appears after you click on the plus sign (shown in Figure 8-7). At this point, OS X will attempt to auto-install the printer drivers. If a pop-up window appears stating that drivers need to be downloaded, click on the Download & Install button in that window (as shown in Figure 8-8). The necessary drivers will be downloaded and installed by OS X.

FIGURE 8-7 Choose a printer from a wireless network or attach a printer via the computer's USB port.

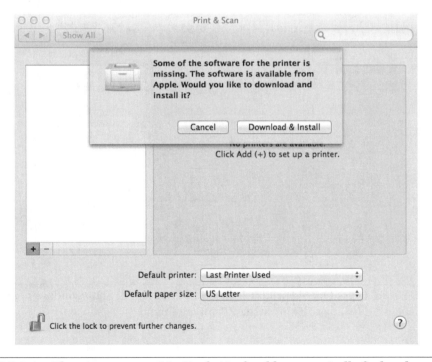

FIGURE 8-8 If necessary, your MacBook Air should automatically find and download the needed printer drivers from the Internet.

Within a few seconds, the printer will be displayed in the Print & Scan window (shown in Figure 8-9). The printer is now ready to use, and will be accessible from any program that has a Print command.

In rare situations when the required printer driver can't be found and installed automatically by OS X, you'll need to first locate and download the necessary drivers yourself (from the printer manufacture's website) and then choose the correct drivers from the Use pull-down menu near the bottom of the Add window (shown in Figure 8-10). Once the proper drivers are downloaded and selected, the printer will become accessible from your MacBook Air.

You'll need to repeat this process, just once, for each printer you plan to use with your MacBook Air. If you have multiple printers connected to your MacBook Air (or the network the computer is connected to), while you're looking at the Print & Scan window in System Preferences, take a moment to select your default printer from the pull-down menu at the bottom of the window.

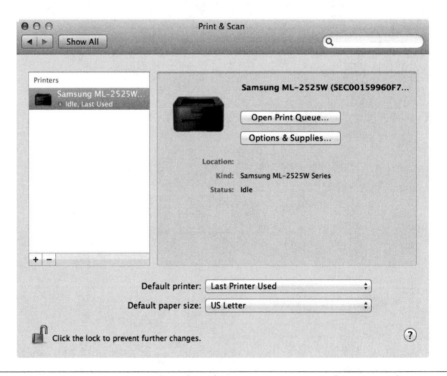

FIGURE 8-9 Once a printer is listed in the Print & Scan window, it can be accessed by any software with a Print command.

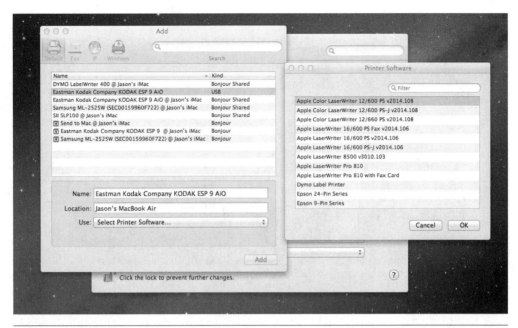

FIGURE 8-10   In some cases, it will be necessary to download printer-specific drivers manually before installing a new printer in OS X.

Instead of selecting a specific printer to be your default printer, you can set up OS X Mountain Lion to use the last-used printer as your default printer. This can be problematic—for example, if you happen to be printing photos on a photo printer (which is something you do only once in a while), but then need to print a text document on your more frequently used laser or inkjet printer, but you forget to switch the printer settings. The computer will send your text document to your photo printer. This winds up wasting paper and ink.

The default printer will be the one the computer automatically selects when you use the Print command from any compatible software or app. To select a printer that's not your default, such as a label printer or photo printer, after executing the Print command, select the printer you want to use from the Printer pull-down menu at the top of the Print window (shown in Figure 8-11).

To speed up the printing process when using the default printer, use the keyboard shortcut COMMAND (⌘)-P, and then press return when the Print window appears as you're using any program (or app) with a Print feature.

FIGURE 8-11   When you click on the Print command in any program, such as Safari (shown here), you will see this Print window appear.

Also from the Print & Scan window in System Preferences, you can select the default paper size. This is necessary if your printer has several paper trays with different paper sizes available, for example. The default paper size for most printers is US Letter (8.5" by 11"). However, if you're using a photo printer, you might opt to use 4" by 6" or 5" by 7" photo paper to create your prints.

The process for setting up a scanner to work with your MacBook Air is identical to setting up a printer. In fact, you can purchase an all-in-one device that includes a printer, scanner, and fax machine and perform setup for all three tools at once.

Using an External Storage Device with Your MacBook Air

Depending on the MacBook Air model you've purchased, your computer has a built-in 64GB, 128GB, or 256GB capacity flash drive. The larger the flash drive's capacity, the more data and files it will be able to store.

You also have the option to connect an external hard drive to your computer. This can be done using a Bluetooth connection, Thunderbolt connection, or through a wireless network (Wi-Fi). Regardless of how you connect an external hard drive, it can be used in the same way as your MacBook Air's primary internal flash drive to store data, files, or content. However, it can also be used in conjunction with OS X's Time Machine feature to maintain a complete backup of your MacBook Air.

External hard drives are available from many different hardware manufacturers, including Apple, Seagate, Western Digital (WD), Verbatim, Iomega, Toshiba, and HP. When choosing a hard drive, you'll have several things to consider, including:

- Its storage capacity, which will range from 256GB to 2TB (or larger). The larger the capacity, the higher the price.
- How the external hard drive will connect to the MacBook Air (using a USB connection, Thunderbolt connection, or wireless connection, for example).
- The read/write speed of the hard drive. This determines how quickly data gets stored on or read from the drive when it's being accessed by your computer. This speed is also dependent on how the drive is connected to the computer. In general, shop for a drive with the fastest read/write speed you can afford, especially if you'll be using the drive with Time Machine or storing large files (such as video files or high resolution digital photos) on the drive.
- The physical size and shape of the hard drive. Some are very tiny and can easily fit in a shirt pocket or purse, which makes them portable enough to carry with your MacBook Air. Others are designed for desktop use and can't easily be transported.
- How the hard drive is powered. Some portable external hard drives operate using power from the MacBook Air's USB port. Others need to be plugged into an electrical outlet or operate using a rechargeable battery.

External hard drives can be purchased online, from Apple Stores, Apple.com, or from any computer, consumer electronics, or office supply superstore. Prices vary greatly, even for similar hardware, so be sure to determine your needs and then shop around for the best price. By shopping online, you can often save 40 percent or more off an external hard drive's suggested retail price.

Almost all external hard drives available these days are both Mac and PC compatible. However, before making your purchase, look at the product's packaging or technical specifications to make sure it's compatible with the Mac and OS X.

 Once data is manually stored on an external hard drive, you can disconnect it from your MacBook Air and plug that drive into another PC or Mac in order to transfer data between computers. Or, if the hard drive is connected to a wireless network, it can be accessed by multiple computers on that network.

Once an external hard drive is connected to or accessible from the computer, an icon for it will appear on the desktop (if the drive is directly connected to the MacBook Air), plus it will be listed in the sidebar of the Finder window (under the Devices heading).

Did You Know?

Time Machine Works with Any External Hard Drive

The Time Machine backup feature of OS X will work with any external hard drive, as long as the available capacity of that drive is larger than the internal hard drive of your MacBook Air. Thus, your best bet is to invest in a 1TB or larger hard drive, so it can be used with Time Machine as well as for other data, file, or content storage.

Because Time Machine accesses your external hard drive regularly to back up newly created or revised data and files, the faster the hard drive's data transfer and read/write speed the better. Whenever Time Machine is actively backing up data, your computer may temporarily slow down. To minimize this inconvenience, use a Thunderbolt-compatible hard drive. However, you can save money by investing in a USB or Wi-Fi-compatible hard drive with a fast read/write speed.

Designed to be used with Time Machine (or as a stand-alone hard drive for other data storage), Apple offers its Time Capsule hard drive (www.apple .com/timecapsule), which can connect to the MacBook Air via Wi-Fi, USB, or Ethernet cable (if the drive will be added to a network). Time Capsule is available with a 2TB ($299) or 3TB ($499) capacity.

Optional external hard drives with similar capabilities are also available (often for less money) from other manufacturers. For example, there's the Seagate GoFlex Satellite Drive, which is Wi-Fi or USB compatible and comes in several different capacities, or there's the Seagate GoFlex Desk for Mac, which is USB and Thunderbolt compatible. It too comes in several capacity configurations. For more information about Seagate drives, visit www .seagate.com/www/en-us/products/external.

To activate Time Machine to work automatically, continuously, and in the background, once an external hard drive is connected to the MacBook Air, access System Preferences and select the Time Machine option. When the Time Machine window appears, on the right side of the window, select the appropriate external drive by clicking on the Select Disk button. Then turn the virtual off/on switch to the ON position. You can customize the options associated with Time Machine by clicking on the Options button that's also displayed in this window (shown in Figure 8-12). For example, you can exclude folders that do not require backing up.

Before disconnecting an external hard drive that is directly connected to the MacBook Air, you'll need to eject the drive. To do this, drag the icon for the drive from the desktop to the Trash on the Dock, or select the drive in Finder and click on the Eject icon that's displayed to the right of its listing on the sidebar. You can also select the drive from within Finder, access the File pull-down menu, and then select the Eject option. Failing to properly eject a drive could corrupt the data stored on it. This applies to USB thumb drives as well.

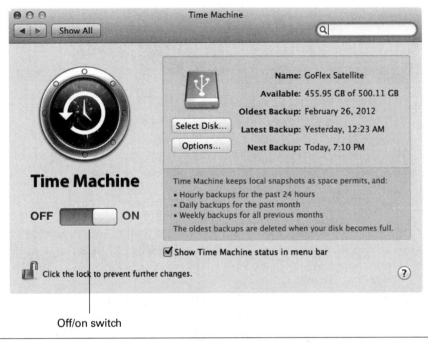

Off/on switch

FIGURE 8-12 The Time Machine window in System Preferences

Using a USB Thumb Drive with Your Computer

A USB thumb drive is a portable storage device that is typically the physical size of your thumb (or smaller). It plugs into the USB port of your computer and can have a storage capacity of between 128KB to 64GB (or larger).

You'll typically find 2GB to 4GB thumb drives available from computer stores, consumer electronics stores, or office supply stores, priced between $10 and $20. If you shop online, these prices will be even lower.

The benefit to using a USB thumb drive is that you can create a backup of important data, files, or content from anywhere, and then store the drive in a pocket or hand it to a friend or coworker. You can easily use these devices to quickly transfer files or data between Macs and PCs, or between multiple Macs.

As you shop for a USB thumb drive, you can find units that are tiny and fit on a keychain, or that have a fun shape, such as an animal or cartoon character. For example, the EMTECH Animal Series of USB thumb drives (www.emtecelectronics.com/products/product.cfm?product=M310), one of which is shown in Figure 8-13, come in 2GB or 4GB capacities. More than a dozen different animal shapes are available. If you're a fan of *Star Wars*, Hello Kitty, or anime, Mimoco offers USB flash drives that resemble popular-culture characters (www.mimoco.com/mimobot-flash-drives/popular-culture/star-wars.aspx) and have capacities between 2GB and 64GB.

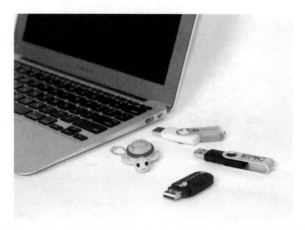

FIGURE 8-13 Shown here is the **EMTECH USB** thumb drive that's shaped like a turtle, as well as several other USB thumb drives from various manufacturers.

 Using a USB thumb drive is ideal for making a backup of important data or files while you're on the go. They're also useful for quickly transferring files between computers. All USB drives are compatible with Macs and PCs.

In terms of functionality, a USB thumb drive works just like an external hard drive when connected to the MacBook Air, but has more limited storage capacity. You can copy and paste or drag and drop files onto or off of the USB thumb drive in Finder. When it's plugged into the computer, an icon for the USB thumb drive will appear on the desktop, and it will be listed under Devices in the sidebar of the Finder window. Remember, when you're ready to disconnect the drive from the computer, it must first be ejected.

PART III

Use Your MacBook Air Anytime and Anywhere

9

Word Processing, Spreadsheets, and Digital Slide Show Presentations on Your MacBook Air

HOW TO...

- Take full advantage of Microsoft Office for Mac
- Use Apple's iWork apps (Pages, Numbers, and Keynote)
- Utilize OpenOffice and other free options for getting work done on the go
- Use popular database management and finance apps

While Apple has gone to great lengths to make the MacBook Air perform more like an iPad, the benefits of using the notebook computer instead of a tablet are that the MacBook Air offers a full-size tactile keyboard, and it is able to run full versions of popular software packages, such as Microsoft Office. This allows you to easily share files and data with other Mac and PC users, while also maintaining full file and data compatibility with other machines and mobile devices. Yet the MacBook Air is lightweight, slim, connects to the Web, and has a long-lasting battery, so you can work from almost anywhere.

Using Microsoft Office with Your MacBook Air

The easiest way to purchase and install Microsoft Office for your MacBook Air is to obtain it directly from Microsoft's website (www.microsoft.com/mac/products). As you'll discover, there are several versions of the popular software suite available, including the Home & Student (starting at $149) and Home & Business (starting at $279) editions.

The Home & Student edition includes full versions of Microsoft Word, Excel, and PowerPoint, while the Home & Business edition also includes Outlook. Both versions come bundled with Microsoft Messenger (for instant messaging using the Microsoft service) and Remote Desktop (which allows you to control your Windows-based PC from a Mac). Both editions are also bundled with Microsoft Lync, a collaboration tool that combines instant messaging with voice-over IP communications and video conferencing (similar to Skype).

In conjunction with Microsoft Office for Mac, Microsoft offers its free SkyDrive service, which serves as a remote, web-based hard drive for storing and sharing files and documents securely. On the Microsoft Office for Mac website (www.microsoft .com/mac/how-to) you'll discover many how-to articles and video-based tutorials for using the Office applications. By clicking on the Templates tab on the website, you'll find hundreds of free application-specific templates for Word, Excel, and PowerPoint (http://office.microsoft.com/en-us/templates) that can help you save time as you create complex documents, spreadsheets, or presentations with minimal formatting effort.

Once you install Microsoft Office for Mac onto your MacBook Air, also install the free (but optional) AutoUpdate for Mac software that's available from the Microsoft website (www.microsoft.com/mac/downloads). It regularly and automatically checks for software updates and installs them, ensuring you're always working with the most current version of the Office software.

If you're already familiar with Microsoft Office for your Windows-based PC, you'll quickly discover that the latest version of Microsoft Office for Mac is virtually 100 percent compatible, but some of the features and functions will appear differently on the screen. For example, Word for Mac now offers both a menu bar and a Ribbon for displaying editing tools on screen. Figure 9-1 shows a sample Microsoft Word screen, while Figure 9-2 shows what Microsoft Excel looks like running on a MacBook Air. In Figure 9-3, you can see a digital slide show presentation being edited using Microsoft PowerPoint.

When porting Office files between a PC and a Mac, the biggest problem you may encounter is the incompatibility of fonts and typestyles, which can ultimately impact document or file formatting. If the fonts and typestyles used in your document or file that was created on a PC are not installed on your Mac, this will often lead to compatibility issues. If this occurs, you'll be notified of the problem when you load an incompatible document or file into the Office software. Microsoft Office will attempt to automatically fix the issues by substituting what it believes to be compatible or similar fonts and typestyles.

To help prevent font or formatting compatibility issues, if you know files will be transferred between PCs and Macs, stick to using common and popular fonts and typestyles, such as Times New Roman, Helvetica, or Arial, for example. Or, if the files won't need to be edited, convert them into PDF files before exporting them to ensure they'll maintain 100 percent compatibility when viewed on any computer or mobile device.

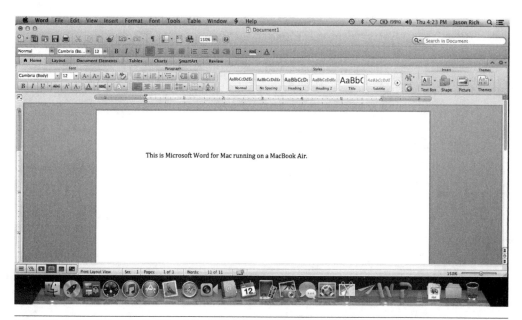

FIGURE 9-1   Microsoft Word for Mac 2011 running on the MacBook Air

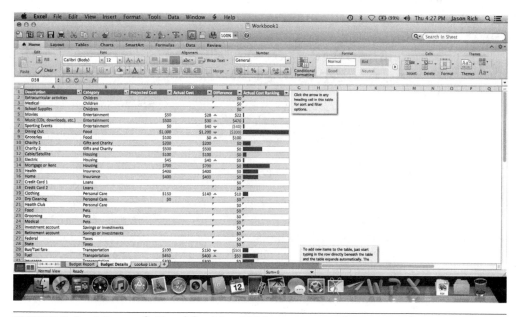

FIGURE 9-2   Microsoft Excel for Mac 2011 running on the MacBook Air

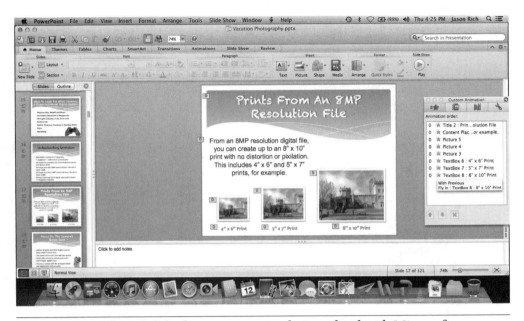

FIGURE 9-3 A digital slide show presentation being edited with Microsoft PowerPoint for Mac 2011

Microsoft Office Works with Microsoft SkyDrive

Similar to iCloud, SkyDrive is a free, cloud-based file sharing service designed specifically for Microsoft Office (for Mac and PC) users. Using Microsoft SkyDrive, you can store, access, and edit your Microsoft Office documents or files from any computer. Unlike iCloud, however, SkyDrive also allows for multiple people to securely access Office documents and files and then collaborate via the Internet. You choose with whom you want to share specific files or documents, and set up password-protected permissions for those people to access certain areas of your SkyDrive account. To help with this collaboration, Microsoft also offers its Microsoft Office Web Apps (online editions of Word, Excel, PowerPoint, and OneNote, which are fully compatible with SkyDrive).

For more information about SkyDrive or to set up a free account, visit http://windows.microsoft.com/en-us/skydrive/home.

Office Offers Application Data and Content Integration

One of the great things about working with the Microsoft Office suite is that each of the applications can be used as a stand-alone product for a specific purpose, such as word processing or spreadsheet management, but all of your data, files, and content can easily be transferred between applications using a variety of methods.

In addition to using OS X's Select, Select All, Copy, Cut, and Paste features or the drag-and-drop method, graphics, photos, clip art, and other elements can be directly imported into or exported from any of the Office applications and easily incorporated into other applications. For example, after you're done crunching numbers with Excel, you can create a stunning multicolor table, chart, or graph that represents your data. Then, with a few clicks, that table, chart, or graph can be imported directly into a Word document or PowerPoint presentation.

As you're working with any of the Office applications, such as Word, access the Insert pull-down menu from the menu bar to import a photo, audio clip, movie clip, clip art, symbol, or shape into the document or file you're working with. You'll discover that Microsoft Office includes an impressive shape and clip art collection that's accessible for free. You can also utilize your own photos or graphics from other sources.

 In addition to the free templates available from the Microsoft website, several companies offer professional templates or themes that work with Word, Excel, or PowerPoint. For example, Presentation Pro (www.presentationpro.com/power _designs.aspx) offers a collection of professionally designed PowerPoint templates that feature many different themes.

Sharing Microsoft Office Files and Data

In Microsoft Word, Excel, and PowerPoint, use the Save command to save your documents and files to the MacBook Air's internal flash drive. Or use the Save As command to store the files on an external storage device such as a USB thumb drive.

From within any of the Office applications, it's also possible to share files by clicking on the File pull-down menu from the menu bar and then selecting the Share option. Shown in Figure 9-4 is Microsoft Word's Share menu option. Doing this will reveal a submenu that allows you to store the document or file you're working with on your SkyDrive account (assuming your MacBook Air is connected to the Internet). Another option is to select the Email Attachment option, and then send the file or document to one or more recipients directly from within the Office program you're using.

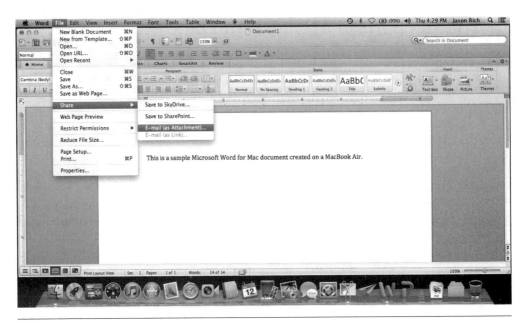

FIGURE 9-4 Export and share a file from Microsoft Word, Excel, or PowerPoint using the Share option.

Of course, once files or documents are stored on your MacBook Air's hard drive (or on an external storage device), it's possible to use Finder to manage those files directly. You can then share those documents or files using any of the file sharing options described in Chapter 6.

There's No OneNote, but Word Offers the Notebook Layout

As you begin working with Microsoft Office for Mac, one application you'll find missing is OneNote, which comes with the Windows edition of the software suite. However, built into the Mac version of Microsoft Word is the Notebook Layout view, which offers the same basic functionality as OneNote (as shown in Figure 9-5).

The Notebook Layout View is a powerful tool for taking notes using a virtual notebook style format. As you type notes, you can incorporate recorded audio clips, flag items, and custom format your document using colored tabs.

Once you launch Microsoft Office, to switch to the Notebook Layout view, click on the View pull-down menu from the menu bar, and then click on the Notebook Layout option (shown in Figure 9-6). Or click on the Notebook Layout icon that's displayed near the lower-left corner of the Word screen.

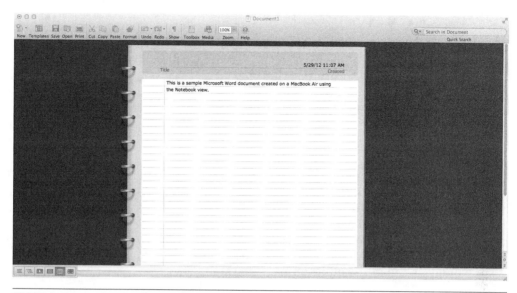

FIGURE 9-5   Microsoft Word 2011 for Mac has a Notebook Layout view that offers additional features not found elsewhere in the Word app.

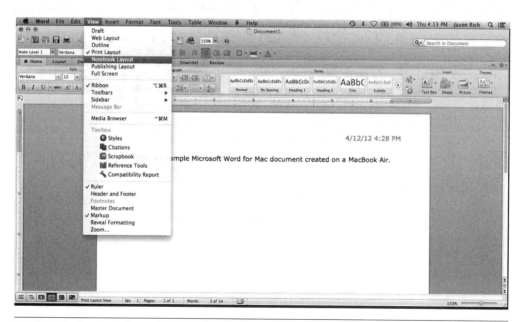

FIGURE 9-6   Switch to the Notebook Layout view in Word by selecting it from the View pull-down menu.

FIGURE 9-7 You can record audio clips and attach then to your text when you use the Notebook Layout view in Word.

In addition to offering full word processing capabilities, the Notebook Layout is perfect for organizing notes, projects, and research, and is ideal for use while participating in meetings, lectures, or seminars.

The built-in audio recorder (shown in Figure 9-7) takes advantage of the MacBook Air's built-in microphone and speakers, allowing you to capture audio content and link the audio files directly to your typed notes, which can take on a traditional format or be created in an outline format with ease.

Did You Know?

OpenOffice Offers Microsoft Office Compatibility for Free

Open source software was created as a free alternative to commercially available, often expensive software. OpenOffice is a suite of applications designed to be 100 percent compatible with Microsoft Office. In fact, OpenOffice mimics Microsoft Office's functionality feature for feature. OpenOffice (and other software like it) is created by a talented team of programmers worldwide who volunteer their talents to create the best software possible. Unlike a commercial software publisher such as Microsoft, which is profit oriented, the goal of open source software is to provide non-copy-protected software entirely free of charge.

To download and install the free OpenOffice for Mac suite of applications, visit www.openoffice.org/porting/mac. Similar to OpenOffice are NeoOffice (www.neooffice.org/neojava/en/index.php) and LibreOffice (www.libreoffice.org), which are also open source suites of Microsoft Office–compatible applications.

Apple's iWork Apps Offer a Microsoft Office Alternative

In addition to creating the Mac computers and the OS X operating system, Apple has developed a selection of popular Mac applications, some of which are bundled free with the Mac (including the software that comprises the iLife suite), and optional software that can be purchased from the App Store.

Apple's iWork suite includes three separate apps—Pages (shown in Figure 9-8), Numbers, and Keynote—that offer similar functionality to Microsoft Word, Excel, and PowerPoint, respectively. The layout and design of the iWork apps are dramatically different from what's offered by Microsoft Office, but the core functionality is the same.

Keep in mind, Pages documents can be exported into Microsoft Word format (or Word documents can be imported into Pages). Likewise, Numbers spreadsheet files can be exported into Microsoft Excel format (or Excel spreadsheets can be imported into Numbers), and Keynote presentations can be exported into Microsoft PowerPoint format (or PowerPoint presentations can be imported into Keynote).

From a price standpoint, the Pages, Numbers, and Keynote apps are sold separately for $19.99 each from the App Store (shown in Figure 9-9). The price of the three apps together, however, comes out to less money than any one of the Microsoft Office suite options.

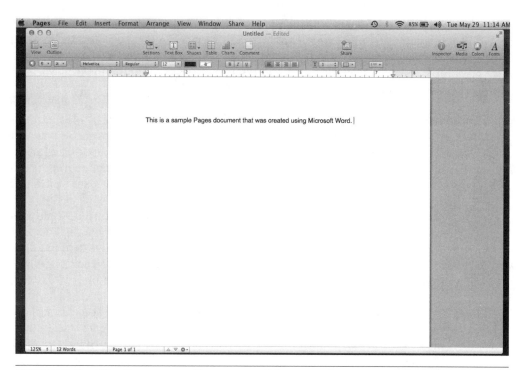

FIGURE 9-8   The Pages app offers many of the same features and functions as Microsoft Word.

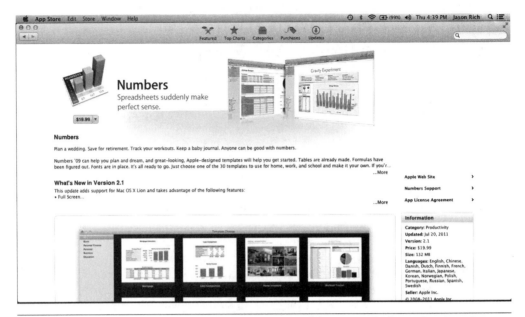

FIGURE 9-9 Pages, Numbers, and Keynote are sold separately from the App Store.

Another advantage to using the iWork apps with your MacBook Air is that they're seamlessly compatible with Apple's iCloud service. So, just as your MacBook Air can automatically sync your Contacts, Calendar, and Reminders data with other computers and iOS mobile devices, this same file syncing functionality works with Pages, Numbers, and Keynote.

If you're an iPhone, iPad, or iPod touch user, iOS versions of Pages, Numbers, and Keynote (which are fully compatible with the Mac versions) are available from the App Store for $9.99 each. Thus, you can create a document in Pages on your Mac, for example, and it will be fully accessible via iCloud on your iPhone or iPad (and vice versa). There's never a need to manually export or import iWork documents or files when transferring them to iWork applications running on other Macs or iOS mobile devices.

Another benefit of iWork is that you can use your MacBook Air's Home Sharing feature in conjunction with an Apple TV device in order to present digital slide presentations on any HD television set wirelessly. The alternative is to use special cables and adapters to connect your MacBook Air to an HD television or LCD projector in order to present PowerPoint presentations, for example.

If you own multiple Macs that are linked to the same iCloud account, such as the MacBook Air and an iMac, you can purchase the iWork apps once, but install them on each of your computers for no extra charge. From the App Store click on the Purchases option from each of your Macs after you've purchased any or all of the iWork apps just once.

Other Software Options to Meet Your Needs

Available from the App Store, as well as directly from the websites of software developers and other online-based sources of Mac software, you'll find a selection of other software for your MacBook Air that's designed for word processing, spreadsheet management, digital slide presentations, and other work-related tasks.

Some of these applications offer very specialized uses. For example, if you want to write the next blockbuster movie or hit Broadway show, you'll find software like Script It!, Final Draft, and Scrivener that are designed specifically for script writing.

Likewise, if you want to use your MacBook Air to keep a digital diary, instead of using a traditional word processor, you could use specialized software like MyDiary 2, Day One, MacJournal, Memories, or iScrapbook.

There are also a handful of other more general purpose word processors available for the Mac such as iA Writer, WriteRoom, Evernote, Write, and Pagesmith. Each offers its own collections of features and functions that set it apart from Microsoft Word or Pages.

When it comes to managing spreadsheets, you also have plenty of options. By visiting the App Store and entering the keyword "spreadsheet" into the Search field, you'll discover third-party software such as Panorama Sheets, Tabulo, and nView.

Database Management on the Go Is Easy Using a MacBook Air

You already know that the MacBook Air comes bundled with software for maintaining a detailed contacts database, as well as a database of to-do lists and your ongoing schedule. In addition, when it comes to creating and managing more complex databases, your options are plentiful.

One of the leading database management applications for PCs and Macs is FileMaker Pro (www.filemaker.com). The latest version of this powerful and versatile software, FileMaker Pro 12, is available for the Mac, but is also fully compatible with PCs and iOS mobile devices. Plus, FileMaker Pro databases can be hosted online and accessed by users from any Internet-enabled device.

Starting at $299, the FileMaker Pro 12 software (shown in Figure 9-10) allows you to create and manage complex databases from scratch. Or you can install and use templates for a wide range of specialized purposes. Using a database created with FileMaker, you can manage people, projects, assets, or images in a very customizable way.

 To discover some of the ways people in hundreds of different industries are using FileMaker Pro as a cost-effective alternative to custom designing software, visit www.filemaker.com/solutions.

With each new version of FileMaker that's released, the process of actually creating the database has become easier, although this still requires a learning curve. Once a database is created, it can be used by anyone, on any computer, intuitively.

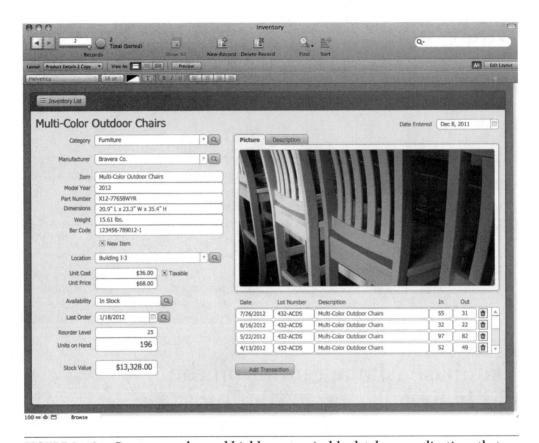

FIGURE 9-10 Create complex and highly customizable database applications that can run on the MacBook Air using FileMaker Pro 12.

Figure 9-11 shows another customized database that was created using FileMaker Pro 12 running on a Mac.

For less complex database management needs that are also highly customizable, FileMaker offers the Bento 4 ($49.99) software, which offers a more straightforward, template-based approach to creating and managing databases. Bento is designed primarily for simpler tasks, such as organizing contacts, tracking projects, or planning events.

From the Bento website (http://solutions.filemaker.com/database-templates), hundreds of free templates are available, so you can begin using the software immediately, without having to create a database from scratch before populating it with your data. For example, there's the Bento Business Organizer (www.bentotrial.com/bbo), a collection of Bento templates designed specifically for small business operators.

 Tip A version of Bento is also available for the iPhone and iPad, so databases and related data can easily be synced between a MacBook Air, other Macs, and your iOS devices.

FIGURE 9-11   FileMaker Pro 12 is an extremely versatile database management application for the Mac.

Manage Financial Data with Quicken or QuickBooks for Mac

In addition to using a spreadsheet application to organize and manage financial data, you can utilize Mac editions of Intuit's popular Quicken and QuickBooks software. Quicken Essentials for Mac ($49.99, http://quicken.intuit.com/personal-finance-software/mac-personal-financial-software.jsp) is a comprehensive tool for managing all aspects of your personal finances. It allows you to manage your bank accounts, credit cards, investments, retirement accounts, and other finance-related data from a single, easy-to-use, and graphic-rich app.

While you can crunch numbers easily without being a mathematical whiz, Quicken Essentials also makes graphing and charting your personal and up-to-date financial data easy, so you can view your entire financial situation at a glance. Then, using the online elements of this software, you can handle online banking tasks, pay bills, and save a lot of time and aggravation when it comes to preparing your taxes.

Meanwhile, for small business operators, QuickBooks for Mac ($229.95, http://quickbooks.intuit.com/mac) offers a complete set of bookkeeping and financial management tools that are highly customizable to meet the needs of your business venture. Using QuickBooks, you can generate customized and personalized invoices, easily keep track of who owes you money, manage your business bank accounts, organize assets, and handle online banking transactions.

 While Quicken Essentials for Mac and QuickBooks will run on any Mac, using this software on your MacBook Air gives you full mobility to manage your personal and/or business finances from virtually anywhere.

Your Data Is Available When and Where You Need It

Regardless of what Mac-compatible software you use, the benefit of running it on your MacBook Air is that you can perform your computing tasks from virtually anywhere, and keep a vast amount of app-specific data at your fingertips. As you now know, the MacBook Air also makes it easy to share data and files with other Macs, PCs, and iOS mobile devices using a variety of methods (many of which are outlined in Chapters 6 and 7), so syncing and sharing files and data securely is always an option, especially if your MacBook Air is connected to the Internet.

The ability to access your personal data and files while on the go, without having to lug around a heavy computer, has changed the way many people do business. As you'll discover, the collection of Mac-compatible software that's available, when combined with the power and capabilities of the MacBook Air, gives you unprecedented computing power at home, at work, and while traveling, without having to give up a nice size screen or full-size keyboard (as is necessary when trying to work with your Mac or PC files on a mobile device).

 When using specialized software on your MacBook Air, you'll discover it's probably compatible with a cloud-based file sharing service, such as iCloud, Dropbox, or SkyDrive. If this is the case, syncing your app-specific data and sharing it with your other computers, mobile devices, and/or other people becomes much easier. So, as you're deciding what software to utilize with your MacBook Air, think about how you'll need to share or sync your data and files, and then consider your best options for doing this securely and easily.

10

Surf the Web on Your MacBook Air

HOW TO...

- Use Safari to explore the Web
- Reduce onscreen clutter with Safari's Reader feature
- Take advantage of Safari's Reading List feature
- Other web surfing options

Anytime you use your MacBook Air within the radius of a wireless network or Wi-Fi hotspot, you can easily access the Internet to manage your email, sync data with iCloud, or surf the Web, for example. If you have access to the Internet via an Ethernet cable connection that isn't wireless, you can purchase the optional Apple USB Ethernet Adapter ($29, http://store.apple.com/us/product/MC704ZM/A), and plug your MacBook Air into an available Internet modem or router.

Surf the Web from Almost Anywhere

Another option for connecting your MacBook Air to the Internet is to plug a wireless data modem into the computer's USB port. Wireless data service and the required modem are available from virtually all wireless data service providers, such as AT&T Wireless, Verizon Wireless, or T-Mobile.

This option will require subscribing to a fee-based wireless data plan. Depending on the service provider, you could sign up for a pay-as-you-go plan for a flat monthly fee for a predetermined wireless data allocation (such as 2GB per month), or sign up for a two-year service plan for access to a 3G or 4G (LTE) wireless data network. If given the option, utilize the much faster 4G (LTE) network.

Once your MacBook Air has access to the Internet, you'll use the Safari web browser (preinstalled with OS X Mountain Lion) to surf the Web. As you'll discover in this chapter, the many commands functions that are built into the Safari web browser are accessible from the app's pull-down menus, as well as from the app's toolbar, or by using keyboard shortcuts.

Tip From the App Store, if you enter the search phrase "Web" or "Internet," you'll discover hundreds of apps that can add features and functionality to your web surfing experience. There are also app-based tools that can enhance your online privacy, or that make storing and organizing information that you acquire from the Web much more efficient. For example, Evernote (free) allows you to gather information from the Web and then organize, store, print, or share it.

Did You Know?

Besides Safari, There Are Other Web Browser Options, as Well as Optional Plug-Ins

Instead of using Safari to navigate the Web, you have the option to download and install an alternate web browser for free, such as Mozilla Firefox (www.mozilla.org), Google Chrome (www.google.com/chrome), or the Opera web browser (www.opera.com). Each of these web browsers offers slightly different features that can alter your web browsing experience.

In addition to the web browser itself, you have the option of installing a wide range of plug-ins for each browser (including Safari) in order to enhance its functionality. For example, the Adobe Flash Player plug-in (www.adobe.com/support/flashplayer/downloads.html) adds Flash compatibility to the popular web browsers for viewing Flash-based animations and graphics.

The Adobe Reader plug-in allows you to view PDF files you acquire from the Internet directly within your web browser. The QuickTime, Java, Real Player, and Windows Media Player plug-ins allow you to view other types of multimedia content as you're surfing the Web.

If you visit a website that requires a special plug-in, you'll be given the opportunity to download and install it for free so that you can fully utilize the website.

Separate and often free apps or browser plug-ins are also available for managing your online presence on services such as Facebook, Twitter, Google+, and LinkedIn, as well as online-based photo sharing services, such as Flickr.

Whether you use Safari as your primary web browser or opt to use another browser, you'll discover it's fast, easy, and efficient to access a wide range of tools for finding, accessing, and utilizing the information that's available on the Web.

Getting to Know the Safari Web Browser

Safari (shown in Figure 10-1) is a powerful web browser developed by Apple. The latest version of Safari that comes preinstalled with OS X Mountain Lion offers a handful of features not found in older versions of this popular browser for the Mac. However, if you're an iPad user, you'll recognize some of these newly added features.

Like all MacBook Air apps, Safari has a series of pull-down menu options available from the menu bar once the app is launched. You can customize your web surfing experience by accessing the Safari pull-down menu and selecting the Preferences option, which you'll learn more about shortly.

Menu bar   Toolbar

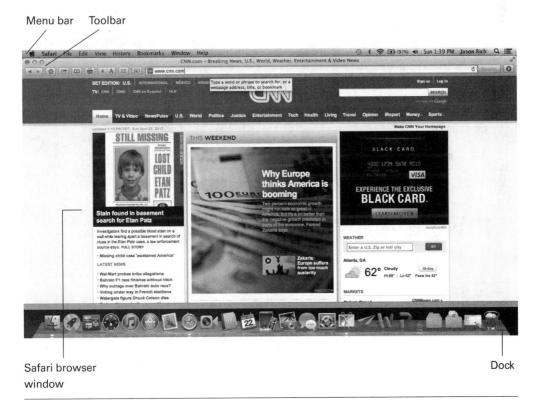

Safari browser
window

Dock

FIGURE 10-1   The Safari web browser allows you to explore the Web from your MacBook Air, assuming an Internet connection is available. Here, the menu bar, toolbar, and Dock are displayed.

Did You Know?

The OS X Mountain Lion Version of Safari Is Chock Full of New Features

At the same time Apple revamped the OS X operating system, the Safari web browser also received a facelift. For example, the older versions of Safari featured a separate Address field and Search field. In the current version, Safari Version 6.0 (or later), there is now just one field that's referred to as a "Smart Search Field."

Thus, if you enter a keyword or search phrase into this field, Safari will access the default search engine and display search results. However, in this same field, you can enter the website address (URL) for the site you want to visit.

Also, like many of OS X Mountain Lion's preinstalled apps, Safari now features a Share button, so it's easy to share web pages with others via email, Messages, Facebook, or Twitter. Plus, the Reading List feature offers a way to store web pages, articles, and content for later review while you're online or offline.

Another new feature added to Safari is called "Do Not Track." This is an up-and-coming web browsing privacy standard that allows you to surf the Web without the websites you visit tracking your actions.

In this chapter, you'll also read about some of the other new Safari features, like tabbed web browsing, which makes switching between web pages faster and easier. When you begin using Safari Version 6.0 (or later) with OS X Mountain Lion, you'll also discover the web browser offers faster performance and smoother scrolling as you're viewing web pages.

Access Safari's Pull-Down Menus from the App's Menu Bar

The pull-down menus available from Safari's menu bar offer a plethora of commands and access to many web surfing features you'll find useful.

The File Pull-Down Menu

From the File pull-down menu (shown in Figure 10-2), you can create and open new browser windows or browser tabs, print content from websites, access the Share menu, and handle a variety of other web surfing tasks.

The Edit Pull-Down Menu

Among the commands available from this pull-down menu are Select All, Copy, Cut, and Paste. You'll also discover the Find command here, which is useful for searching for a keyword or phrase within the text that's featured on a website.

File pull-down menu

FIGURE 10-2   The File pull-down menu that's available from the menu bar offers a handful of commands accessible while surfing the Internet.

The Speech option allows the MacBook Air to read out loud whatever text is displayed onscreen in the active browser window. A computer voice is used. Start Speech and Stop Speech commands are submenu options.

The View Pull-Down Menu

The commands found under the View pull-down menu allow you to better control what you see on the screen while you're navigating your way around the Web. For example, you can access the Zoom In or Zoom Out commands; show/hide the browser's bookmarks bar, tab bar, or status bar; or view your Reading List. From this pull-down menu (shown in Figure 10-3), it's possible to better utilize your MacBook Air's screen by entering Full Screen mode (shown in Figure 10-4) as you explore the Web.

In addition to accessing Safari-related commands and features via the options listed under the app's pull-down menus, you can often use keyboard shortcuts. Plus, many of the popular Safari commands are accessible from the app's icon-based toolbar as well.

When surfing the Internet using Safari, to switch to Full Screen mode and maximize onscreen real estate, click on the Full Screen icon that's displayed near the top-right corner of the screen. Another option is to select the Enter Full Screen option from the View pull-down menu, or use the CONTROL-COMMAND (⌘)-F keyboard shortcut.

View pull-down menu

FIGURE 10-3   Safari's View pull-down menu

FIGURE 10-4   Fully utilize your MacBook Air's screen when surfing the Web by entering Full Screen mode to view a website. Notice the menu bar and Dock are not displayed.

The History Pull-Down Menu

On the History pull-down menu (shown in Figure 10-5), you'll see a listing of websites you've visited during the current web surfing session, earlier in the day, or on previous days. You can use the Clear History command to delete this stored data.

The Bookmarks Pull-Down Menu

Most people have a selection of favorite websites they frequent. To save time accessing these sites, you can create and store bookmarks for them, and then access those bookmarks from the Bookmarks pull-down menu (shown in Figure 10-6). In addition to using Bookmarks, a handful of your most-frequented or favorite websites can be saved and displayed within Safari's bookmarks bar.

The bookmarks bar can be displayed along the top of the screen, before the toolbar, for easy access.

From the Bookmarks menu, it's possible to access the web browser's Reading List feature, which will be explained in detail shortly.

History pull-down menu

FIGURE 10-5   The History pull-down menu offers commands for easily revisiting websites you've already accessed.

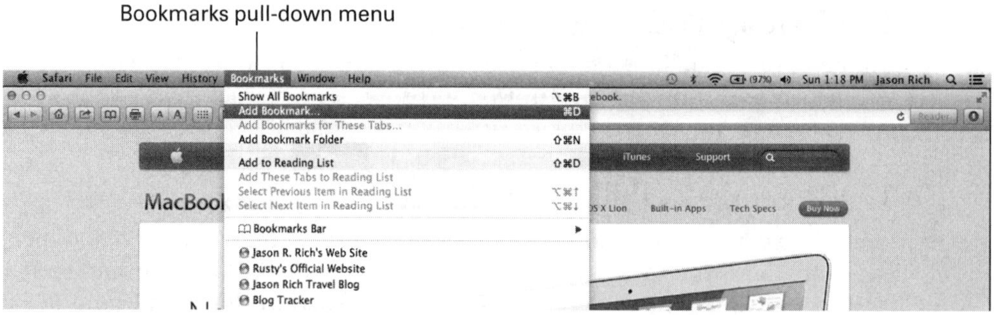

Bookmarks pull-down menu

FIGURE 10-6   Safari's Bookmarks pull-down menu allows you to manage your saved bookmarks, as well as your bookmarks bar.

The Windows Pull-Down Menu

The Windows pull-down menu offers commands for managing tabs within the browser. Instead of opening separate web browser windows, each of which can display one website, and then having to switch between active browser windows if you want to access multiple websites simultaneously, it's possible to use tabbed-based web browsing.

When you create multiple tabs within Safari, each tab is displayed along the top of the Safari window, just under the toolbar. Each tab represents one browser window (which displays a website). Simply by clicking on a tab, you can make it the active browser window. This makes it easy to quickly switch between websites or web pages. One benefit of using separate browser windows (as opposed to tabs), however, is that you can position two or more windows side by side on the computer screen and view them simultaneously.

 If you need help using the Safari web browser, access the Help pull-down menu to utilize the app's built-in Help feature.

Finding Your Way Around Safari's Toolbar

Displayed just below the Safari menu bar, at the top of the Safari app window, you'll discover the toolbar. The toolbar is fully customizable and comprises command icons and fields that make it easier and more efficient to navigate your way around the Web. You also have the option to hide the toolbar altogether.

By customizing the toolbar, you will have the command icons you want or most frequently use displayed along the top of the screen in locations that are convenient for you.

 You have the option to conserve onscreen real estate and remove the toolbar display altogether. To do this, access the View pull-down menu from the menu bar and select the Hide Toolbar option.

How to... **Customize Safari's Toolbar**

Like most things in Safari, you can customize the appearance of the toolbar. To do this, launch the Safari web browser. Access the View pull-down menu, and make sure the Show Toolbar option is active. You'll know it's active because you'll see the toolbar displayed in the Safari app window, plus the pull-down menu option will say Hide Toolbar, as opposed to Show Toolbar.

Next, select the Customize Toolbar option in the View pull-down menu. Displayed within the window that appears (shown in Figure 10-7) are a series of command icons and interactive fields.

One at a time, drag the command icons or fields from the Customize Toolbar window to the exact location where you want each to appear on the actual Safari toolbar (displayed along the top of the Safari window).

As you're customizing the layout of the toolbar, you can also drag command icons that already appear within the toolbar out of it. Doing this allows you to determine not just which command icons are displayed along the toolbar but also the order in which they appear. It's also possible to rearrange command icons that are currently displayed in the toolbar by dragging them from one position to another.

To return the appearance of the Safari toolbar to its default settings, look near the bottom of the Customize Toolbar window under the Or Drag The Default Set Into The Toolbar heading, and drag the precreated toolbar layout from the window onto your Safari's toolbar.

When you're done with your customizations, click on the Done button that's displayed in the lower-right corner of the Customize Toolbar window.

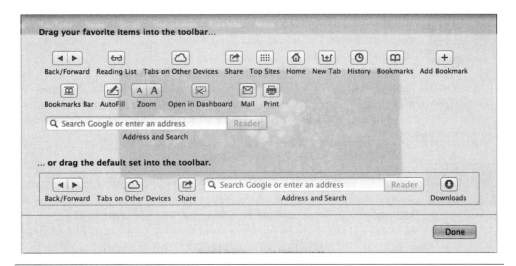

FIGURE 10-7 Drag icons from the Customize Toolbar window onto your toolbar that's displayed near the top of the Safari app window.

Discover What Each Toolbar Command Icon Is Used For

As you'll see when you access the Customize Toolbar window, there are 17 different command icons available that you can use to customize the layout of your Safari toolbar. The following is a quick summary of what each command icon is used for.

- **Back/Forward** Click on the Back or Forward icon to revisit a web page that you recently accessed within the same Safari browser window.
- **Show/Hide Reading List** This command serves the same purpose as the Show Reading List option from the View pull-down menu. It's used to display a list of web pages or articles you've manually saved on your Reading List. This feature is described in greater detail later in this chapter.
- **Tabs on Other Devices** If you become a fan of tabbed-based web browsing, and use this feature, you can set up Safari to sync your active tabs with your other Mac and iOS devices (including your iPhone or iPad). So you can begin exploring the Web on your MacBook Air, for example, open up multiple browser tabs, and then continue your web surfing experience on another Mac or iOS device and see those same tabs displayed. This feature works on all computers or iOS devices linked to the same iCloud account.
- **Share** Quickly access the Share menu, which is a new feature added to Safari for the Mac. The Share menu is explained in greater detail later in this chapter. You can also access the Share menu from the File pull-down menu.
- **Top Sites** Instead of accessing your History listing to view a text-based summary for the web pages you've recently visited, you can click on the Top Sites icon to view current thumbnail images of the same websites (shown in Figure 10-8). At the top of the Top Sites screen, click on the Top Sites tab or the History tab. The Top Sites listing can be customized, just like the Bookmarks menu. Click on any website's thumbnail image to access that site from the Top Sites display.

 To customize your Top Sites screen, click on the Edit button displayed in the lower-left corner. This allows you to pick and choose which 12 websites will have thumbnails displayed.

- **Home** Quickly access the web page that you have selected to be your home website. Many people set their home website to be their favorite search engine (such as Yahoo!, Google, or Bing), their company's home page, or their favorite website.

 To set the home website, access the Safari pull-down menu and select the Preferences option. Click on the General button at the top of the Preferences window. Within the General window, type the home page URL within the Homepage field. Be sure to enter the complete URL, starting with "http://".

- **New Tab** If you opt to use Safari's tabbed browsing feature, click on the New Tab command to open a new tab with Safari, which in turn opens a new browser window.

FIGURE 10-8   The Top Sites view shows thumbnail previews of favorite or recently visited websites.

- **History**   Clicking the History icon serves the same purpose as accessing the History pull-down menu from the menu bar.
- **Bookmarks**   Clicking the Bookmarks icon serves the same purpose as accessing the Bookmarks pull-down menu.
- **Add Bookmark**   Quickly save the web page you're currently viewing in the active browser window as a bookmark in your Bookmarks menu or the bookmarks bar.
- **Bookmarks Bar**   Along the top of the Safari app window, under the toolbar, you can choose to display a handful of bookmarked website links for your favorite or most frequented websites. Displaying the bookmarks bar on the screen takes up an extra line of screen space. Clicking on the Bookmarks Bar icon will show or hide the bookmarks bar, making it available only when it's needed.
- **AutoFill**   When visiting a website that requires you to fill in a form with your name, address, phone number, or other information that's already stored in your personal entry in the Contacts database, click on the AutoFill option so Safari will automatically plug in the appropriate information into each field without you having to retype it.

 Using the AutoFill feature, Safari can also store your usernames and passwords for websites, and then fill in this information automatically every time you revisit a website. To customize how the AutoFill feature operates, access the Safari pull-down menu from the menu bar, select the Preferences option, and click on the AutoFill button. You can then turn on or off, as well as edit, specific AutoFill functions.

- **Zoom**   Quickly decrease or increase the size of website text being displayed in the browser window by clicking on the "a" or "A" icon, respectively.
- **Open In Dashboard**   If there is a particular part of a website, such as a news headline box, that constantly updates, you can add a window for that web page content within your MacBook Air's Dashboard. When you click on this icon, you'll be able to choose what content you want displayed on your Dashboard by selecting highlighted content and clicking on the Add icon. That content will be displayed whenever you access the Dashboard.
- **Mail**   Send emails directly from the Safari app without manually having to first launch the Mail app. When you use this feature, the active website's URL will automatically be embedded within the email, so you can easily share details about a website with one or more other people by sending them an email message about the site.
- **Print**   If you have a printer connected to your MacBook Air, you can print web pages or website content from within Safari using this Print command icon. Or access the Print command from the File pull-down menu. You can also use the COMMAND (⌘)-P keyboard shortcut.
- **Address and Search**   With this version of Safari, you can perform a web search or manually enter a website's URL in the Address and Search field. To perform a web search using the default search engine you select, simply type in a keyword or search phrase and press RETURN. To visit a specific web page, manually type the website's URL. When doing this, you can use one of the following formats:
  - *http://www.websitename.extension*   Example: http://www.jasonrich.com
  - *www.websitename.extension*   Example: www.jasonrich.com
  - *websitename.extension*   Example: jasonrich.com

When manually entering a website address (URL), you can mix uppercase and lowercase letters or just use lowercase letters. However, it is essential that you enter the correct website extension in order to access your intended website. There are many website extensions, the most popular of which is ".com". The website you're visiting may have .org, .gov, .info, .biz, or .tv, or one of countless other extensions.

Displayed on the right side of the toolbar are the Refresh, Reader, and Download icons, as well as the Full Screen icon. These can't be moved or removed when customizing the toolbar.

The Refresh icon, which looks like a circular arrow, is used to reload or update the current web page you're viewing within the active browser window. If information on the website you're viewing updates regularly, it may be necessary to click on the Refresh icon to reload the web page to view those updates or changes.

Using the Reader Feature of Safari

When the Reader icon becomes active, it means you're currently viewing a web page that's compatible with this Safari feature. Not all web pages are compatible, however.

The Reader icon is used to clear away the onscreen clutter that may be present on a particular website, and then automatically reformat the text-based content (and related photos) into something that's easy to read on the screen (or print out).

Reader is ideal for reading long articles, for example, when ads and other distracting content are also displayed on the Safari screen. Figure 10-9 shows a Reader-compatible web page without this feature being activated. Once the web page is loaded into a browser window in Safari, click on the Reader icon to reformat the web page content into a format that's less cluttered (as shown in Figure 10-10).

Using the Download Icon

Located to the extreme right of the toolbar is the Download icon. When you click on a file or document in a web page and have it downloaded to your computer, by default it will be stored in the Downloads folder (accessible using the Finder). Click on the Downloads button to view the progress of a file download, and to access a listing of recently downloaded files, photos, or documents (shown in Figure 10-11).

 Click on the Clear button in the upper-right corner of the Downloads window to clear this listing. To quickly access the Downloads folder, click on the magnifying glass icon to the right of a recently downloaded file. You can also access a downloaded file by double-clicking on its listing in the Downloads window.

FIGURE 10-9 Many websites for newspapers, for example, are compatible with Safari's Reader feature. This is what the *New York Daily News* web page looks like regularly.

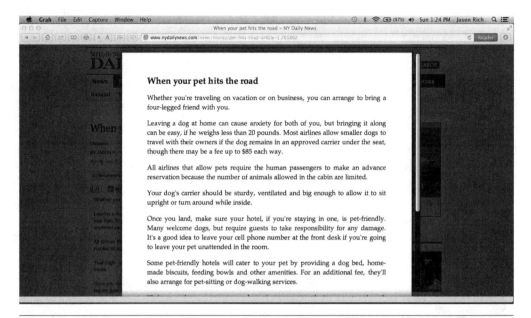

FIGURE 10-10 The same web page content is shown here using the Reader feature.

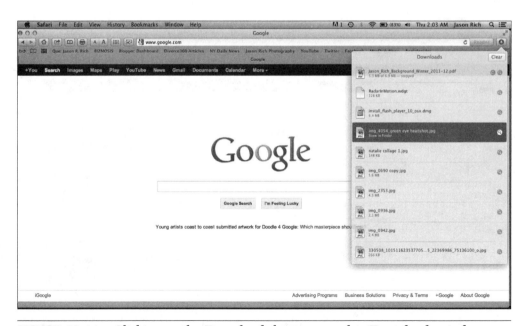

FIGURE 10-11 Clicking on the Downloads button reveals a Downloads window on the right side of the screen. This displays recently downloaded files, as well as the progress of files currently downloading, if applicable.

If you want to change the default location where files, documents, photos, or other content that's downloaded from Safari is saved, access the Safari pull-down menu from the menu bar and select the Preferences option. Click on the General button that's displayed near the top of the Preferences window (shown in Figure 10-12). Near the bottom of this window, click on the Save Downloaded Files To option and set your new default location.

Using the Remove Download List Items option, you can determine when downloaded content is removed from the Download list that appears when you click on the Download icon as you're surfing the Web. You can do this manually by clicking on the Clear button that's displayed within the Downloads window, or you can have Safari automatically delete the listings when you quit the Safari app, or immediately after the file is successfully downloaded.

Using the Full Screen Icon

At any time when exploring the Web using Safari, you can click on the Full Screen icon (that's displayed near the upper-right corner of the Safari app window) to enter Full Screen viewing mode. Doing this removes the menu bar and Dock from the screen, allowing you to view just the Safari app window on your MacBook Air's display.

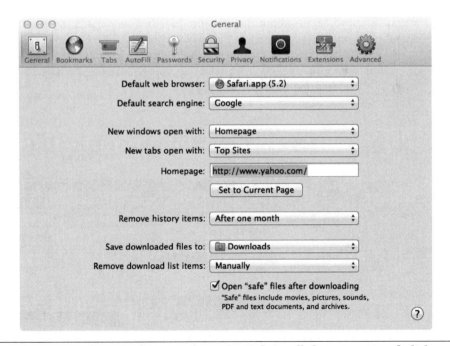

FIGURE 10-12   Select Preferences from the Safari pull-down menu and click on the General button to determine the default location where downloaded files will be saved on your MacBook Air.

To exit out of Full Screen mode, press the ESC key on the keyboard.

Using Safari's Share Menu

There will be times when surfing the Web that you come across something you want to share with friends, family, or coworkers. Thanks to the new Share menu that's built into Safari, you can quickly share information about the website you're currently viewing without having to leave the Safari web browser.

 If you have Facebook integration set up on your MacBook Air, when you click on the Share button within Safari (or many of the other preinstalled apps), you'll have the opportunity to publish app-specific content directly to your Facebook page from within Safari.

As you're viewing a website that you want to share with others, simply click on the Share icon (shown in Figure 10-13), or select the Share menu from the File pull-down menu. You'll then be given the option to add the web page to your Reading List (for later viewing), or add it to your Bookmarks menu (or bookmarks bar). From the Share menu, you can also email the URL of the website that's active from directly within the Safari web browser (without first having to manually launch the Mail app), or you can send details about the website via iMessage or text message using the Message command.

Finally, if you have one or more active Twitter accounts, and you've set up Twitter integration with your MacBook Air, you can compose and send a tweet with the website link embedded within it from Safari.

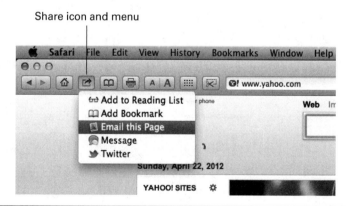

FIGURE 10-13 Click on the Share icon on the toolbar to access the Share menu in Safari and quickly share details about the website you're viewing with other people via the Message app, email, or Twitter.

FIGURE 10-14   Send a tweet from within Safari and have the active website's URL that you're viewing automatically be embedded within that tweet.

When you select the Twitter option from the Share menu in Safari, a tweet window will appear. The website link will already be embedded in the outgoing tweet message (as shown in Figure 10-14). Simply enter additional text using the keyboard and then click the Send button. You can also add your exact location to the tweet, or if you have multiple Twitter accounts set up to work with your MacBook Air, choose which Twitter account the tweet will be sent from (by clicking on the From field).

Store Articles and Web Content for Later Viewing Using Reading List

Another common occurrence when you're exploring the Web is that you'll come across an article, website, or online content that's of interest to you, but that you don't have the time to read at the moment. One option when this happens is to save the website's URL as a bookmark in your Bookmarks menu or bookmarks bar.

Using Safari's Reading List feature, you can also store the article on your Reading List and then easily refer back to it later without having to first locate that web page again. To add a web page or article to your Reading List, as you're viewing it within an active browser window, select the Add To Reading list command from the Bookmarks pull-down menu (from the menu bar). Or select the View Reading List option, and then click on the Add Page button at the top of the Reading List window (shown in Figure 10-15).

As you're viewing your Reading List window, you can sort the stored listings and view all of them, or click on the Unread button to display only unread articles or stored web pages. From the Reading List window, click on any listing to view that article or website in a new browser window.

When using the Reading List feature of Safari, you can later view web pages, articles, or content offline, meaning that the content you save in your Reading List will be automatically downloaded and stored on your MacBook Air, so it can be viewed later, without an Internet connection being present.

Reading List window

FIGURE 10-15   The Reading List window displays all articles or web pages stored on your Reading List.

In some cases, when you open an article from the Reading List in a Safari browser window, you can then click on the Reader icon to display that content in an uncluttered, easier-to-read format.

Taking Advantage of Safari's Privacy Features

If you've ever seen the hit Broadway musical *Avenue Q*, you probably remember a song from that show called "The Internet Is for Porn." Well, if you're one of those people who use the Internet for this purpose, or you simply want to keep your web surfing activities private so other people who access your MacBook Air can't easily determine what you've been up to, there are a handful of things you can do to cover your tracks, including:

- Access the History pull-down menu when you're done surfing the Web and click on the Clear History command.
- Turn on the Private Browsing feature from the Safari pull-down menu. When you do this, Safari will no longer keep track of the pages you visit, nor will it remember your search history or retain AutoFill information. When you access the Private Browsing option, click on the OK icon to confirm your decision to activate this feature. Even with this feature turned on, you can still use the

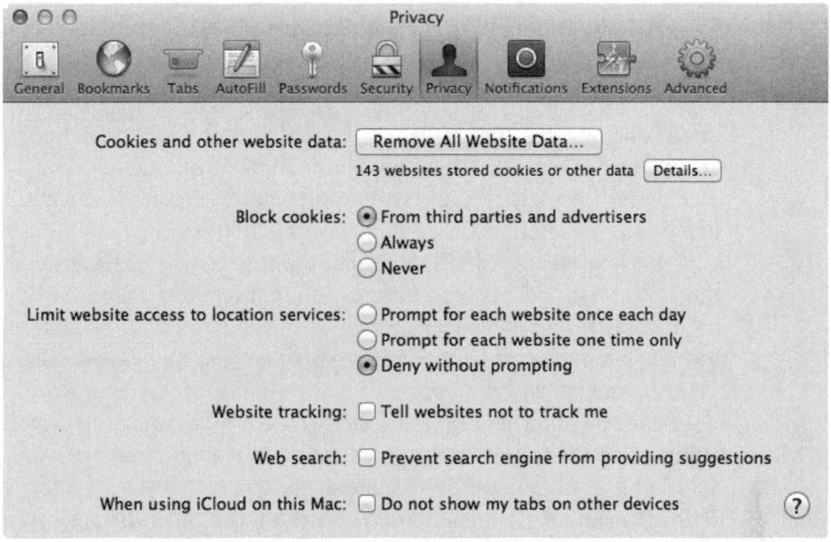

FIGURE 10-16   There are multiple options that you can customize within the Privacy window of Safari to keep your web surfing activities confidential.

Forward or Back button while browsing, as long as the same active browser window remains open.

- From Safari's Preferences menu, click on the Passwords button at the top of the Preferences window, and then select all of the stored website URLs, usernames, and passwords that are listed, using the Remove All command to delete them.

- From Safari's Preferences menu, click on the Privacy button at the top of the Preferences window (shown in Figure 10-16), and then click on the Remove All Website Data option. You can also turn on the Block Cookies option, which will prevent Safari from storing any information related to any websites you visit on your computer (such as website-specific preferences). There are several other options available within the Privacy window that can be turned on or adjusted to enhance the level of web surfing privacy you'll have when using your MacBook Air and Safari.

- Access the Downloads folder using Finder and delete any files, photos, documents, or other content that you have manually downloaded from the Internet. Once you send these items to the Trash, be sure to use the Empty Trash command to delete the items from your computer altogether. Otherwise, someone could view them from the Trash folder.

- Turn off iCloud functionality for your Safari bookmarks so any bookmarks or Reading List items you save will not be synced with iCloud or made accessible from your other Macs, PCs, or iOS devices that are linked to your iCloud account. How to do this is covered in Chapter 7.

Did You Know?

Some Websites Can Tap into Notification Center to Display Alerts

One of the new features built into OS X Mountain Lion is the Notification Center. Through the Notification Center window, as well as through banners and alerts, the various apps running on your MacBook Air can alert you of important information that requires your attention.

A growing number of websites are now Notification Center compatible. As those sites get updates with information that requires your attention, you'll be notified by having an alert displayed within the Notification Center window, or by having a banner or alert window pop up on the MacBook Air's screen.

To customize which compatible websites can access your MacBook Air's Notification Center functionality, and to determine what types of alerts, alarms, or notifications those websites will be able to generate, access the Safari pull-down menu from the menu bar and select the Preferences option. Then, from the Preferences window, click on the Notifications button.

Within the Notifications window, a list of Notification Center compatible websites, if any, will be displayed. For each listing, you can adjust its settings, or you can adjust all Safari-related settings at once by clicking on the Notification Center Preferences icon. Next, select Safari from the left side of the Notifications window within System Preferences, and then make your adjustments.

- The Do Not Track feature prevents the websites you visit from tracking your online actions. You can turn on this feature by launching Safari, accessing the Safari pull-down menu from the menu bar, selecting the Preferences option, and then clicking on the Privacy tab. When the Privacy window is displayed, add a checkmark to the checkbox that's associated with the Website Tracking option. When turned on, the Do Not Track feature will prevent websites you visit from tracking your online actions.

 Keep in mind, if you have iCloud's Photo Stream feature turned on and then download photos from the Internet and view them using iPhoto (or an iCloud compatible app), those images will automatically be added to your Photo Stream and become accessible from your other computers, Apple TV, and iOS mobile devices.

 Unless you manually turn on the Private Browsing feature and adjust the other privacy-related settings in Safari Preferences, someone who uses your account on your MacBook Air can easily determine what websites you've visited. Plus, if you've stored your usernames and passwords for those websites in Safari, other people can log into those websites as you and access your personal (and often private) accounts.

Sync Your Saved Bookmarks with Other Computers and Mobile Devices

Thanks to iCloud, you can automatically sync your Safari bookmarks, bookmarks bar, and Reading List between your MacBook Air and your other Macs, PCs, and iOS mobile devices. This way, when you add a bookmark on one computer or device, for example, it will become accessible from the bookmarks bar, Bookmarks menu, and/or Reading List on all of your linked computers or devices.

To set this up, once you have your iCloud account established, launch System Preferences, and click on the iCloud option. Add a checkmark next to the Bookmarks option in the iCloud menu. You must do this on all of the computers or devices that are linked to the same iCloud account and with which you want to sync your bookmarks.

For computers that are not linked via iCloud, you can manually import or export your web browser bookmarks using the Import Bookmarks and Export Bookmarks commands that are available from the File pull-down menu (accessible from the menu bar) in Safari. You'll discover that your stored bookmarks can be imported from other Macs running Safari or other compatible web browsers, as well as PCs running Microsoft Internet Explorer (or other compatible web browsers).

To export browser bookmarks to be imported into Safari on your MacBook Air, use the Bookmark Export command offered by the web browser on your other computer. Next, transfer the exported file to your MacBook Air using one of the methods outlined in Chapter 6. Then, on your MacBook Air, launch Safari and use the Import Bookmarks command.

11

Set Up Existing Email Accounts for MacBook Air

HOW TO...

- Use Safari to access your email account(s)
- Set up and use the Mail app to manage multiple email accounts
- Effectively manage email using the Mail app

The MacBook Air's ability to easily access the Internet makes it simple to manage one or more email accounts from virtually anywhere, as long as an Internet connection is available. When it comes to managing your preexisting email accounts, you have multiple options.

For example, you can:

- Access web-based email accounts using the Safari web browser (or any other web browser)
- Use the Mail app to manage multiple email accounts simultaneously
- Use Microsoft Outlook or another third-party app for managing email accounts

Regardless of which option you choose, to set up your MacBook Air to manage your preexisting email accounts, you'll need to know your email address, username, password, and potentially the address of your email account's incoming mail server and outgoing mail server. This is information you can easily obtain from your email service provider.

If you opt to use the Mail app that comes preinstalled on your MacBook Air, or Microsoft Outlook, for example, you'll need to set it up just once by providing details about each of your preexisting email accounts.

The benefit to utilizing the Mail app is that it's fully integrated with other apps such as Safari and iPhoto, so you can send emails from those apps without first manually launching the Mail app.

Did You Know? **You Can Access Your Web-Based Email Accounts Using Safari**

Use the Safari web browser (or any other web browser) to access the portal for your web-based email account(s). If you have a Yahoo! Mail account, for example, you'd point your web browser to https://login.yahoo.com. To access your Google Gmail account, visit http://mail.google.com, or to access your AOL Mail account, visit www.aol.com. For Microsoft Hotmail accounts, visit https://login.live.com, or to access your free Apple iCloud Mail account, visit www.icloud.com/#mail.

   If you want to set up a free email account for any of these services, simply visit the appropriate website and click on the icon or option for setting up a new account. These same email accounts can also be managed using the Mail app on your MacBook Air.

Note   The Mail app also works seamlessly with Notification Center and the Notification Center window, so you can be alerted of new incoming emails without having the Mail app running.

Discover the Features and Functions Offered by the Mail App

The Mail app that comes preinstalled with OS X Mountain Lion offers all of the functions needed to efficiently manage one or more preexisting email accounts simultaneously. You can read incoming emails, organize messages into separate and customized folders, prioritize messages, and compose outgoing emails from within the app.

   The Mail app also includes a wide range of other features, such as email signatures, and the ability to format outgoing messages by selecting the font, font color, typestyle, and paragraph alignment.

Did You Know? **The Mail App (Version 6.0 or Later) That Comes Preinstalled with OS X Mountain Lion Offers a Handful of Useful New Features**

For example, the VIP feature allows you to indicate which people you receive email from are the most important to you. Once you do this, the Mail app will flag those incoming messages as important by displaying a star-shaped icon to the left of those incoming messages.

(continued)

To add someone to your VIP list, as you're reading one of their emails, wave the cursor over the sender's name, and then click on the star-shaped icon that appears to the left of their name. A new VIPs inbox (Smartbox) will be created the first time you do this, allowing you to view all of your incoming messages from VIPs in one place.

In the future, as you're viewing your main inboxes, new (unread) messages from VIPs will have a blue star to the left of them, instead of a blue dot.

Like many of the preinstalled apps that come with OS X Mountain Lion, the Mail app is fully compatible with Notification Center. As a result, you can customize how you receive alerts, alarms, and notifications from the Mail app by accessing the Notifications option within System Preferences, and then choosing the Mail app.

The Mail app is also fully compatible with iCloud, so all of your Mail app preferences can be synced with your other Macs. These are among the new features added to the Mail app that make managing one or more email accounts from your MacBook Air that much easier.

Set Up Your Preexisting Email Accounts to Work with the Mail App

There are two ways to set up the Mail app to work with your preexisting email accounts. One involves configuring the app to work with your email accounts from your MacBook Air's System Preferences.

The second method involves adding or editing email account information from within the Mail app itself by selecting the Mail pull-down menu, choosing the Preferences option, and then clicking on the Accounts button that's displayed near the top of the Preferences window that appears. Either method will work fine for setting up a preexisting email account to work on your MacBook Air.

Setting Up Your Email Accounts from Within System Preferences

To set up your preexisting email accounts to work with the Mail app from within System Preferences, launch System Preferences from the Dock, Launchpad, or the Applications folder. When the main System Preferences window appears, click on the Mail, Contacts & Calendar option that's displayed under the Internet & Wireless heading (shown in Figure 11-1).

To add details about a preexisting email account, click on the plus sign icon that's displayed near the lower-left corner of the Mail, Contacts & Calendars window. Then on the right side of the window, click on the type of email account you're setting up.

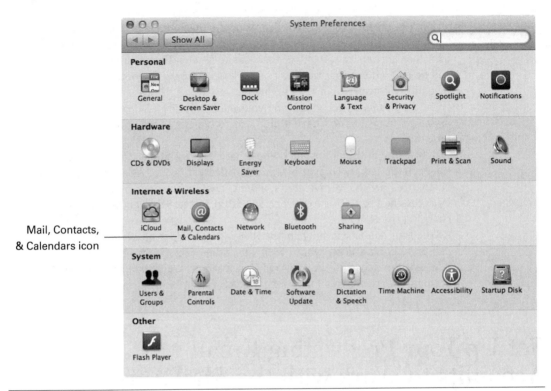

Mail, Contacts,
& Calendars icon

FIGURE 11-1 Click on the Mail, Contacts & Calendar option in System Preferences to set up a preexisting email account to work with the Mail app.

The menu options (shown in Figure 11-2) include iCloud, Microsoft Exchange, Gmail, Yahoo!, AOL, and a handful of others. If your email account type is not listed, click on the Other option that's displayed at the bottom of the list.

 If you select the Other option, select the Add A Mail Account option from the pop-up window that appears, and then click on the Create button that's also displayed within that window.

Depending on the type of email account you selected, you'll be prompted to enter your name, username, email address, and/or password. For your name, enter your first and last name exactly how you'd like it to appear in the From field when you compose and send new email messages or reply to messages from others.

In the Username field, if applicable, enter the username that's associated with that email account. If you're prompted to enter your email address, enter the complete email address. Within the Password field, enter your current password for accessing the email account.

Again, depending on the type of email account you're setting up, you may be required to enter details about the account's incoming mail server and outgoing mail server.

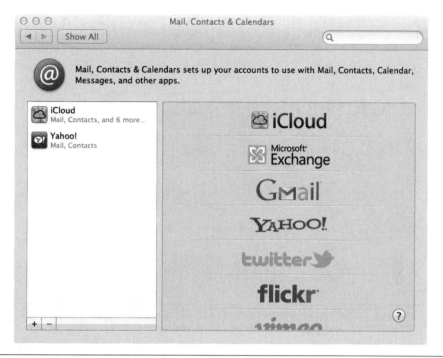

FIGURE 11-2   Select the type of preexisting email account you want to set up to work with the Mail app.

When you've entered all of the requested information about one email account, that information will be verified. Your MacBook Air will need access to the Internet to do this. Once the account has been verified, you may also be prompted to choose what type of related information you want saved or synced in conjunction with that account, such as Notes or Calendar information. Then a listing for the account will be displayed on the left side of the Mail, Contacts & Calendars window. It will now function properly within the Mail app.

Repeat this process for each of your separate email accounts.

 If you have already set up an iCloud account, you'll discover details about your free iCloud email account are already listed in this window.

Setting Up Your Email Accounts from Within the Mail App's Preferences Window

To set up a preexisting email account to work with the Mail app, from within the Mail app access the Mail pull-down menu from the menu bar and select the Preferences option. At the top of the Preferences window, click on the Accounts tab. Then click on the plus sign icon that's displayed near the lower-left corner of the window (shown in Figure 11-3).

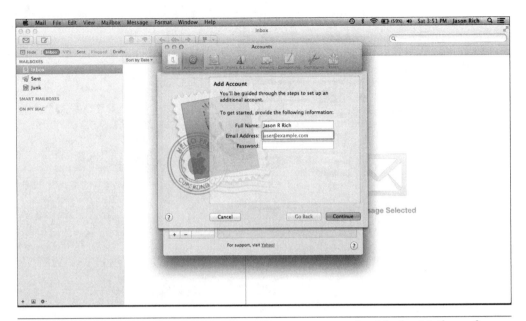

FIGURE 11-3 You can also set up an email account to work with the Mail app from within the Mail app.

When prompted, enter your full name, email address, and password that's associated with the preestablished email account, and then click on the Continue button.

For some types of email accounts that only require you to enter your email address and password, a Create button will be displayed instead of a Continue button.

Follow the onscreen prompts and enter any other requested information. When the process is completed, the inbox for your newly added email account will be listed on the left side of the Mail window under the Mailboxes heading, and the other folders associated with the account will be displayed in the Mailboxes column.

If you need help setting up your preexisting email account to work with the Mail app, contact your email service provider to obtain the setup information you need (such as the incoming mail server and outgoing mail server addresses). You can also contact AppleCare for assistance in setting up and using the Mail app.

Navigating Your Way Around the Mail Apps Menu Bar and Toolbar

Like all Mac apps, Mail displays a menu bar along the top of the screen (shown in Figure 11-4). With the exception of the Apple icon pull-down menu, all of the menu bar options, including Mail, File, Edit, View, Mailbox, Message, Format, Window,

FIGURE 11-4   The menu bar of the Mail app gives you access to a wide range of commands and features for managing your email accounts, accessing emails, composing, and sending emails.

and Help, relate specifically to the Mail app and allow you to access commands and features for reading, composing, organizing, and sending email messages from one or more accounts.

Running along the top of the Mail app window below the menu bar is the toolbar. It offers a series of command icons that correspond to commonly used features found with the various pull-down menus on the menu bar. The toolbar, however, is fully customizable so you can pick and choose exactly what command icons will appear on it, and in what order they appear.

 To customize the toolbar and determine which command icons are displayed along it, select the Customize Toolbar option from the View pull-down menu. This process is covered later in the chapter.

By default, the main Mail app window is divided into three columns (shown in Figure 11-5). On the left is the Mailboxes column. From here, you can access your Inbox, Sent, Trash, Junk, and/or Drafts folders, as well as other folders you create or that are utilized by your specific email account(s).

To make the Mailboxes list disappear, select the Hide Mail Box List option from the View pull-down menu that's found on the menu bar.

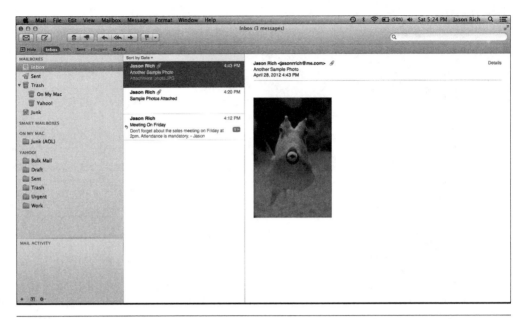

FIGURE 11-5 By default, the Mail app's program window is divided into three columns, although you can opt to hide the Mailboxes column.

 Under the Inbox heading, you can opt to view all incoming messages from all of your mailboxes simultaneously, or select one inbox related to one email account at a time. Simply select and highlight either the Inbox listing or the listing for a specific email account's inbox that's displayed below the main Inbox heading.

Incoming emails are listed in the middle column. If you have the main Inbox option from the left column selected, the incoming emails from all of your accounts will be listed with the most recent message first (and the rest in reverse chronological order, based on when they were received), and/or sorted by conversation thread. Or from the Mailboxes column you can select and highlight just one email account's inbox to view its contents.

The Anatomy of an Incoming Email Listing Within the Mail App

Each email listing displayed in the middle column represents one incoming email. To view that email in its entirety, select and highlight it. The entire message will then be displayed in the right column of the Mail app's program window.

An email listing (as shown in Figure 11-6) includes the sender's information, the date, subject, and up to five lines of the incoming message's body text. A paper-clip icon is also displayed within an incoming message listing if it contains an attachment.

> **Jason Rich**   4:12 PM
> **Meeting On Friday**
> Don't forget about the sales meeting on Friday at   [1▸]
> 2pm. Attendance is mandatory. - Jason

FIGURE 11-6   A typical incoming email message listing within the Mail app

If the incoming message is part of a message thread (where one person sent an email, the recipient replied to that message, and then the original sender posted a response, etc.), a number in a gray rectangle will be displayed on the right side of the listing that indicates how many messages that particular message thread (the email conversation) contains.

When a message listing is selected and highlighted, you can press the DELETE key on the keyboard to delete it. Or from the Messages pull-down menu, you can use the Reply, Reply All, Forward, Forward As Attachment, Redirect, Mark, Flag, Archive, Move To, Copy To, or other commands to handle that message as needed. Many of these commands are also accessible from the command icons along the toolbar, and some have keyboard shortcuts associated with them.

In the left margin of an email message listing, one of several small graphic icons can be displayed (shown in Figure 11-7). A blue dot indicates a message is new and unread. An arrow icon that curves and points to the left indicates an incoming email message that you've already replied to, while an arrow icon that points to the right means you have forwarded that message to others.

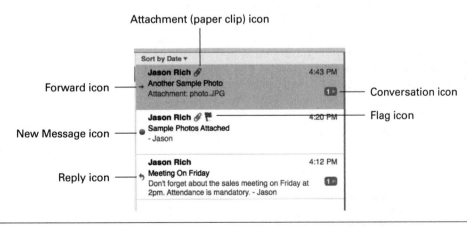

FIGURE 11-7   Several graphic icons may be displayed to the left of an incoming message listing.

You Can Create a VIP List for Incoming Emails

One new feature of the Mail app that's been added to Mountain Lion is the ability to create a VIP list. When you do this, when you receive an email from someone on your VIP list, it will be flagged with a star icon. Plus, that email will be placed within a Smart Mailbox that's labeled VIPs under the Mailboxes list on the left side of the screen.

To add someone to the Mail app's VIP list, look to the immediate left of the From field in an incoming email. A gray star icon will appear when you hover the mouse over the From field. Click on the star icon to add that person to your VIP list. All future emails that you receive from that person will be labeled with a star icon in the inbox, and appear within the VIP Smart Mailbox that will automatically be created. You can add as many people to your VIP list as you like.

The VIP list combines incoming messages from all of the email accounts you have set up to work with your Mac and displays the VIP emails in one place. However, the Mail app still keeps the emails properly sorted, based on which email account each was sent to.

To remove someone from your VIP list, access one of their incoming emails and again click on the star icon that appears to the immediate left of the From field.

If a flag icon is displayed to the right of an incoming email's Subject heading, this indicates the message has been marked by you as urgent or important. To flag an email, simply click on the flag icon that's displayed within the toolbar, or select the Flag option from the Message pull-down menu. You can then select the color of flag that will be associated with the email. Flag colors include red, orange, yellow, green, blue, purple, and gray. You can associate colors with a level of importance, or with specific friends, customers, clients, or family members, for example.

The Conversation icon that appears to the right within an email message listing (under the time) indicates that the message is part of an ongoing conversation. The number in the Conversation icon indicates how many incoming messages and replies there have been thus far.

As you're looking at an email message listing (in the middle column of the Mail app), you can use any of the commands from the Message pull-down menu, the command icons displayed along the toolbar, or keyboard shortcuts to manage that listing.

For example, you can reply to the message, forward the message to others, mark the message (as unread, junk mail/spam, or as a low, normal, or high priority), flag the message, or archive the message. You also have the option to move or copy the message from the inbox of the email account in which it was received to another folder.

By opting to move an incoming email, that message will be removed from your inbox and placed in the destination folder. If you choose to copy the message, however, a copy of it will remain in your inbox as well as in the folder you assign it to.

Another way to move a message from the Inbox listing to a specific folder is to highlight and select it from the center column and then drag and drop it into a specific folder that's displayed in the Mailboxes column.

Note   Messages that are deleted are sent to the Trash folder, where they remain until you empty that folder. This can be done manually or you can set the Mail app to automatically empty the Trash folder at predetermined intervals, such as daily, weekly, or monthly. Depending on how your email account is set up, the message you delete may be erased from your MacBook Air (and the Mail app), or it could be retained on the email account's server indefinitely.

When viewing your incoming email listings, you can select and highlight one message at a time, or you can select and highlight multiple messages by clicking on one message and then holding down the SHIFT key when clicking on additional listings. With one or more email messages highlighted, you can delete, move, or copy them, for example.

Reading Your Incoming Emails Using the Mail App

By selecting and highlighting an email listing in the middle column of the Mail app, the entire email message will be displayed on the right side of the screen (shown in Figure 11-8). At the top of the message, the header information (From, Subject, Date, To, and Reply-To) is displayed. You can click on the Hide icon to condense some of this information on the screen.

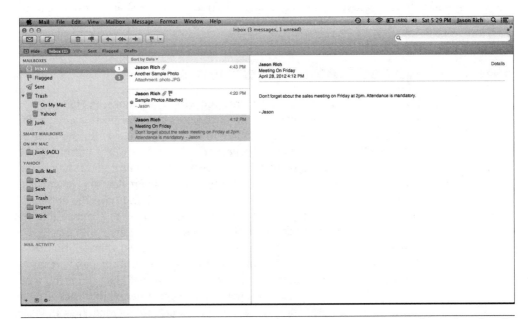

FIGURE 11-8   A sample incoming message shown in its entirety on the right side of the Mail app's program window

FIGURE 11-9   Move the cursor over the divider line between a message header and message body to reveal these command icons.

From the Preferences window within the Mail app, you can determine how often the Mail app will automatically check for new emails. To adjust this setting, access the Mail pull-down menu, select the Preferences option, and then click on the General button. Access the pull-down menu that's associated with the Check For New Messages option and choose between Every Minute, Every 5 Minutes, Every 15 Minutes, Every 30 Minutes, Every Hour, or Manually.

Along the divider bar between the heading and the message body will be a horizontal line. In the center of this line, you'll see command icons for the Trash, Reply, Reply All, and Forward commands when the cursor is dragged over it (shown in Figure 11-9).

If the incoming message is part of a thread, the most recent message will be displayed first, but as you scroll down, all of the other messages in that message thread will be displayed, making it easier to track an email-based conversation.

How to...   # Access Email Attachments

If an email has an attachment associated with it (as shown in Figure 11-10), an icon for that attachment will be displayed within the email message. At the top of the email, a paper-clip icon will also be displayed to the right of the sender's name in the message header.

Depending on the type of file the attachment contains, you may be able to open and view it within the Mail app or the Preview app (that also comes preinstalled with OS X Mountain Lion). You'll also have the option to download and utilize the attached file in conjunction with a compatible app.

To view PDF files, graphics, or photos that are associated with email attachments, double-click on the attachment icon to view the content using the Preview app. Or, highlight and select the attachment icon and press the CONTROL key while clicking on the trackpad to reveal a pop-up menu that offers the following commands: Open Attachment, Open With, Quick Look Attachment, Save Attachment, Save To Downloads Folder, and View In Place.

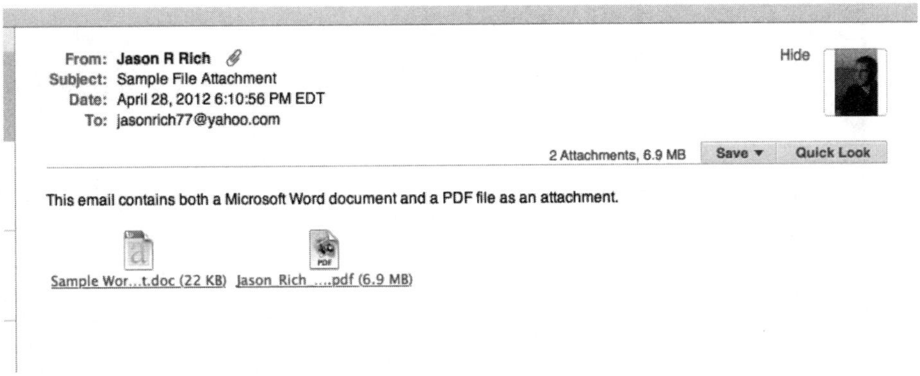

From: **Jason R Rich** 🖉   Hide
Subject: Sample File Attachment
Date: April 28, 2012 6:10:56 PM EDT
To: jasonrich77@yahoo.com

2 Attachments, 6.9 MB | Save ▼ | | Quick Look |

This email contains both a Microsoft Word document and a PDF file as an attachment.

Sample Wor...t.doc (22 KB)   Jason_Rich_....pdf (6.9 MB)

FIGURE 11-10   Displayed within an incoming email will be icons that represent attachments that are associated with that message. The Mail app can display a wide range of attachment file types for documents, files, apps, photos, music, movies, etc.

As you're reading emails or reviewing email listings, if you receive an unsolicited spam message (which is a common occurrence), you can click on the Spam command icon and immediately send that message to your Junk or Spam folder. In the future, all other incoming emails from that same sender's email address will also automatically be sent to your Spam/Junk folder so that they don't clutter your inbox.

The Spam icon displays a thumbs-down ("boo") icon.

To manually check for new messages, click on the Get New Mail icon that's displayed on the toolbar, or access the Mailbox pull-down menu and select the Get New Mail option.

Printing Email Messages Within the Mail App

As you're reading an email, you can send it to a printer that's connected to your MacBook Air (via a cable or wirelessly) using the Print command. The Print command can be found under the File pull-down menu on the menu bar. You can also click on the Print command icon on the toolbar, or use the COMMAND (⌘)-P keyboard shortcut. When you use the Print command, a Print window is displayed that allows you to adjust various printer options (shown in Figure 11-11).

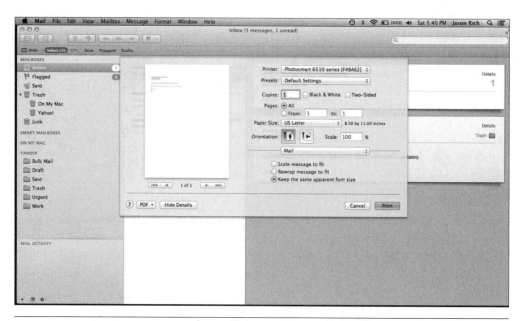

FIGURE 11-11 When you choose to print something from the Mail app, you can adjust a variety of printer options or select which printer you want to use.

Customizing the Mail App's Toolbar

The toolbar that appears below the menu bar contains command icons. Using the Customize Toolbar command that's found under the View pull-down menu, you can pick and choose among more than 25 command icons, each of which represents a commonly used command for managing emails or email accounts.

One at a time, drag and drop each command icon from the window that appears after selecting the Customize Toolbar option to the exact location on the app's toolbar where you want it displayed (shown in Figure 11-12). You can choose to display only the most commonly used command icons, such as Delete, Junk, Reply, Reply All, Forward, Flag, New Message, Get Mail, and/or Print, or you can add as many command icons as will fit on the toolbar.

Keep in mind, each command icon that can be displayed on the toolbar corresponds to a command that's accessible from the pull-down menus along the menu bar, and is also often associated with a keyboard shortcut.

When you're done customizing the toolbar, click on the Done button.

Tip To save onscreen space, you can opt to hide the toolbar altogether. To do this, select the Hide Toolbar option from the View pull-down menu. To make it reappear, choose the Show Toolbar command.

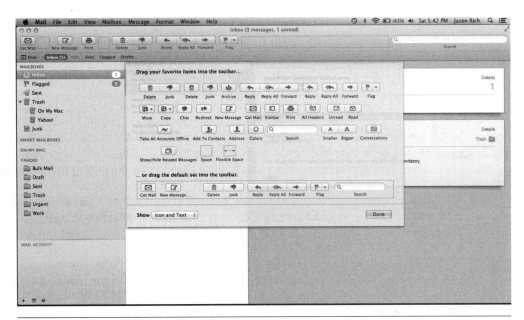

FIGURE 11-12   Customize the toolbar within the Mail app by dragging and dropping the command icons from the window into the actual toolbar.

Composing Outgoing Emails from the Mail App

By clicking on the Compose New Message command icon on the toolbar, by selecting the New Message command from the File pull-down menu, or by using the COMMAND (⌘)-N keyboard shortcut, you can compose a new outgoing message using the Mail app (shown in Figure 11-13).

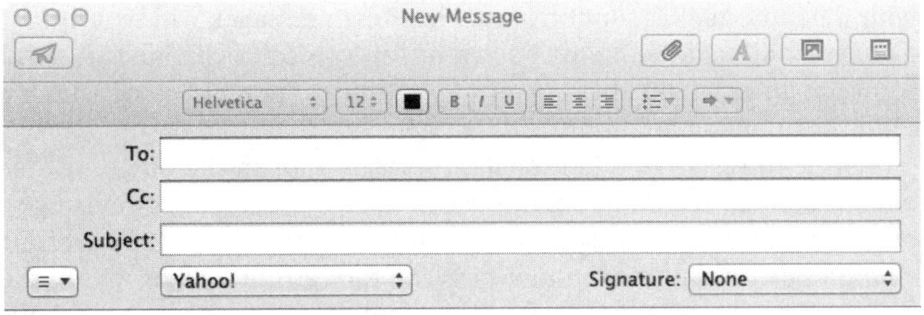

FIGURE 11-13   From the Mail app, you can compose and send emails with or without attachments.

When you choose to compose a new message, near the top of the New Message window that appears, fill in the To field with the recipient's email address. You can add multiple recipients to one email by entering multiple email addresses in the To field and separating them with commas. You can also add email addresses to the Cc: field.

 The Mail app works seamlessly with the Contacts app. If you are sending an email to someone who has an entry in your Contacts database, instead of manually entering the recipient's email address in the To field, you can begin typing their name and then select the appropriate email address from the listing that's displayed.

For any outgoing email, filling in the To field is mandatory. You also have the option to fill in the Cc: field to send a copy of the email to other people as well. When you list email addresses (recipients) in the Cc: field, all of the message's recipients will see who else the message was addressed and sent to.

However, by clicking on the icon to the left of the From field, you can select to add a Bcc: field to the outgoing message. This allows you to forward the outgoing message you're composing to multiple people, but those people will not be visible to the other recipients.

While filling in the Subject field of an email is optional, it's considered proper email etiquette to fill in this field so the message recipients know what the email message is about and don't confuse it with spam.

 When composing an email message's Subject line, include information that's short but descriptive and relevant.

If you're managing multiple email accounts using the Mail app, click on the From field pull-down menu to choose which of your email addresses the outgoing message will be sent from. If you don't choose an email address, the default email account will be used. To set your default email account, access the Mail pull-down menu and select the Preferences option. When the Preferences window appears, click on the Composing tab at the top of the window. Near the middle of the Composing window, look for the Send New Messages From option, and from the pull-down menu, select your default email account from which new messages will be sent.

Even with a default email account set, you can override this option anytime you compose an email by clicking on the From field and choosing which email account to send the outgoing email from.

Once you have filled in the appropriate fields in the outgoing email message's header, click in the main email message body and begin composing your email message. Click on the Attachment icon (the paper clip) to add an attachment to the email. Click on the "A" icon to access the formatting toolbar within the New Message window to choose your font, font size, font color, typestyle (bold, italics, underlined, etc.), as well as the paragraph justification. You can also format bulleted or numbered lists in the body of an email, or indent/outdent text by clicking on the right-most icon that's displayed along the formatting toolbar.

To insert a photo or graphic into the email (either as an attachment or embedded within the email message), click on the Photo icon (which looks like a picture frame). You can then find and select the images you wish to attach or embed, and choose the file size for those graphic/photo attachments.

Click on the Show Stationery button (the icon to the extreme right) to use one of the Mail app's templates to format your outgoing message using virtual "stationery." As you'll discover, there are specialized templates (stationery designs) for birthdays, announcements, to send photos, to simulate personalized stationery, or to send special themed sentiments (such as thank you, love, get well, or congratulations messages).

When you're ready to send the outgoing email, click on the Send icon that's displayed near the upper-left corner of the New Message window. The Send icon looks like a paper airplane. A copy of your outgoing message will be retained in your Sent folder.

If you compose an email, but choose to not send it right away, it can be stored in the Drafts folder that's associated with your email account. You can then go back and edit and/or send that email at a later time.

Thanks to OS X Mountain Lion, when an app has a Share menu associated with it, you can compose emails from directly within those apps that contain app-specific attachments. When you select the Send Email option within a compatible app, the Mail app will launch automatically and a customized New Message window will appear.

Using Email Signatures at the End of Outgoing Messages

If you have email signatures set up, you can have the Mail app automatically insert your default signature at the end of your email messages. Or you can pick and choose from multiple signatures that you've created and stored in the app. Within the email signature, you can include your name, address, phone number(s), website URL, and other contact information, and/or an inspirational quote or any other text you deem appropriate.

To set up email signatures, from the Mail pull-down menu, select the Preferences option. In the Preferences window, click on the Signatures button that's displayed along the top of the window (shown in Figure 11-14). Then click on the plus sign icon to compose and save a new signature. You can opt to associate signatures with a specific email account or all of your email accounts, and give each signature a name for easy reference.

From the Choose Signature field within the Signature window of Preferences, you can also select a default signature that will be displayed automatically at the end of your outgoing emails.

Once set up, a Signature field will be displayed in the New Message window to the right of the From field.

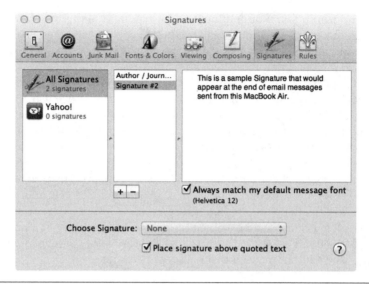

FIGURE 11-14 Set up signatures that will appear at the end of your outgoing emails.

Setting Up the Mail Account Preferences

Like all of the apps that come preinstalled with OS X Mountain Lion, the Mail app is fully customizable. In addition to customizing the toolbar, for example, by accessing the Mail pull-down menu and selecting the Preferences option, you can personalize a wide range of the app's other commands and features.

As you'll discover, at the top of Mail's Preferences window (shown in Figure 11-15), there are eight tab buttons. They're labeled General, Accounts, Junk Mail, Fonts & Colors, Viewing, Composing, Signatures, and Rules. By clicking on each button, you'll reveal a separate tab that includes a handful of customizable options.

Invest a few minutes to click on each command button and review each of the customizable options available. Make changes as you deem appropriate to fully personalize how the Mail app manages your email accounts and individual incoming and outgoing emails. Keep in mind, the options available in each submenu will vary based on the type of email account you're using.

Like many apps for the MacBook Air, you can maximize the screen of the computer by running the Mail app in Full Screen mode. To do this, click on the Full Screen icon that's displayed near the upper-right corner of the Mail app's window. You can also select the Enter Full Screen command from the View pull-down menu or use the CONTROL-COMMAND (⌘)-F keyboard shortcut.

FIGURE 11-15   The Mail app's Preferences window

How to...

Manage Your Email Accounts Efficiently

Whether you're managing one or more email accounts from your MacBook Air, the more messages you store on your computer (within the Mail app), the more internal storage space on your computer's hard drive will be required.

It's a good strategy to set up the Mail app to automatically delete junk/spam messages at predetermined time intervals and to erase deleted items from your Trash folder. You can also archive older messages in your inboxes or other folders to conserve storage space.

To manage your email accounts and delete unimportant messages, access the Mailbox pull-down menu and use the Erase Junk Mail option to get rid of unwanted junk mail or spam. Also, utilize the Erase Deleted Items option to permanently delete messages moved to your Trash folder.

In addition to accessing these commands from the Mailbox pull-down menu, you can click on the Action menu icon (it looks like a gear) that's displayed near the lower-left corner of the Mail app's program window to display a menu of commands used for managing email accounts.

Using the Notification Center Window with the Mail App

Even if you're proficient using the Mail app on your MacBook Air or other Macs, if you recently upgraded your MacBook Air's OS X to OS X Mountain Lion, you'll discover a few new features added to this app. For example, you can set up the Mail app to work with Notification Center so that details about new incoming emails appear in your MacBook Air's Notification Center window.

To set up this feature, launch System Preferences and then choose the Notifications option. From the Notifications window in System Preferences, click on the Mail option that's displayed on the left side of the window (under the In Notification Center heading). Then, on the right side of the screen, set up banners or alerts to work with the Mail app so notices of new email messages are displayed in banner or alert form, of for the Mail Alert Style select None.

If you want new incoming emails to be summarized in your Notification Center window, place a checkmark next to the Show In Notification Center option, and then choose how many messages you want details to be displayed about. Your options include 1, 5, 10, or 20 recent items.

 By adding a checkmark to the Badge App Icon With Notification Count, the Mail app's icon that appears within the Dock will display a badge that shows how many new incoming emails are waiting for you. You can also set up an audible alert to be generated when a new email is received.

12

Bring the iLife Apps into Your Life

HOW TO...

- Upgrade your iLife apps that come preinstalled on your MacBook Air
- Use iPhoto to view, edit, print, share, and work with your digital photos
- Use iMovie to create, edit, and share movies
- Make music with GarageBand

While OS X Mountain Lion comes with a handful of apps preinstalled that work seamlessly with the operating system, Apple also offers a suite of three apps, called iLife, that dramatically enhance your ability to create, edit, and share photos, videos, and music. The iLife '11 suite also comes preinstalled on all Macs, but is separate from the OS X operating system.

 iLife '11 includes the iPhoto, iMovie, and GarageBand apps. If you have an older version of this app suite, you'll definitely want to upgrade to the most current version of each app in order for them to work seamlessly with the OS X Mountain Lion operating system and iCloud. To do this, visit the App Store and click on the Updates button that's displayed near the top-center of the screen. While minor updates to the iLife apps are free, purchasing the latest edition of each app, the most recent of which are iPhoto '11 (version 9.3 or later), iMovie '11 (version 9.0.6 or later), and GarageBand '11 (version 6.0.5 or later), costs $14.99 each. The apps are now sold separately.

As you'll discover, each of the iLife apps has a very distinct purpose, and includes a robust set of tools and features. Here's a quick summary of what each iLife app is used for:

- **iPhoto** This app is designed to handle all aspects of digital photography, except for actually taking photos. Use this app to import digital images from your digital camera, iPhone, iPad, the Web, or other sources, and then organize your photos into albums or events (shown in Figure 12-1) so that you can view, edit, enhance, print, and/or share them. You can also easily create a wide range of photo projects—from slide shows to printed calendars—that allow you to showcase your favorite digital images.

 When you import photos into iPhoto, the app automatically places them into new events based on when they were shot. You can custom name events, or you can create albums, which are your own collections of images stored in iPhoto. To automatically split events by day, access the iPhoto's Preferences pull-down menu and click on the General button. Next to the Autosplit Into Events pull-down menu, select the One Event Per Day option.

- **iMovie** If you enjoy shooting home videos or creating original video content to share on YouTube, for example, the iMovie app offers a powerful video editing toolset that allows you to import raw video footage and then edit it using professional-quality features. Adding animated titles, special effects, transitions,

FIGURE 12-1 Use iPhoto to organize all of your digital images into related groups, which are then stored in albums or events.

How to...   ## Set Up iCloud Photo Stream to Work with iPhoto on Your MacBook Air

iPhoto is designed to work seamlessly with iCloud's Photo Stream feature, which gives you access to up to 1,000 of your most recent digital photos on all of your Macs, PCs, Apple TV, and iOS mobile devices that are linked to the same iCloud account. Once set up, Photo Stream works automatically and in the background.

To turn on iCloud's Photo Stream feature, launch System Preferences and click on the iCloud icon. Then, add a checkmark to the checkbox that's associated with the Photo Stream option. Once this is done, launch iPhoto on your MacBook Air. From the iPhoto pull-down menu (accessible from the menu bar), select Preferences.

Next, click on the Photo Stream tab that's displayed near the top-center of the window. Make sure a checkmark appears in conjunction with the main Photo Stream option. You can then decide whether or not to automatically download images from your Photo Stream to your MacBook Air, plus decide whether you want to automatically upload new images from iPhoto on your MacBook Air to your Photo Stream. You can also add or delete images manually from your Photo Stream.

Since Photo Stream was first introduced, it's been given a handful of new enhancements and features, which keep coming every few months. As you read this, you'll probably discover a handful of additional features that aren't mentioned here.

sound effects, music, and voiceovers to your movies is easy using the app's drag-and-drop interface. Then, once a video is edited, iMovie offers the tools needed to export the file into a variety of formats so you can share your productions online or transfer them to an iPhone, iPad, or Apple TV, for example (as shown in Figure 12-2). Videos can also easily be published to YouTube or other online-based video services, or burned onto DVDs using an optional MacBook Air SuperDrive.

- **GarageBand**   This app is designed for amateur musicians and is used to compose, record, play back, edit, and share music and audio content. GarageBand transforms your MacBook Air into a portable, multitrack recording studio that allows you to record and edit instruments and vocals, plus create and share digital music or audio content.

This music creation-oriented app has a handful of different components that are displayed on the main menu when you launch the app (shown in Figure 12-3). For example, if you select New Project, you can compose or record and edit music from scratch. If you select the Learn To Play option, the app will transform into a digital music instructor and teach you how to play guitar or piano.

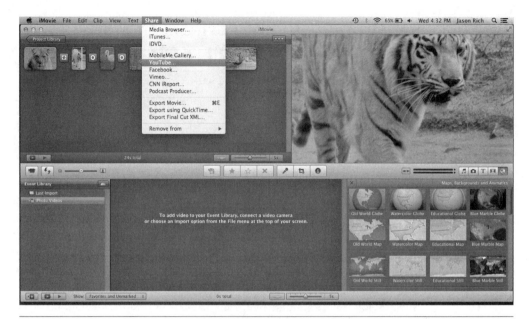

FIGURE 12-2 Edited movies can be exported into a wide range of popular video file formats and resolutions based on how they'll be viewed or later utilized.

FIGURE 12-3 The main menu of the GarageBand app, which is part of iLife

The Magic GarageBand option allows you to control virtual instruments to create and record music, even if you have no musical talent whatsoever. You can pick and choose a musical genre, such as blues, rock, jazz, country, reggae, funk, Latin, roots rock, or slow blues, and then choose virtual instruments and prerecorded musical samples to create and play original compositions.

The iPhone Ringtone module of GarageBand allows you to edit, record, and format ringtones for your iPhone using prerecorded music or music you compose and record yourself.

What's nice about GarageBand is that many of its features are very easy to use, so you can utilize the app's various features with a minimal learning curve. However, for more experienced musicians, GarageBand can serve as a feature-packed digital recording studio. To fully utilize these more complex features, some familiarity with music composition and digital recording, not to mention some musical talent, are necessary.

Did You Know?

There Are Many Alternatives for Editing, Organizing, and Sharing Digital Photos

iPhoto offers some very easy-to-use digital photo editing, enhancing, and organizing tools. However, if what's offered by this app isn't enough to meet your needs, you can purchase and install Apple's Aperture 3 software ($79.99, www.apple.com/aperture), which offers vastly more powerful photo editing and organizational tools.

There are also many optional photo editing software packages available for the Mac, such as Adobe Photoshop Elements 10, Adobe Photoshop CS 6, and Adobe Lightroom CS 6, which can be used to edit and organize your photos.

Photoshop Elements 10 ($99.99) is designed for amateur photographers and offers many of the same functions as iPhoto, in terms of it being an all-in-one tool for importing, viewing, organizing, editing, enhancing, printing, and sharing digital photos. However, Photoshop Elements 10's photo editing and enhancement tools and features are dramatically more powerful than what's offered by iPhoto. To learn more about Adobe's photo editing tools, visit www.adobe.com/products/photoshopfamily.html.

If you want to edit portraits of people and create truly professional-quality results after spending less than five minutes editing each photo, the Portrait Professional 11 software ($39.95, www.portraitprofessional.com) is incredibly powerful but very simple to use. It's ideal for amateur and professional photographers alike.

From the App Store, if you enter the keyword "photography" into the Search field, you'll discover many other third-party photography-related apps. Plus, if you surf the Web, you'll find free, online-based tools, like Google Picasa (http://picasa.google.com), that also offer features for organizing, viewing, editing, enhancing, printing, and sharing digital photos.

The iLife apps (iPhoto, iMovie, and GarageBand) are designed for average consumers and offer a lot of basic functionality with a minimal learning curve. However, if you're looking or more professional-level features, you'll need to upgrade to more advanced software.

For example, Apple's Aperture ($79.99, www.apple.com/aperture) software offers professional level photo editing capabilities. When it comes to editing video like a pro, Apple's Final Cut Pro ($299.99, www.apple.com/finalcutpro) is available. And to truly transform your MacBook Air into a digital recording studio, Apple's Logic Pro ($199.99, www.apple.com/logicpro) app offers functionality that's vastly superior to what's possible using GarageBand.

Keep in mind, professional photographers, videographers, or recording engineers (and musicians) can spend considerable time learning how to harness and master the capabilities of Aperture, Final Cut Pro, and Logic Pro, respectively. These apps are more powerful and more complex than their consumer-oriented counterparts.

 If you're also an iPad user, you'll discover that the iPhoto, iMovie, and GarageBand apps for your tablet (sold separately from the App Store) are fully compatible with the Mac versions of these apps. Thus, data from your projects are fully interchangeable. For example, you can begin editing a movie on your MacBook Air, and then transfer the project in order to continue working on it on your iPad.

Discovering All that the iPhoto App Is Capable Of

Taking photos with a digital camera is fun. You can capture memories by snapping pictures of your friends, family, pets, vacations, special events in your life, nature, or anything else that's around you. You can purchase a feature-packed, point-and-shoot digital camera that's easy to use from dozens of different companies, such as Nikon, Canon, Sony, or Olympus. Or if you have a smartphone (such as the iPhone 4S), chances are it has a digital camera built in that allows you to take pictures just about anywhere.

iPhoto is designed to handle all aspects of digital photography, except actually taking the pictures. Thus, begin by importing photos (your digital images) into the app from your digital camera or any other source. You can then view your photos using iPhoto, either one at a time or in groups. As you're viewing images, if you click on the Edit icon, you can enhance an image using the app's basic photo editing and enhancement tools. Then you can share your images using the various tools built into the app.

 The camera that's built into your MacBook Air can also be used for snapping digital photos, using the Photo Booth app, for example. It too comes preinstalled with OS X Mountain Lion.

Once you've shot digital photos or acquired images from the Web or other sources, iPhoto is designed to make it very easy to import, organize, view, edit, enhance, print, and share your images—all from a single app.

iPhoto not only integrates nicely with the OS X operating system, but it can also be used in conjunction with iCloud. Plus, using the app's Share button, you can quickly share your favorite photos via email, Twitter, Facebook, or Flickr, for example. As you're viewing a single image or have multiple image thumbnails highlighted and selected, click on the Share icon to view your options for sharing the selected image(s) with others. This is shown in Figure 12-4.

Ordering Prints from iPhoto Using Apple's Photo Lab

iPhoto links directly to Apple's own photo lab service (assuming your MacBook Air is connected to the Internet). With a few clicks, it is possible to order prints (shown in Figure 12-5), greeting cards, photo books, printed calendars, and a wide range of other photo products that feature your digital images. Your prints and photo products can be paid for using your Apple ID and will be shipped directly to your door within a few business days.

As an alternative, your images can be sent to other online-based photo labs to be processed into prints and mailed to you, or you can save the digital files to an external USB thumb drive and take them to any one-hour photo lab to have prints created while you wait. Apple's photo lab service is competitively priced compared to other online-based and one-hour photo labs.

FIGURE 12-4   iPhoto has a Share button that allows you to send images via email or publish them online via Twitter, Facebook, or Flickr.

FIGURE 12-5 Order professionally created prints in a variety of popular sizes directly from your MacBook Air. Apple's photo lab will create your prints and ship them to your door.

The prices for various photo products, such as printed calendars and photo books, are also very competitive. However, when it comes to creating photo products, you also have a wide range of options. For example, the Blurb.com service allows you to create visually stunning and inexpensive photo books using your digital photos and their free, easy-to-use photo book layout software.

Using iPhoto's Various Organizational and Editing Features

iPhoto's usefulness begins after you've shot photos using any digital camera (including the camera that's built into your smartphone or tablet). You can also import digital photos into iPhoto from the Web or other sources. For example, you can directly connect your digital camera to your MacBook Air via a USB cable, and then transfer images from your camera's memory card into iPhoto.

Whenever you import new images into iPhoto, the software automatically creates a new digital event, which can be customized with a unique title. This allows you to easily keep all of your photos organized. Over time, your personal photo collection could grow to include thousands of images, and being able to find specific images quickly and efficiently is just one of the things that iPhoto does well.

However, beyond just sorting your images into events, iPhoto has face recognition technology built in. This allows you to sort your image library based on who appears in your photos, because the app can identify faces.

 To utilize the Faces feature of iPhoto, you'll need to teach the app who the people that often appear in your photos are. Once the app is taught, it will begin to identify those people and group images they appear in together.

To teach the app how to identify the people in your photos, such as your kids, load the images into iPhoto and view the images one at a time (either as a thumbnail or large on-screen image). As you're viewing images that contain people (faces), click on the Info button that's displayed near the lower-right corner of the screen. Along the right margin of the screen, the Info window will appear. In this window, the Faces option is displayed. Click on the Add A Face option (displayed under the Faces heading). When you do this, a box will appear around each face in the photo in the main image viewing area with a button labeled Unnamed displayed below it. Click anywhere in the box and type the person's name who appears in the photo.

If multiple people appear in your photo, click on the Add A Face option on the right side of the screen (when the Info window is visible) to connect additional names to faces in your photos.

iPhoto learns as you associate names with people's faces. Over time, the software will automatically detect who is in your photos and label them accordingly, but ask for your confirmation to ensure accuracy. Instead of an Unnamed label, you'll see a message under a face frame that says "Is this [name]?" Click on the checkmark to confirm the identification.

Like many apps, iPhoto pulls information from your Contacts database (and can access information from your Facebook friends list), so as you begin entering someone's name manually, if they're already listed in Contacts, the app will auto-insert their full name as you're typing.

Plus, if your photos have geo-tagging information associated with them, simply click on the Places icon in iPhoto (shown in Figure 12-6) to sort your images based on where they were shot. You can view locations on a map. You can also sort or search for images based on keywords, date, filename, personal rating, or a variety of other criteria.

After importing and organizing your photos using iPhoto's often fully automated tools, you can view thumbnails of your images on the MacBook Air's screen. This allows you to quickly display a handful of images simultaneously. Or you can click on an image's thumbnail to view a single image using almost the entire screen, which is shown in Figure 12-7 (or the entire screen if you place iPhoto into Full Screen mode by clicking on the Full Screen icon that's displayed near the upper-right corner of the screen).

As you're viewing single images in an album or event, use the left or right directional arrow keys on the MacBook Air's keyboard to scroll through the images. You can also click on an image thumbnail that's displayed on the filmstrip at the bottom of the screen to view a particular image.

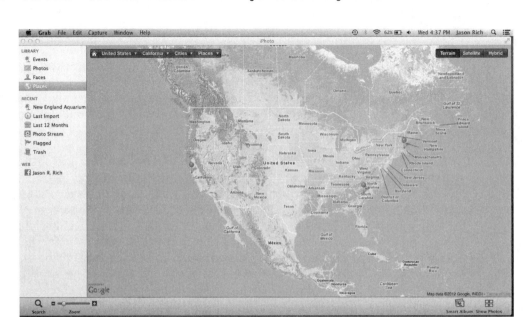

FIGURE 12-6 iPhoto allows you to display a map showcasing where your images were taken.

FIGURE 12-7 Using iPhoto, you can utilize almost the entire screen to view one image at a time.

Tip As you're viewing a single image, click on the Info button that's displayed near the lower-right corner of the screen to view details about that image. You can also click on the Edit, Create, Add To, or Share buttons to edit, work with, or share the image.

Editing and Enhancing Photos Using iPhoto

Organizing and viewing digital images is only part of what iPhoto is capable of. As you're viewing albums, events, image thumbnails, or full-screen images, click on the Edit icon to access iPhoto's collection of photo editing and enhancement tools (shown in Figure 12-8).

Upon clicking the Edit icon, click on the Quick Fixes, Effects, or Adjust command tab that's displayed near the top-right corner of the screen, or use the Rotate, Enhance, Fix Red Eye, Straighten, Crop, or Retouch command icons to utilize a wide range of quick and easy photo editing and enhancement tools.

Using these tools, you can crop and rotate images, alter their lighting, fix problems with images, correct red eye, implement color correction, adjust contrast, and perform a variety of other tasks—often with just one or two clicks.

Note Most of iPhoto's photo enhancement tools must be applied to an entire image. So if you need to apply an enhancement to only part of a photo rather than the entire image, you'll need to use a different application than iPhoto, such as Apple's Aperture or Adobe's Photoshop Elements or Photoshop CS6.

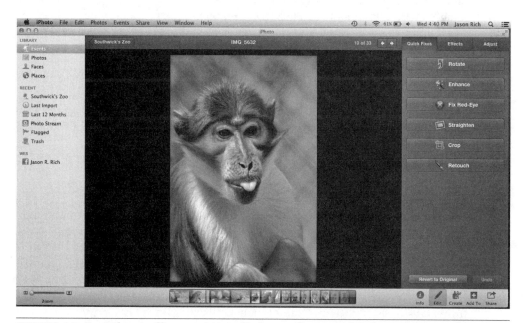

FIGURE 12-8   iPhoto offers a variety of photo editing and enhancement tools.

FIGURE 12-9 The Create button allows you to use your digital images to create photo products, such as prints, photo books, or greeting cards.

Using iPhoto, it's possible to print images directly to your photo printer using the app's Print command, order prints from Apple, share your edited images online (via email, Twitter, Facebook, or Flickr), or create various types of photo projects with your images. Before doing this, however, it's a good idea to use a few of iPhoto's photo editing and enhancement tools to ensure the image looks as amazing as possible.

 Clicking on the Create button (shown in Figure 12-9) that's displayed in iPhoto as you're viewing images allows you to quickly and easily create an album, photo book, greeting card, calendar, or slide show using your digital images. A charge applies to order these items from Apple's photo lab. The charges are billed directly to the credit card that's linked with your Apple ID.

Sharing Your Photos from Within iPhoto

The great thing about iPhoto is that the software is powerful, yet extremely intuitive. It's designed to offer the core functionality you need to organize and manage all of your digital photos from your MacBook Air.

Once photos have been imported, each newly created event will be named "Untitled Event," and below this event name will be the date range during which the photos were taken (shown in Figure 12-10). To customize an event name, click on the title and simply type a new name, such as "Emily's Birthday Pictures" or "Summer 2012 Vacation Photos."

FIGURE 12-10   Easily organize your images by creating customized album and event names that describe the photos stored in these folders.

Keep in mind, when you import digital images into iPhoto, the app creates a new copy of each image that gets stored specifically for use by the iPhoto app. This utilizes some of the computer's internal storage. Then, as you edit or enhance an image, the app automatically saves your alterations, but allows you to revert back to the original image at any time.

 The number and resolution of the digital images you have stored on your MacBook Air in iPhoto will determine how much internal storage is required. Using iPhoto to store hundreds or thousands of high-resolution digital images will utilize a significant portion of your MacBook Air's internal storage.

When using iPhoto, you can view many images in an Event folder at once by viewing their thumbnails. Double-click on any thumbnail to view the image so it fills the entire app window. You can also enter into Full Screen mode when using iPhoto (by clicking on the Full Screen icon that's displayed in the upper-right corner of the app window) and view an even larger version of the image. You also have the option of viewing images as an animated slide show and can select background music and slide transitions for the presentation.

If you opt to create prints of your favorite images using your own photo printer, from within iPhoto, you can choose a print size, plus add a border, theme, caption, and other enhancements (shown in Figure 12-11) before sending the digital file(s) to the printer. Your available options will vary based on the photo printer you're using.

Sharing your images via email, Twitter, Facebook, or Flickr is also very easy. When doing this, be sure to select an image size. By lowering the resolution of an image, you create a smaller file size that makes emailing or uploading them much faster, but the quality (resolution) of those images will suffer.

FIGURE 12-11 You can create your own prints from digital images using iPhoto's Print command.

 Choosing the Small image size is fine for viewing images online or in an email, for example, but is not adequate for creating a print or enlargement.

When sharing digital photos online using iPhoto's Share command (and then selecting Email), from the pull-down menu that's displayed near the lower-right corner of the app window, you can choose the Optimized file size (default), or select a Small, Medium, or Large file size (resolution). Another option is to select Actual Size (Full Quality) in order to leave the digital image and its resolution unaltered. These options are shown in Figure 12-12.

If you've shot an image using a high-resolution digital camera, you will discover that a single image's file size will be between 3MB and 6MB (or larger). As a result, it will take a long time to upload or send it via email. Plus some email services don't allow for extremely large file attachments. Instead of sending multiple images in a single email, if you choose Actual Size, you may only be able to email one photo at a time.

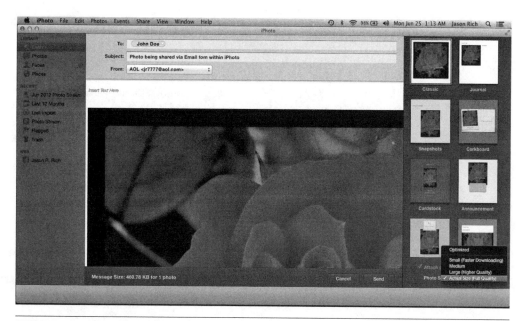

FIGURE 12-12   When sharing images from iPhoto via email, you can choose their image quality.

 When sharing images via email from iPhoto, you can embed images in an email and send one or more of them simultaneously from within the iPhoto app (without launching the Mail app). At the same time, you can click on the Attach Photos To Message option to include the photo(s) as an email attachment as well. You also have the option of launching the Mail app and attaching photos to your outgoing emails manually.

Depending on how you want to share your digital images, it may be necessary to export them out of iPhoto (after they've been edited). To do this, select and highlight the image thumbnails or images you want to export, and then use the Export command that's found under the File pull-down menu on the menu bar. You'll then be able to determine where the file will be exported to (such as a USB thumb drive), as well as the image size for the exported file. When exporting images, you can also change their file format.

 If you are exporting images and saving them on a USB thumb drive to take to a photo lab in order to create prints, export the images in Maximum file size to ensure the highest quality print can be created.

How to... **Delete Images from iPhoto**

iPhoto stores all of your images in master albums or events, which are created when you import the images into the app. Albums and events are created based on date. To delete images from any album or event, drag their thumbnails to the left side of the screen to the Trash icon. You can also highlight and select images and then use the Move To Trash command that's found under the Photos pull-down menu. Another option is to highlight and select an image thumbnail and press the DELETE key.

Keep in mind, iPhoto maintains a separate Trash folder from the main Trash folder that's found on your MacBook Air's Dock. To view the images that have been moved to the Trash in iPhoto, click on the Trash option that's displayed on the left side of the screen.

To then empty the Trash and actually delete the images from your MacBook Air, select the Empty iPhoto Trash option from the iPhoto pull-down menu on the menu bar. Until you do this, the discarded images will remain in the Trash folder and will continue to take up storage space in your computer.

Creating a Backup of Your Digital Image Library

It is absolutely essential that you maintain a reliable backup of your personal digital image library. If your MacBook Air gets lost, stolen, or damaged, or the internal storage gets corrupted, for example, you always want to have copies of your digital images stored somewhere safe. This can be on CDs or DVDs, on an external hard drive, or on an online-based server.

Keep in mind, iCloud's Photo Stream does not permanently store (archive) your images online. They only remain in your Photo Stream for up to 30 days, or are replaced sooner once you reach the 1,000 image cap. Once 1,000 images have been added to your Photo Stream, older images are replaced by newer ones.

Likewise, if you opt to use Facebook to share photo galleries or albums online, this should not be considered an online backup option either. When you upload digital photos to Facebook, their resolutions and file sizes are automatically decreased dramatically.

If you opt to back up or archive your digital photos online, choose a service, such as Flickr (www.flickr.com) or SmugMug (www.smugmug.com), for example, that does not reduce the file size or resolution of your images when they're uploaded.

Don't forget, the OS X Mountain Lion operating system also comes with Time Machine preinstalled. This can be used to maintain a complete backup of your MacBook Air on an external hard drive. This is a viable option for maintaining a backup of your personal digital image library, but like everything else, it has a few potential drawbacks. For example, if your MacBook Air and the external hard drive are kept together, both could be stolen or damaged at the same time.

For your most important images, such as wedding or honeymoon photos, consider maintaining a Time Machine backup, but also using an online-based remote photo backup/archive service.

Discovering How iMovie Can Make You a Skilled Home Movie Producer

Just as iPhoto offers the tools needed to manage just about all aspects of digital photography except for actually snapping the photos, Apple's iMovie app offers a comprehensive toolset for editing, viewing, and sharing home videos.

iMovie allows you to import raw video footage that was shot using a video camera, smartphone, tablet, or the camera that's built into your MacBook Air. You cannot import or edit copyrighted or copy-protected video content such as movies or TV show episodes acquired from iTunes.

In the past, editing video was a very technical and time-consuming process. It also required a computer with tremendous processing power and a massive hard drive. Apple has streamlined the video editing process, making it possible to import, edit, and share video footage on your MacBook Air and create high-definition movies.

The iMovie app (shown in Figure 12-13) requires more of a learning curve than iPhoto because it involves editing the raw video footage and related sound.

FIGURE 12-13   iMovie is a robust video editing toolset for your MacBook Air.

Using this app, you can also add professional-quality animated titles, special effects, transitions, sound effects, music, voiceovers, and other elements to your video productions using a drag-and-drop process.

While theoretically iMovie allows you to edit and produce movies of any length in high definition, the hardware limitations of your MacBook Air (based on how much RAM and hard drive space you have, as well as the speed of your computer's microprocessor) will dictate the length that movies can be.

Trying to edit an extremely long movie could require more RAM, processing power, or internal storage space than your MacBook Air has available. This will result in your MacBook Air operating very sluggishly while the large video files are being processed or utilized.

 When editing movies, consider storing the video footage on an external hard drive and working from that storage device as you edit your movie. This will keep the internal storage space free on your MacBook Air and help keep the computer running efficiently.

The iMovie app is ideal for putting together video clips under 10 minutes in length that can then be shared online, via YouTube or on Facebook, for example. However, editing and producing longer videos is certainly possible.

In addition to editing your home videos from scratch, iMovie allows you to use templates to create extremely impressive and personalized movie trailers, or you can use other templates to add customizable themes to your movies (shown in Figure 12-14).

 As you're producing a movie, you can use the app's library of prerecorded music and sound effects, or just as easily import music from iTunes or that you've recorded from scratch using GarageBand.

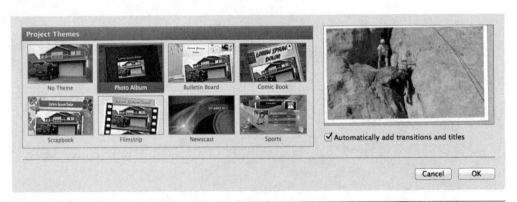

FIGURE 12-14   iMovie offers a handful of precreated themes, as well as a large music and sound effects library.

However, the first step is to import raw video footage into your MacBook Air. This can be done in a variety of ways. For example, you can connect your digital video camera directly to your MacBook Air via a USB cable.

 Raw video footage shot using an iPhone or iPad can be imported into iPhoto automatically. From there, it can be transferred into iMovie and edited into a final video production that can ultimately be viewed and shared online.

Once your raw video footage is imported into iMovie, you can edit it, and then drag and drop various types of titles, visual effects, and graphic scene transitions (shown in Figure 12-15). You can also add music or sound effects, custom record voiceovers, or manipulate the audio that was recorded in conjunction with the video footage itself.

While editing a photo using iPhoto takes just a few minutes, it's easy to spend considerably more time editing and producing videos using iMovie. After the potentially time-consuming editing process is complete, with a few clicks it's possible to view and then share your finished movies.

You can watch your edited productions on your MacBook Air's screen, stream them to your home theater system via Apple TV, or share them with others via email, YouTube, Facebook, or another online service. Edited videos can also be burned to DVDs using the optional MacBook Air SuperDrive and then played on any DVD player. Using iCloud or the iTunes Sync process, your video creations can be specially formatted and then transferred to an iPhone, iPad, or iPod touch (shown in Figure 12-16) to be viewed and enjoyed while on the go.

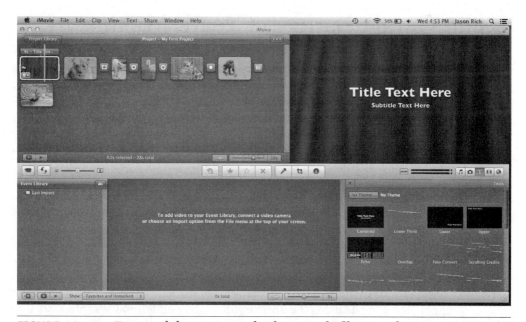

FIGURE 12-15   Drag and drop animated titles, visual effects, and scene transitions into your movie.

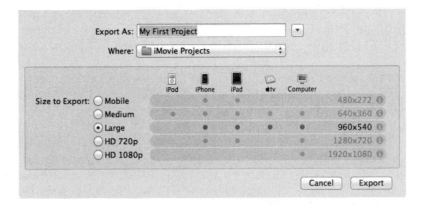

FIGURE 12-16   iMovie allows you to export your edited video and choose from a variety of popular file formats and resolutions based on how the movie will be viewed.

 To learn more about what iMovie can do and what features it offers, visit www.apple.com/ilife/imovie. All of the Apple Stores offer free iMovie workshops. To learn about how to participate in a free group training class near you, visit www.apple.com/retail/workshops. To learn how to use specific features in the iMovie app in order produce your own home videos that look visually amazing, visit www.apple.com/support/imovie.

Using GarageBand to Create Music

Whether you're a skilled musician or someone with only the most rudimentary musical skills, the GarageBand app is a comprehensive toolkit for composing, recording, editing, and producing music on your MacBook Air. Basically, this app transforms your computer into a feature-packed home recording studio (shown in Figure 12-17).

The goal behind GarageBand is to make digital music production achievable by just about anyone. This includes recording and producing music using live instruments and/or vocals, or composing digital music using digital instruments that come preinstalled in the GarageBand app.

Once raw audio tracks are imported into GarageBand or recorded directly using the app, an assortment of editing tools is available. Then you can export your digital audio files so they can be stored and played on your MacBook Air (using iTunes) or any other digital music player. You can also share your recordings via email or an online service, burn them onto audio CDs, or import your music productions into your iMovie videos. They can also be added to your iTunes digital music library and listened to using your iPod, iPhone, or iPad.

People with no musical knowledge whatsoever can enjoy hours of fun composing original digital music using the app's intuitive drag-and-drop user interface. However, someone who invests the time to learn basic music production skills will find this app extremely useful for composing and recording music.

FIGURE 12-17   GarageBand is an app used to compose, record, edit, and share music.

Some of the new features incorporated into GarageBand include interactive lessons for learning how to play the piano or guitar, as well as tools for composing, recording, and editing original music. If you're a singer, you can also use GarageBand to record, edit, and share vocals, or to produce a song from scratch.

The Magic GarageBand component of the app is ideal for someone with no musical training who wants to create original music. To do this, first select a musical genre. When prompted, choose which virtual instruments you want to add to your composition. This is all done by dragging or clicking on icons or instruments that are displayed on the screen. To take your composition (which uses presampled music) a bit further, click on the Open In GarageBand button. You can then edit and create individual tracks and add your own musical accompaniment.

If you're an iPhone user, GarageBand allows you to load in your favorite prerecorded music (or compose and record your own music) and transform that content into iPhone-formatted ringtones that can be transferred directly into your Apple smartphone.

Each module of GarageBand is used for a different purpose, although all revolve around creating, composing, recording, and sharing your own music. Whether you're an accomplished musician or a "wannabe" rock star with minimal musical talent or training, you can use this app to discover or fine tune your musical skills in a fun and creative way.

Tip   To learn the basics about what GarageBand can do and how it can be used to record and compose music or audio, visit www.apple.com/ilife/garageband. Online tutorials and other how-to information related to GarageBand can be found at www.apple.com/support/garageband.

13

Get Organized with the Contacts and Calendar Apps

HOW TO...

- Use the Contacts app
- Use the Calendar app
- Sync Contacts and Calendar data

The Address Book and iCal apps that have historically been part of the OS X operating system on all Macs were used to manage your personal contacts database and your schedule. In conjunction with the launch of OS X Mountain Lion in summer 2012, these two powerful apps were dramatically revamped. Address Book is now called Contacts, and the iCal app is now called Calendar. However, the name changes are only the beginning of what's new and different.

Both the Contacts and Calendar apps have been redesigned to now closely resemble the Contacts and Calendar apps that come with iOS 6.1, and that are used with the iPhone, iPad, and iPod touch. Now Contacts and Calendar on your Mac look and work almost identically to the iPad versions.

Plus, the two apps are now fully integrated with iCloud, which makes it even easier to wirelessly and automatically keep your personal contacts database and calendar data synchronized between your MacBook Air, other Macs, iOS mobile devices, and even your PC (running Microsoft Outlook, for example), without using the iTunes sync process.

 The OS X version of the Contacts and Calendar apps are fully compatible with their iOS edition counterparts. However, data can easily be imported into these two apps from other contact management and/or calendar apps, such as Microsoft Outlook, that are running on a Mac or PC. Likewise, data from these apps can be exported from Contacts or Calendar into other third-party apps.

How to... **Create a Personal Card for Yourself**

Because the Contacts app shares information with other apps, including Safari, it's useful to create a personal card for yourself with as much detail as possible, keeping in mind that this is information that will potentially be shared by the app when filling in forms or sharing your personal contact information with others, for example.

Instead of constantly entering your mailing address when you order products from various websites on the Internet, in Safari you can utilize the AutoFill option, which will import appropriate data from your My Card entry in the Contacts app.

To create a personal card, create a new contact entry as you normally would and include all of your personal information. Then, from the Card pull-down menu in the Contacts app, select the Make This My Card option. Once you do this, you can easily share your personal contact information with others using the Share My Card command. It's also found under the Card pull-down menu.

One of the biggest benefits of utilizing Contacts and Calendar on your MacBook Air to manage your contacts database and schedule is that these apps seamlessly integrate with other OS X apps. For example, data from your contacts database is accessible by the Mail, FaceTime, Safari, and Messages apps. Plus, when you enter a contact's birthday into their contacts entry in the Contacts app, for example, it can automatically be displayed in the Calendar app, and you can be notified in advance of the upcoming event.

When using the Mail app to compose an outgoing email, if the recipient's contact information is already stored in your contacts database, instead of manually entering their email address, simply type their name into the To field, and the Mail app will automatically insert their email address.

The Contacts app refers to individual contacts entries as "cards." You can view, add, edit, share, or link cards in your contacts database when using Contacts.

Syncing Contacts and Calendar Data from Other Apple Devices via iCloud

If you're already using the Contacts and Calendar apps on your iPhone, iPad, iPod touch, or another Mac, and you have an iCloud account set up, syncing your existing Contacts and Calendar app data is very easy. You can also sync data with Macs that are still running Address Book and iCal.

On your MacBook Air, launch System Preferences, and then click on the iCloud option (shown in Figure 13-1). From the left side of the iCloud window, make sure you sign into your existing iCloud account using your Apple ID and password. Then, from the right side of the iCloud window in System Preferences, add a checkmark to the checkboxes associated with the Contacts and/or Contacts & Reminders options.

Once you do this, exit out of System Preferences. As long as your MacBook Air has access to the Internet, your preexisting Contacts and Calendar data currently stored in your iCloud account (and synced with your other Macs and/or iOS mobile devices) will automatically load into and then remain synced on your MacBook Air as well. Thus, within a few minutes, your preexisting Contacts and/or Calendar data will be accessible from the Contacts and/or Calendar apps on your MacBook Air.

From your MacBook Air, you can also access your Contacts and Calendar data that's stored in your iCloud account by launching Safari (or any web browser) and visiting the iCloud website (www.icloud.com). Click on the Contacts or Calendar online app icon after signing in. This will allow you to access free, online-based Contacts and Calendar apps that are also almost identical to the Mac and iOS versions of these apps. This can be done from any computer or mobile device with Internet capabilities, even if it's not linked to your iCloud account.

FIGURE 13-1   Set up iCloud to work with the Contacts and Calendar apps and automatically sync your data.

Once your Contacts and/or Calendar data is being synchronized with iCloud, if you make a change to a contact card or appointment entry (event), or delete an entry from your MacBook Air, Mac, iOS mobile device, or from the iCloud website, that change will instantly be synced and applied to all versions of your databases that are stored on all of your various devices and linked to the same iCloud account. As a result, if you accidently delete an appointment or contact entry, within a few seconds it will be deleted on all of your devices that are connected to iCloud.

On your other computers and/or mobile devices, if you use a contact management app other than Contacts, you can manually import or export your entire contacts database or individual entries (cards).

For example, if you've already created a Contacts database on your MacBook Air, but want to use Microsoft Outlook or another app on your iMac, you can export your entire contacts database from your MacBook Air using the Export command that's displayed under the File pull-down menu.

You'll discover that the Contacts app supports the industry-standard vCard format. Thus, when you export your contacts database using this command, it can then be imported into any other app that supports the vCard format. The vCard format is a standardized file format for storing business card data in a contact management application. A contact entry stored in this format can be saved using one app and easily opened and viewed in another with no file conversion process required.

Likewise, you can export your preexisting database from another app on another PC or Mac, save it in the vCard format, and then import the database into the Contacts app on your MacBook Air. Using the Import and Export commands offered in the Calendar app, you can also easily exchange data with other software or computers that are not linked to your iCloud account. However, this is a manual process, while iCloud syncing happens automatically and in the background.

 It's a good strategy to periodically create a backup of your entire Contacts and Calendars databases, and save them on an external hard drive or USB thumb drive, for example. Thus, if for some reason your database gets accidently erased or corrupted, or your computer is lost or stolen, you have a reliable backup. This is particularly important if you do not use iCloud. To create a backup of your Contacts or Calendar database, use the Export command from the File pull-down menu, and select an external hard drive or USB thumb drive as the save location.

Maintaining Detailed Contact Records Using the Contacts App

In addition to the Contacts app working seamlessly with other OS X apps, one of the great features that Contacts offers is its flexibility and customizability. When you first launch the app and create your first contact entry, a default set of data fields is displayed for a contact card. It includes a first name, last name, company name, phone number, mailing address, email address, website URL, and notes field.

FIGURE 13-2   Customize the Contacts app to meet your personal or work-related needs by adding various data fields to each entry.

However, you can customize the default fields that appear (shown in Figure 13-2). Built into the Contacts app are over a dozen different fields. Plus, you can just as easily create your own custom fields to meet your needs as you create and maintain your personalized contacts database. To do this, from the Contacts app's Contacts pull-down menu, select the Preferences option and then click on the Templates button that's displayed near the top-center of the window.

Tip   In addition to editing the default contact template that will apply to all contact entries in your database, as you're creating a single new contact entry (card), you can add custom fields for that specific entry. To do this, access the Card pull-down menu, select the Add Field option, and then choose the type of field you want to add. You also have the ability to add multiple phone numbers, mailing addresses, email addresses, and/or website URLs to each contact entry. This allows you to include someone's home and work information, for example.

Viewing Contact Entries in Your Contacts Database

When you launch the Contacts app on your MacBook Air, the Contacts app window is displayed, if you select the List and Card view from the View pull-down menu. It is divided into two sections (shown in Figure 13-3). On the left, a master list of contacts in your database is displayed in alphabetical order. This listing can be sorted by last name, first name, or company name. To make this determination, access the Preferences

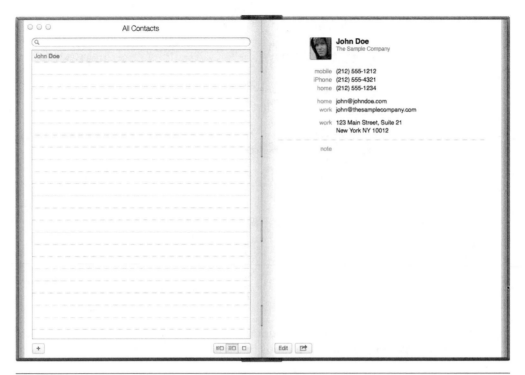

FIGURE 13-3 The Contacts app window is divided into two main sections.

option from the Contacts pull-down menu (that's displayed on the menu bar), and then click on the General tab that's displayed near the top of the window. Use the pull-down menu that's associated with the Sort By option to make your selection.

 In addition to the List and Card view, from the View pull-down menu in the app, you can choose the Card Only option, which displays one contact entry at a time. You can also choose the Groups option, which adds a third column to the app screen and allows you to view various contact groups you've created using the Contacts app.

Also displayed on the left side of the Contacts app window, near the top, is a Search field. Use it to quickly locate any contact entry in your database. You can search the database using any keyword that appears in any field of the database.

 Another option for quickly finding information stored in your Contacts or Calendar databases is to use the Spotlight Search feature that's built into OS X. This feature can be used anytime by clicking on the Spotlight Search icon that's displayed in the upper-right corner of the screen along the menu bar. It looks like a magnifying glass. Use the Spotlight Search feature to locate contact or scheduling data whether or not the Contacts or Calendar apps are running.

To create a new entry in your database from scratch, click on the plus sign icon that's displayed near the lower-left corner of the Contacts app window.

Tip Displayed to the right of the plus sign icon, near the bottom-center of the app window, you'll see three View buttons. Each will display your contacts database on the left side of the window using a slightly different format.

As you're viewing the contacts listing on the left side of the Contacts app window, highlight and select any single entry listing in order to view that entire listing on the right side of the app window.

Displayed below an individually selected Contact listing are two command buttons. The Edit icon allows you to edit or delete the selected listing. The Share icon (shown in Figure 13-4) allows you to share the individual contact entry with other computers and mobile devices, or with other people via email, Messages, or AirDrop. This feature is useful for sharing contact information with computers or mobile devices that are not linked to your iCloud account.

Note The AirDrop feature is not available on older Macs or on Windows-based PCs. When AirDrop is not available, use the email or Messages option to share individual contact cards.

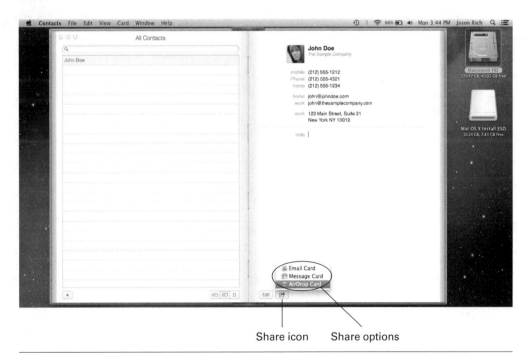

Share icon   Share options

FIGURE 13-4   Use the Share icon to easily share information from the Contacts app with other computers or mobile devices that are not linked to your iCloud account.

Creating a New Contact Entry

Whether you're using the Contacts app on your MacBook Air (running OS X Mountain Lion), on another Mac, or on your iOS mobile device, the process for creating a new contact entry (card) is virtually identical.

Begin by clicking on the plus-sign icon that's displayed near the lower-left corner of the app window. On the right side of the window, a blank card entry will be displayed. One at a time, fill in the data fields (as shown in Figure 13-5).

Keep in mind, it is not necessary to enter information into each of the data fields. For example, if a contact is not associated with a company, you can leave the Company field blank. Or if you want to include someone's phone number and/or email address, but not their mailing address, that's okay too.

Begin by entering the contact's first name, followed by their last name. You can then continue on to fill in the Company, Phone, Email, Home Page, User Name, and Mailing Address fields, as well as any other fields you set up to be defaults in a contact entry.

 Just below the contact's First Name, Last Name, and Company fields is a checkbox labeled Company. When you add a checkmark to this field, the contact entry will be stored and alphabetized based on the company title, as opposed to the person's last name.

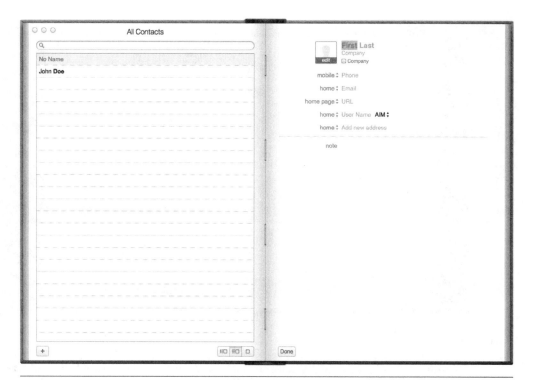

FIGURE 13-5 Fill in the data fields as prompted to create a new card entry in the Contacts app.

Tip   To add an additional field to the specific entry, access the Card pull-down menu from the menu bar and select the Add Field option. From the submenu that appears, choose the type of field you want to add to that entry. You'll have almost 20 options (shown in Figure 13-6) to choose from, plus you can create your own field types.

As you're entering information into some fields, you'll discover that by clicking on the field's label, you can modify it. For example, as you're entering someone's phone number, click on the Mobile field label to access a submenu of different phone number types, such as Home, Work, iPhone, Fax, or Other. Once again, you also have the option to create a custom phone number field by clicking on the Custom option.

Field labels can be customized related to phone numbers, email addresses, home pages, and mailing addresses, for example. Then, once one phone number, email address, or mailing address is entered, additional fields of that type but with different labels will be displayed, allowing you to enter someone's work, home, mobile number, and other details separately, but in the same card.

Tip   When entering someone's phone number, there is no need to enter parentheses around the area code, or to use a dash between the three-digit exchange and four-digit phone number. Just enter the 10-digit phone number and the Contacts app will format the field automatically. It's also useful to use the iPhone label in contact cards as opposed to the Mobile label when you know someone has an iPhone. The FaceTime and Messages apps (as well as others) look for the iPhone label in a card when you're using these apps and look up someone's contact information.

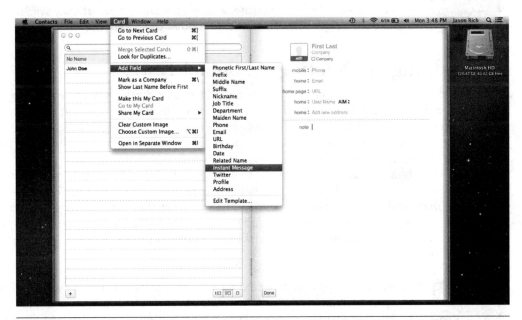

FIGURE 13-6   You can add any of almost 20 customizable fields to a Contacts entry or create your own field(s) from scratch.

In addition to filling in the text-based fields, when creating a new contact or editing an existing one, you have the option of linking a digital photo to a card. This can be a photo that's currently stored on your MacBook Air or that you take using the computer's built-in camera.

To link a photo with a contacts entry as you're creating or editing an entry, click on the Photo Box that's displayed to the left of the First Name, Last Name, and Company fields. Then, choose between Defaults, Recent, or Camera. The Defaults option allows you to associate a graphic icon with a contact entry, while Recent allows you to choose a photo that's stored on your MacBook Air. Camera allows you to snap a new photo using the computer's built-in camera.

 If you have iPhoto or a Finder window that has images open, you can also drag and drop an image into the photo box in Contacts to link an entry with a photo.

One other field that's available as you create or edit a contact entry is the Notes field. Here, you can cut and paste or type freeform notes of any length, and have them stored in a Contacts entry (card). Use this field to include any information about a contact that doesn't fit into one of the other fields. For example, you can include details about your most recent business conversations or meetings, driving directions to their location, or other information that's relevant and that would be convenient to have at your fingertips.

 As soon as you're finished creating or editing a contact entry, be sure to click on the Done button that's displayed near the bottom-center of the app window. This will save the entry in your database, and, if applicable, automatically sync the new additions or changes with iCloud and your other computers/devices.

Editing or Deleting a Contact Entry

Once a card has been added to your personal contacts database, you can update or alter the information in a specific card at any time. To do this, find and select the entry from the left side of the Contacts app window. When the appropriate card is displayed on the right side of the screen, click on the Edit icon that's displayed near the bottom-center of the app window.

One field at a time, enter the desired changes to the card entry. When you're finished, click on the Done icon. To delete a card altogether from your database, highlight and select its listing from the left side of the Contacts app window and press the DELETE key on the keyboard. Confirm your deletion decision when the "Are you sure you want to delete the card for [contact name]?" appears in the dialog box. Do this by clicking on the Delete icon.

 Remember, when you delete a card from your Contacts database on your MacBook Air, if your computer is linked to your iCloud account and has access to the Internet, that entry will also be deleted from your other computers and iOS mobile devices that are linked to same iCloud account.

Group Contact Entries (Cards) Together for Easier Access

While the Contacts app allows you to automatically sort the entries (cards) in your database alphabetically, there may be times when you'll want to link two or more cards together into groups. For example, you can link individual cards containing information about family members or relating to employees from the same company.

To create a new group, access the File pull-down menu and select the New Group, New Group From Selection, New Smart Group, or New Smart Group From Current Search option. You can then give the group a custom name and associate individual contact entries (cards) with it.

From the View pull-down menu, you can then opt to view contacts sorted into your groups by selecting the Groups option as opposed to the List and Card or Card Only option.

A Smart Group is created by first searching your database for individual entries that contain specific information, such as the same company name or last name, or finding cards that contain related information based upon parameters you establish. After selecting the New Smart Group option from the File pull-down menu, a pop-up window (shown in Figure 13-7) will appear.

Another way to link entries is to select the Related Name option when you're creating or editing a card. To do this, access the Card pull-down menu and choose the Add Field option. Select the Related Name option, and select the appropriate field name. Then include the name of the contact you want to link.

Another method for deleting a card is to select and highlight its listing on the left side of the Contacts app window and then utilize the Delete Card command that's found under the Edit pull-down menu on the menu bar.

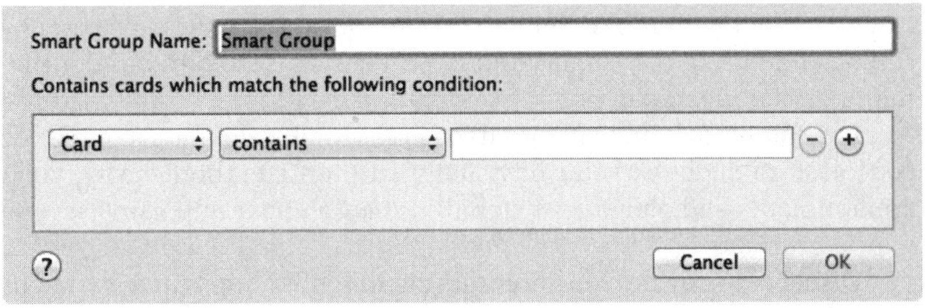

Smart Group Name:	Smart Group

Contains cards which match the following condition:

Card ⬍	contains ⬍		⊖ ⊕

⑦   Cancel   OK

FIGURE 13-7   Use the pull-down menus and data fields in the Smart Group pop-up window to set the parameters for the creation of the new Smart Group.

Managing Your Schedule Using the Calendar App

Just like the Contacts app, the Calendar app is designed to be easy to use, fully customizable, work seamlessly with the OS X Mountain Lion operating system and other apps, plus sync data automatically with iCloud. And, just like the Contacts app, the Calendar app that comes preinstalled with OS X Mountain Lion now looks and functions almost identically to the iPad version of the app, as well as the online-based Calendar app that's accessible via www.iCloud.com.

To view the current day in the Calendar app, regardless of which Calendar view you're using, click on the Today button that's displayed near the top-right corner of the screen. You can then use the directional arrow buttons displayed next to the Today button in order to scroll day by day, week by week, month by month, or year by year, depending on which view you're looking at.

The Calendar app can be set up so you can maintain multiple calendars on your MacBook Air, and then keep all of your scheduling-related data fully synchronized with iCloud automatically. Thus, your Calendar data also remains synchronized with your other Macs and iOS mobile devices.

To create a new calendar, which will have its own color coding, from the File pull-down menu in the Calendar app, select the New Calendar option. When prompted, give the calendar a unique name, such as Work, Family Obligations, Travel, etc. You can then view each individual calendar in the Calendar app separately, or view the color-coded calendars simultaneously by clicking on the Calendars button that's displayed near the top-left corner of the app window.

In the Calendar app, each individual appointment or item is referred to as an event.

You can also manually import and export your Calendar database so the information can be synced with non-Calendar apps on other computers or mobile devices. This can be done using the Import and Export commands found under the File pull-down menu on the menu bar.

In addition to being able to manage multiple calendars simultaneously and color code each calendar so you can visually differentiate them easily, you can view your appointments and obligations stored in the Calendar app using several different viewing formats.

Displayed near the top-center of the Calendar app window are command tabs labeled Day, Week, Month, and Year (shown in Figure 13-8). Click on any of these to view your scheduling information using a specific format.

As you've probably surmised, the Day view (shown in Figure 13-9) allows you to view your appointments and events one day at a time, using an hour-by-hour display.

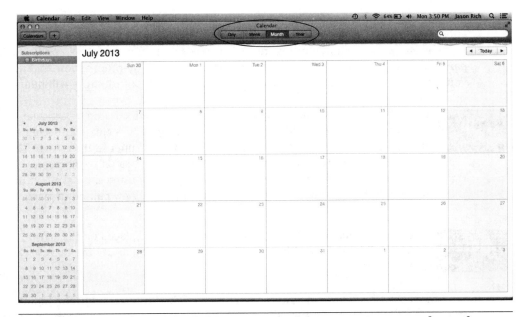

FIGURE 13-8   With a single click you can switch between viewing modes in the Calendar app. Shown here is the Month view with no events yet added.

FIGURE 13-9   The Day view in the Calendar app

On the left side of the app window, a more comprehensive listing of upcoming appointments or events is simultaneously visible.

The Week view (shown in Figure 13-10) shows your appointments and items for a particular week, while the Month display shows a month-by-month view that displays your appointments. The Year view displays a year's worth of monthly calendars.

 Regardless of which calendar view you select, when you click on a particular appointment or event, full details for it are displayed. To increase or decrease the text size of information displayed in the Calendar app, use the COMMAND (⌘)-+ keyboard shortcut to increase the text size, or the COMMAND (⌘)-– keyboard shortcut to shrink the text size. This is also adjustable using the Make Text Bigger or Make Text Smaller options that are found under the View pull-down menu.

 As you're viewing any calendar view, to print what's displayed on the screen, select the Print command from the File pull-down menu or use the COMMAND (⌘)-P keyboard shortcut.

Like most apps that come preinstalled with OS X Mountain Lion, the Calendar app has a Full Screen mode that allows you to utilize the entire MacBook Air's screen to display your calendar information. To enter into Full Screen mode, click on the Full Screen icon that's displayed near the upper-right corner of the app window, or use the Enter Full Screen option from the View pull-down menu. This also works when using the Contacts app.

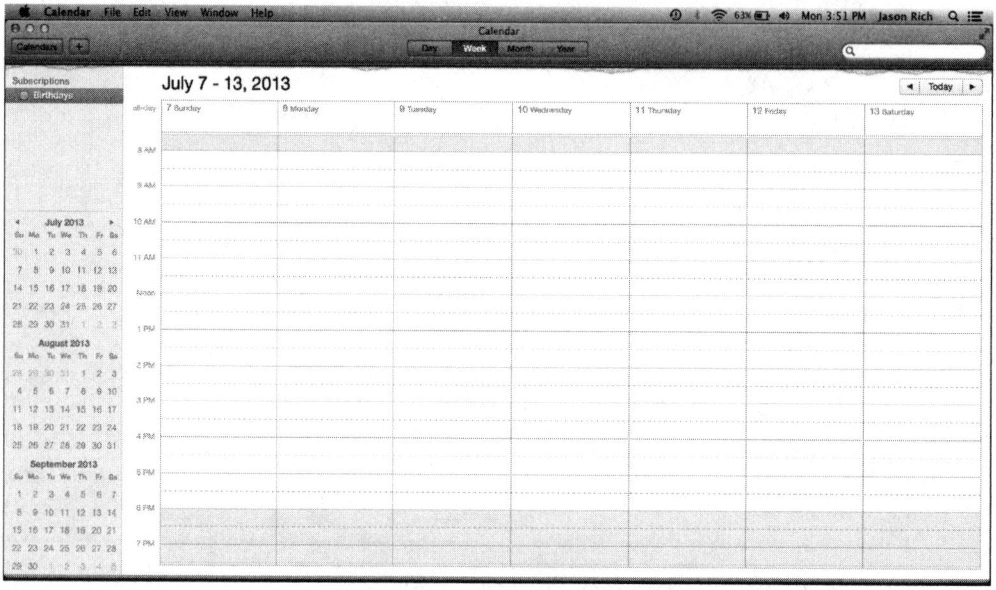

FIGURE 13-10 The Week view in the Calendar app.

The COMMAND (⌘)-CONTROL-F keyboard shortcut also works for quickly entering into or exiting out of Full Screen mode.

To exit out of Full Screen mode, press the ESC key on the keyboard.

Adding Events to Your Calendar(s)

The Calendar app refers to individual appointments or items as events. To add a new event to your calendar, you can create a Quick Event by clicking on the plus sign icon that's displayed near the upper-left corner of the app window (shown in Figure 13-11).

Then, when the Create Quick Event pop-up window appears, enter your event-related information using plain English. For example, you could type "Lunch meeting with Natalie at 2pm on Friday, July 2nd at Morton's Steak House." The Calendar app will format this information accordingly and automatically add it to a New Event window, which you can approve and save as a new event in your calendar.

The other option is to add an event using the more detailed New Event window. To access this, double-click on any day in a calendar, regardless of which calendar view you're using. The New Event window (shown in Figure 13-12) provides a handful of fields to fill in, one at a time, in order to enter a new event into your calendar.

At the top of the New Event window, enter the name or title for the meeting or event. Below that, click on the Location field to enter the event's location. Next, you

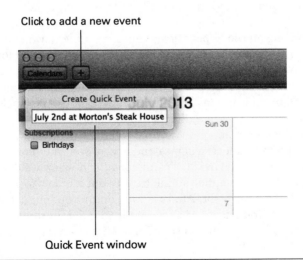

FIGURE 13-11 To quickly add an event to the Calendar app, click on the plus sign icon that's displayed near the upper-left corner of the app window.

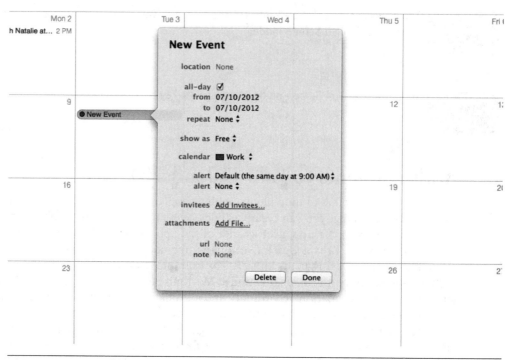

FIGURE 13-12   The New Event window allows you to enter detailed information about a new event to be added to the Calendar app.

can either add a checkmark to the All-Day option, if the event will last all day, or click on the From and To fields to manually enter the start and end times and dates for the event.

By clicking on the Repeat field, you can set the new event to recur every day, week, month, or year, for example. The default, however, is for the event to happen just once. You then have the option to click on the Show As field. This determines how the time period during which you have the event scheduled will be displayed on your calendar. Your options are customizable and can be labeled Work, Personal Time, Busy, In Meetings, Vacation, Business Travel, etc.

Then, if you're managing multiple calendars from the Calendar app, click on the Calendar option to select which calendar you want the new event to be listed in. This will determine how the event is color coded and when it's displayed.

Click on the Alert option in the New Event window to associate one or two alarms with the new event. After clicking on this option, determine how you want to be alerted. If you choose Message With Sound, for example, next select how far in advance an audible alarm will sound in conjunction with a notification message.

By associating two alarms with an event, you can remind yourself of the pending obligation several hours (or even days) prior to the event, and then again just minutes or hours before it, based on your personal needs.

By clicking on the Invitees option in the New Event window, it's possible to invite others via email to attend an event. Click on the Attachments option to link a file with the event listing. Finally, you have the ability to click on the URL option to associate a website link with a new event listing, or click on the Note option to add freeform notes to the listing.

When you're done entering all of the information that pertains to a new event, be sure to click on the Done button that's displayed in the lower-right corner of the pop-up window to save the event and add it to your calendar.

Once you click on the Done button, the event will be displayed in the Calendar app, plus the information will be automatically synchronized with your iCloud account. Thus, your new event will be displayed on your other Macs, as well as in the Calendar app running on your iPhone, iPad, or iPod touch.

As you fill in the various fields in the New Event pop-up window, you have the option to leave any of the fields blank and only include details that you deem relevant. However, the more information you add, the more helpful the app can be later.

How to...

Display Alerts and Alarms from Calendar in the Notification Center Window

The Notification Center feature that's built into OS X Mountain Lion is designed to work seamlessly with the Calendar app. Thus, you can set up the app to display all upcoming events, alerts, alarms, and notifications related to Calendar. To do this, launch System Preferences and click on the Notifications option.

From the left side of the Notifications window, click on the Calendar option. Then, on the right side of the Notifications window, make sure you add a checkmark in the checkbox that's associated with the Show In Notification Center option. Next, from the pull-down menu displayed to the immediate right of this option, select how many events you want displayed simultaneously in the Notification Center window. Your options include 1, 5, 10, or 20. Keep in mind, these settings apply only to your MacBook Air. They can be set differently on your other Macs or iOS devices.

In addition to having alerts, alarms, and notifications displayed in the Notification Center window, you can also set up the Calendar app to display this information as alerts or banners, plus set up the app to add badge alerts to the Calendar icon that's displayed in your MacBook Air's Dock. These options can also be customized from the Notifications window in System Preferences.

Editing and Deleting Events from Your Calendars

When viewing any individual event in your Calendar, double-click on the event listing itself and then click on the Edit icon to modify the information. When you do this, the New Event window for that event will again be displayed and you can change any of the fields in the window. Be sure to click on the Done button to save your changes.

To delete an event from in the Calendars app, simply select and highlight the event and press the DELETE key on the keyboard. You can also select the Delete command from the Edit pull-down menu.

Keep in mind, you can only edit or delete events that are created on your MacBook Air or that you have permission to alter. If you use the Calendar app to subscribe to a calendar (which is a way multiple people can share their scheduling information), you cannot edit or delete information from this type of calendar.

To subscribe to a new calendar, access the New Calendar Subscription option from the File pull-down menu. You'll then need to manually enter the appropriate URL for that calendar. Or, if you receive an email from someone else allowing you to subscribe to their calendar, simply click on the link that's embedded in the email.

 If you're managing multiple calendars using the Calendar app, click on the Calendars icon that's displayed near the upper-left corner of the app window to display the names of each calendar as well as their corresponding color code. You can then place checkmarks in the checkboxes associated with each calendar to decide what information you want to view at any given time.

As you make changes to your events stored in the Calendar app on other devices, if the app doesn't immediately showcase those changes, you can manually refresh the calendars on your MacBook Air by selecting the Refresh Calendars option from the View pull-down menu. (You can also use the COMMAND (⌘)-R keyboard shortcut to refresh your calendars.) This may be necessary if changes were made to your Calendar entries while Internet access was turned off on your MacBook Air.

Customizing the Calendar App

The Calendar app is customizable in many ways. To personalize the various settings in the app in order to display your event-related information in a format that best meets your needs, access the Calendar pull-down menu and select the Preferences option. You can then adjust the various Preferences settings one at a time. This only needs to be done once.

Once you access the Preferences window in Calendar, you'll see four command tabs displayed near the top of the window (shown in Figure 13-13). Upon clicking on each tab, a handful of submenu options are displayed. The four tabs are labeled General, Accounts, Advanced, and Alerts.

Click on the General tab to set up the Calendar app based on your typical work schedule. For example, you can set the number of days in your personal work week,

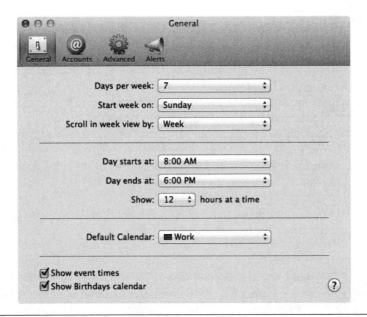

FIGURE 13-13 Access the Preferences option from the Calendar pull-down window to customize the app.

the day each work week begins, and the hours during the day you typically work. You can also show the default calendar that new events will be added to.

From the General window, add a checkmark to the checkbox associated with Show Birthdays Calendar to access birthday information from the Contacts app and display this information in the Calendar app.

Click on the Accounts tab at the top of the Preferences window to set up iCloud to work with the Calendar app and determine how often the app will sync with iCloud. The default option is Push, which means that as changes are made to a calendar, they will be synced in almost real time with iCloud (as long as your computer is connected to the Internet).

You can also set up the Calendar app to automatically sync data with Google Calendar or other services.

By clicking on the Advanced tab in the Preferences window, it's possible to turn on or off time zone support. This feature is useful if you will be traveling between time zones, or if you'll be attending virtual meetings taking place in a different time zone. When turned off, the Calendar app will not compensate for travel between time zones.

For example, if you're based in New York and set up a 1:00 PM (Eastern Time) lunch appointment for next Wednesday but you plan to be in Los Angeles on that day, with the time zone support turned off you will be alerted of that event at 10:00 AM (Pacific Time). However, with time zone support turned on, you will be alerted about the event at 1:00 PM (Pacific Time) while you're in Los Angeles.

From the Advanced window, you can also adjust other features associated with the Calendar app's functionality, including when and if events will be automatically deleted from the app after a predetermined time period.

By clicking on the Alerts icon in the Preferences window, it's possible to set up defaults for when you will see or hear alerts and alarms associated with specific events. For example, you can set up the app to alert you of upcoming birthdays several days in advance, as well as about upcoming events a predetermined number of minutes, hours, or days before they're scheduled.

 Alerts can also be customized on a per-event basis as you're creating or editing a specific event entry in the Calendar app.

 Instead of using the Calendar app to manage to-do lists with deadlines associated with them, consider using the Reminders app that also comes preinstalled with OS X Mountain Lion. Like the Calendar app, data from the Reminders app automatically synchronizes with iCloud.

Especially if you use your MacBook Air in conjunction with other Macs and/or iOS mobile devices, you'll discover that utilizing the Contacts and Calendar apps and syncing your databases via iCloud will not only make you more efficient and organized, it'll also ensure that your contact and scheduling-related information is always up to date and available whenever and wherever it's needed.

PART IV

Entertain Yourself with iTunes Content, Games, and More

14

Find and Enjoy Music, Movies, TV Shows, and More with iTunes

HOW TO...

- Use iTunes to find, purchase, and download music, movies, TV shows, and other multimedia content
- Listen to music or watch video content using the iTunes software on your MacBook Air
- Access iTunes content purchased on other computers or devices that are linked to the same iCloud account

Two of the primary uses for the iTunes software that comes preinstalled on your MacBook Air are to find, acquire, and download content from the online-based iTunes Store, and then to listen to and/or view that content on your computer (in this case, your MacBook Air).

The iTunes Store is operated by Apple and it offers one of the largest collections of multimedia content available on the Internet. The majority of the content available from the iTunes Store can be purchased using the credit card that's associated with your Apple ID account, and some free content is also available.

 In order to shop for content from the iTunes Store or to retrieve past purchases via iCloud, you'll need a valid Apple ID account set up. Your Apple ID will also need to be linked to a major credit card or debit card, or you'll need to prepurchase iTunes Gift Cards. To create or manage your Apple ID, visit: https://appleid.apple.com.

Thanks to the iTunes Store and the iTunes software, your MacBook Air can easily be transformed into a feature-packed and very mobile entertainment center. From the online-based iTunes Store, you can:

- Purchase music (more than 28 million songs are available)
- Purchase or rent movies

- Purchase TV show episodes (or complete seasons of your favorite TV series)
- Purchase eBooks from Apple's iBookstore online-based bookstore to be read on an iOS mobile device
- Purchase apps for your iPhone, iPad, or iPod touch (to be transferred to your device later)
- Access free podcasts
- Access free iTunes U educational content

Once you've acquired content from the iTunes Store (or other sources), you can then experience it using the iTunes software, which is also used to manage your multimedia content, as well as to play it.

Making an Online Content Purchase from the iTunes Store

When you opt to purchase content from the iTunes Store, upon clicking on the listing for the song, album, TV show episode, movie, etc., you will see a price icon for it displayed. To initiate the purchase, click on that price icon.

When prompted, enter the password that's associated with your Apple ID. The content you've selected will then be downloaded directly to your MacBook Air, and also be made available via iCloud on your other computers, iOS devices, and Apple TV (if applicable) that are linked to the same iCloud account. Keep in mind that due to copyright issues, you cannot easily share with a friend a TV show episode, song, or movie that you purchase. You can only transfer content between devices linked to your Apple ID account.

As soon as you enter your Apple ID password, confirm the purchase, and begin the download process, you will be charged for the content you've purchased. Thus, if you have a debit or credit card linked to your Apple ID account, it will be charged.

However, if you have redeemed an iTunes Gift Card and have a positive balance associated with your Apple ID account, the purchase price of the content will be deducted. If you have a positive balance, it will be displayed near the upper-right corner of the iTunes Store window next to your Apple ID (as shown in Figure 14-1).

To redeem an iTunes Gift Card, which can be purchased from Apple Stores, Apple .com, directly from the iTunes Store (and sent via email), or many other retail stores that sell gift cards (including supermarkets, pharmacies, and convenience stores), scratch off the silver line on the back of the gift card to reveal the redemption code. Next, launch the iTunes software and access the iTunes Store. From under the Quick Links heading that's displayed on the right side of the screen, click on the Redeem option and follow the onscreen prompts.

 Note iTunes Gift Cards come in $15, $25, $50, and $100 denominations. They are used for purchasing online content from the iTunes Store, iBookstore, App Store, Newsstand, and Apple's other online businesses. They are different from Apple Gift Cards (which can be used to make purchases from Apple Stores or Apple.com). For more information about iTunes Gift Cards or how to redeem them, visit www.apple .com/gift-cards.

FIGURE 14-1 If you have redeemed iTunes Gift Cards, the remaining balance from the card(s) is displayed near the upper-right corner of the iTunes Store window next to your Apple ID.

If the price icon for what you want to acquire displays the word Free or Download in it, that content is offered for free from iTunes, and can be downloaded directly to your MacBook Air.

To view what's currently being offered on iTunes for free, from the main iTunes Store screen, under the Quick Links heading that's displayed on the right side of the screen, click on the Free On iTunes option (shown in Figure 14-2).

FIGURE 14-2 Every week, iTunes offers a different selection of music, TV show episodes, Featurettes, apps, and other content for free.

The iTunes Store Offers a "Complete My Album" Feature

From the iTunes Store, you can purchase one or more singles at a time from a particular music album. After purchasing one or more singles, if you later decide that you want to purchase the entire album, be sure to use the iTunes Complete My Album feature. This allows you to purchase all of the remaining songs from the album at a discounted price, based on how many singles you've already purchased. In other words, if you have purchased one or more songs from the album already, you don't need to repurchase that music if you opt to acquire the entire album later.

When you view an album listing in the iTunes Store for an album that you already partially own, look for the Complete My Album option. It will display the discounted price of the album. You should also scroll down in the listing to view other Complete My Album offers, if applicable.

As you shop for TV show episodes from the iTunes Store, if you acquire individual episodes of your favorite TV shows that aired in the same season, but later decide to purchase that entire season of episodes from the series, the iTunes Store offers a Complete My Season option, which works just like the Complete My Album feature. It allows you to purchase the episodes in a particular TV season that you haven't yet purchased individually at a discounted price.

Note The process for acquiring free content from the iTunes Store is the same as purchasing content, but you will not be charged for it when you enter your Apple ID password. The free content you select will be added to your personal collection and become available via iCloud on all of your computers or devices that are linked to the same account, just as if it were purchased.

One drawback to buying and owning digital content, as opposed to an audio CD or video DVD, for example, is that you can't lend the content to other people or move the content easily between computers or devices that are not linked to the same iCloud account. When you purchase digital content, it is a digital file. There is no physical CD or DVD to store on your shelf at home.

The Cost of Purchasing Music, Movies, and TV Shows from iTunes

The cost of purchasing music, movies, individual TV show episodes, complete seasons of TV shows, music videos, and made-for-television movies varies. However, prices for the majority of the multimedia content in these categories that's available from the iTunes Store are listed in Table 14-1.

TABLE 14-1   The Average Cost of iTunes Content

Type of Content	Standard Definition Price*	High Definition Price*	Audio File Price*
Music (Single Song)	N/A	N/A	$0.69 to $1.29
Music (Complete Album)	N/A	N/A	$9.99 to $12.99
TV Show Episode	$1.99	$2.99	N/A
Complete TV Series Season	Varies	Varies	N/A
Music Video	$1.99	$1.99	N/A
Made-for-Television Movie	$3.99	$4.99	N/A
Movie	Varies	Varies	N/A
In Theaters Now Movie Rental	$9.99	$9.99	N/A
Regular Movie Rental	$3.99	$4.99	N/A

*Some content may be priced higher or lower.

Accessing the iTunes Store from Your MacBook Air

To access the iTunes Store, your MacBook Air needs access to the Internet. Begin by launching the iTunes software on your computer (shown in Figure 14-3). This can be done from the Dock, Launchpad, or from the Applications folder, for example. Especially if you'll want to access past iTunes purchases that were made from other computers or iOS devices, you'll want to make sure you're using the most current version of the iTunes software.

Tip   To make sure you're using the latest version of iTunes, upon launching the iTunes software access the iTunes pull-down menu and select the Check For Updates option. If a newer version of the iTunes software is available, allow it to be downloaded and installed on your MacBook Air. However, if the latest version of iTunes is currently running, a pop-up window will be displayed with a message that says, "This version of iTunes [insert version number] is the current version."

FIGURE 14-3 You can launch the iTunes software from the Dock or Launchpad (shown here), or from the Applications folder, for example.

Once the iTunes software is running on your MacBook Air, click on the iTunes Store option that's displayed on the left side of the screen under the Store heading. The main iTunes Store screen (shown in Figure 14-4) will be displayed in the iTunes program window.

Displayed near the top-center of the iTunes Store screen are nine command tabs. The Home tab will return you to the main iTunes Store screen. To search for and acquire digital music from the iTunes Store, click on the Music tab. To find, purchase, or rent full-length movies, click on the Movies tab. To find, purchase, and download individual TV show episodes or complete seasons of your favorite TV series, click on the TV Shows tab. These tabs are shown in Figure 14-5.

If, in addition to your MacBook Air, you have an iOS mobile device, such as an iPhone, iPad, or iPod touch, you can find and shop for apps for that device from Apple's App Store, and then transfer those apps to your mobile device later.

 The App Store that's accessible from the iTunes Store using the iTunes software is for finding, purchasing, and downloading apps for your iPhone, iPad, or iPod touch. If you want to access the App Store to acquire software or apps for your MacBook Air, use the separate App Store app that comes preinstalled on your computer. Refer back to Chapter 5 for more information about installing software on your MacBook Air.

FIGURE 14-4   The main iTunes Store screen

Through the iTunes Store, Apple offers one of the largest collections of digital music, TV shows, and movies available on the Internet. In addition, Apple operates iBookstore (which is accessible from iTunes), one of the world's largest online-based ebookstores. To shop for ebooks, click on the Books tab that's displayed along the top of the iTunes Store screen. Ebooks purchased from iBookstore can be viewed (read) on an iOS device such as an iPhone, iPad, or iPod touch using the iBooks app, or can be purchased from your MacBook Air and later transferred to your iOS mobile device.

Beyond the free and paid music, TV shows, and movies that are available from the iTunes Store, you can also access a vast and ever-growing library of free audio- and video-based podcasts by clicking on the Podcasts tab. Or by clicking on the iTunes U tab, you'll be able to access an extensive multimedia library of educational content created by some of the leading high schools, colleges, universities, and academic scholars from around the world.

FIGURE 14-5   Choose the type of content you wish to shop for using the command tabs displayed near the top-center of the iTunes Store screen.

Note For people who enjoy music, Ping is an online community that allows you to discover news and information about your favorite bands and recording artists, plus interact with other fans. It's a free service that can be accessed through iTunes using your Apple ID account. It is believed that in mid-to-late 2012, Apple will discontinue the Ping online service, at which time a new version of iTunes will be released that will no longer offer this feature.

It's important to understand that while the iTunes Store does offer some free content, the majority of what's offered must be purchased and paid for using your Apple ID account. However, once content is purchased, it can then be accessed from any computer or iOS mobile device that's linked to the same iCloud account.

Thus, if you purchase a song from the iTunes Store on your iPhone, for example, within seconds after that purchase is made you can also download and enjoy it on your MacBook Air (or vice versa). This applies to music, TV shows, and purchased movies, as well as ebooks and apps. Rented movies are handled slightly differently, but this will be explained later in the chapter.

Acquiring Music from the iTunes Store

When it comes to shopping for music, Apple's iTunes Store offers a vast online music selection, but it's not your only option. There are other online-based music stores, such as the Amazon MP3 Store, that allow you to purchase and download music, and then enjoy that music on your MacBook Air. You can also stream music from a wide range of online sources.

Tip If you know the name of the music, TV show, or movie, for example, that you're looking for and want to acquire from the iTunes Store, or you want to browse for content based on a keyword or search phrase, use the Search field that's displayed near the upper-right corner of the iTunes Store window. Enter exactly what you're looking for and the related search results will be displayed in the main iTunes Store window. The results will be sorted by media type.

If you opt to shop for and acquire digital music from the iTunes Store, click on the Music tab at the top of the iTunes Store screen (shown in Figure 14-6). From the main iTunes Store Music screen, you can view listings for new and soon-to-be-released albums or singles from bands and recording artists from virtually every music genre imaginable.

Tip By clicking and holding your cursor on the Music tab at the top of the iTunes Store screen, not only can you search for music in a specific genre, you can also browse the vast collection of music videos available from this service.

In the main area of the iTunes Store Music screen, you can browse through various music listings that are being featured by Apple. However, from the charts that are displayed along the right margin of the screen, you can see the most popular music based on sales. By default, you'll see Top Charts displayed for the Top Songs (shown in Figure 14-7), Top Albums, and Top Videos compiled from all genres.

FIGURE 14-6   Shop for music in any genre from the iTunes Store.

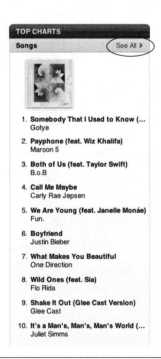

FIGURE 14-7   The Top Songs Chart is displayed on the right side of the iTunes Store's Music screen.

To view the top 200 selections from one of these charts, click on the See All button that's displayed to the right of the Top Charts heading. Or to view a Top Charts listing for music in a particular genre, first click and hold the cursor on the Music tab at the top of the screen, then select which music genre is of interest. Once the genre is selected, refer to the genre-specific Top Charts that are displayed along the right margin of the iTunes Store Music screen.

As you browse the iTunes Store's music selection, what you'll see is a selection of individual listings for singles or albums. Each listing includes an album graphic, the artist's name, and the album/song title. Click on any listing to view more details about that music selection.

If you click on a music listing for a single song, details about that one song will be displayed (shown in Figure 14-8). However, if you click on an album listing, details about all of the songs on that particular album will be displayed (shown in Figure 14-9). From the album listing, you can then purchase individual songs of your choice or purchase the entire album at once.

 Tip Before purchasing any music from the iTunes Store, from a song or album's listing, it's possible to listen to a short preview of the music by clicking on a song's title or the Preview icon. To purchase the song, click on the Price icon that's displayed to the right of the song listing.

In addition to the title of a song, the artist, and the album it's from, each listing also includes a star-based rating and displays how many ratings it has received. These ratings are from your fellow iTunes customers. Plus, you can access detailed reviews also written by iTunes Store customers.

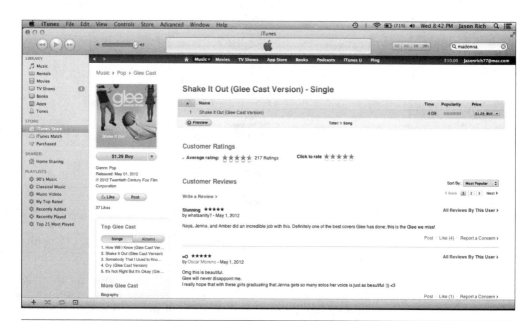

FIGURE 14-8   A sample listing for a single song offered from the iTunes Store.

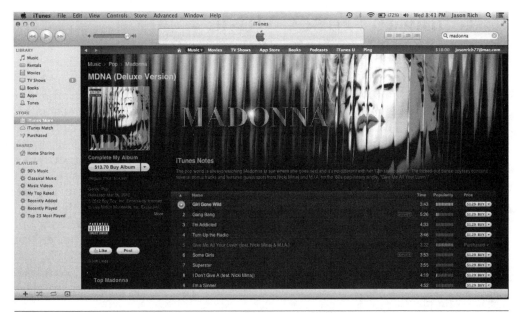

FIGURE 14-9 A sample listing for an album offered from the iTunes Store

 From the listing screen, you'll discover links to other music recommendations recorded by that artist/band or similar artists/bands.

How to... Authorize Your Computer to Work with iTunes and iTunes Match

The first time you try making a purchase or downloading content from iTunes on your MacBook Air, it will be necessary to authorize the computer. Up to five computers can be authorized for each iTunes (Apple ID) account.

To authorize your computer, launch the iTunes software, access the Store pull-down menu from the menu bar, and then select the Authorize This Computer option. When prompted, enter your Apple ID password.

The authorization process needs to be done just once on your MacBook Air. After the computer is authorized to work with iTunes, you can also turn on the iTunes Match service (if you're a subscriber). To do this, click on the iTunes Match option that's displayed on the left side of the iTunes screen under the Store heading. Next, click on the Add This Computer icon that's displayed near the center of the screen.

Listening to iTunes Music Purchases Using the iTunes Software

In addition to serving as a conduit for accessing the iTunes Store and purchasing music, the iTunes software on your MacBook Air is used to manage your personal digital music library and to listen to the music you currently have stored on your computer. This includes iTunes Store music purchases, music acquired from other online sources, music you've composed on your computer, as well as music you've "ripped" from traditional CDs and have converted into digital music (.MP3) files.

To manage your personal digital music library, launch the iTunes software on your MacBook Air, and then click on the Music icon that's displayed on the left side of the screen under the Library heading (shown in Figure 14-10).

In the main iTunes window, a listing of all music that's currently stored on your computer will be displayed. To play one of the songs listed, double-click on its listing.

Along the top of the iTunes screen, onscreen music controls are displayed. Near the upper-left corner of the screen you'll discover the Rewind/Track Back, Play/Pause, and Fast Forward/Track Forward buttons. They're used for controlling the music you want played.

FIGURE 14-10 Play music using the iTunes software that's stored on your MacBook Air, plus manage your digital music library.

To the right of these three buttons is the volume slider. Near the top-center of the screen, you'll see the active song display and timer slider. To the right of that are the Music View icons. These determine how the music listings are displayed on the iTunes screen.

There are four Music View options in iTunes. The leftmost button offers a text-only-based listing of the songs and/or albums and related information. It's sorted by song title. To the right of it is an enhanced text listing button that sorts music by album title. The third option displays album artwork and allows you to sort your music library by album title, artist, genre, or composer. The fourth Music View is an animated carousel option that showcases album artwork along the top of the screen, plus offers a text-based listing on the bottom half of the iTunes screen.

Finally, near the upper-right corner of the iTunes screen is the Search field that you can use to quickly find music that's stored on your computer by entering a song title, artist name, album name, or any keyword/search phrase that's associated with the music you're looking for.

In the Song Display window, the active song's title, artist, and album name are displayed. On the timer slider, displayed to the left is the amount of the song you've heard thus far, while on the right the timer displays how much time remains in the song.

In addition to being able to click on and play a single song, you can create and play customized playlists from within iTunes. To create a new playlist, access the File pull-down menu and select the New Playlist option. Also from this pull-down menu, you'll discover commands for rating your music, editing playlists, and managing your music library.

Once a new playlist is created, you can name it and then drag and drop songs from your main Music library in iTunes to the new playlist that is listed on the left side of the screen. You can add as many songs as you want to a playlist, from any album or music genre, as long as each song is stored on your MacBook Air.

Another option is to create a Smart Playlist. Using a series of pull-down menus and search fields, you can automate the playlist creation process and include songs that meet predetermined criteria, such as an artist name, music genre, or personal rating. To create a Smart Playlist, select the New Smart Playlist command from the File pull-down menu.

Once you create a custom playlist, a listing for it will be displayed on the left side of the iTunes screen under the Playlists heading. You can create, save, and sync as many custom playlists as you desire, and each can contain any number of songs from any music genre that's stored on your computer.

Clicking on the Music option under the Library heading allows you to access music that's already stored on your MacBook Air. To access music you've purchased from iTunes and that's stored on iCloud, but that has not yet been downloaded to your computer, click on the Purchased icon that's displayed on the left side of the iTunes screen under the Store heading.

FIGURE 14-11 Using the iTunes software, you can download and play music that you've previously purchased and that's stored in your iCloud account.

When the listing of songs that you own (and have purchased from iTunes) is displayed (shown in Figure 14-11), click on the iCloud icon to download individual songs to your MacBook Air.

Keep in mind, you can also set up iTunes to automatically download all new music purchases, regardless of which device they were purchased on. To set this up, from the iTunes pull-down menu, select the Preferences option. When the Preferences window appears, click on the Store option. You can then opt to automatically download music, apps, and/or books.

 If you've subscribed to the premium iTunes Match service, your entire music collection can be synced with your MacBook Air, regardless of where the music was originally purchased. This means that music from your Mac(s), PC(s), and iOS mobile devices can also be accessed and downloaded to your MacBook Air. To learn more about the iTunes Match service, visit www.apple.com/itunes/itunes-match.

Shopping for TV Show Episodes from the iTunes Store

There are many ways to access TV shows and watch them on your MacBook Air. You can purchase TV show episodes or entire seasons of your favorite shows from the iTunes Store. When you do this, you own those episodes and can then view them, commercial-free, whenever and wherever you'd like, as often as you'd like.

TV show episodes purchased through iTunes on your MacBook Air get downloaded to your computer, but also become accessible on your other computers, iOS mobile devices, and via your Apple TV device, as long as they're linked to the same iCloud account. You can also download to your MacBook Air and then watch TV show episodes you've previously purchased on other devices that are linked to the same iCloud account.

From the iTunes Store, you can purchase individual TV show episodes in standard definition or high definition for $1.99 or $2.99, respectively. New episodes of current shows are typically made available 24 hours after they air on television.

In addition to purchasing individual episodes, it's possible to purchase entire seasons of TV shows that have already aired, and download those episodes all at once at a discounted price. If you acquire a season pass for a currently airing TV series, you can set up your MacBook Air to download new episodes automatically as soon as they become available.

To find, purchase, and download TV show episodes, launch the iTunes software and access the iTunes Store. Next, click on the TV Shows tab that's displayed near the top-center of the screen. You'll then be able to browse through featured shows, access Top Charts that list popular shows, or search for shows using a wide range of criteria (as shown in Figure 14-12).

FIGURE 14-12 From the iTunes Store, you can purchase individual TV show episodes or entire seasons of your favorite TV series to watch on your MacBook Air.

Tip   If you know the exact TV show you're looking for, enter its title or keywords related to it in the Search field that's displayed near the upper-right corner of the screen. From the TV Shows Quick Links menu that's displayed on the right side of the screen, you can browse for shows based on categories. Click on the Free Episodes option to see a listing of shows currently being offered for free (this selection changes weekly), or click on the Get The Latest Episodes option to access the most recent episodes of popular shows that have aired within the past seven days. Also from the Quick Links menu, you can select the Networks & Studios option to find TV shows based on what network they are broadcast on or which studio they are produced by.

Just like when shopping for music from the iTunes Store, each show listing includes a graphic icon, the name of the series, and the title of an episode. When you click on a listing, a more detailed information screen for a particular TV series is displayed, listing all of the seasons available and each of the episodes available in those seasons. You can then preview each episode, or opt to purchase and download individual episodes or entire seasons.

Shopping for Movies from the iTunes Store

The iTunes Store offers an ever-growing selection of feature-length movies from major studios, as well as many independently released films. Typically, when a movie is released on DVD or Blu-ray, it's also made available from the iTunes Store for purchase and download and/or rental. However, you'll discover some iTunes Store movie selections available exclusively from iTunes that are not yet on DVD or Blu-ray.

Note   Not all movies available from the iTunes Store are available for purchase and rental. Some can only be purchased, while others can only be rented. The purchase price and rental fee for movies vary.

To browse the available selection of movies for rent or purchase, click on the Movies tab that's displayed near the top of the iTunes Store screen (as shown in Figure 14-13). The process for browsing what's available is very similar to searching the iTunes Store for music or TV shows. Just like music, movies are searchable by genre. To view the various movie genres, click on the All Categories option that's displayed under the Quick Links menu, or click and hold down the trackpad when the cursor is on the Movies tab.

New releases and featured movies are promoted on the main iTunes Store Movies page. You can also search for movies using the Search field, or access the Quick Link menu options that are displayed on the right side of the screen to help you find what you're looking for.

When you purchase a movie from iTunes using your MacBook Air, the digital file for that movie gets downloaded to your computer and will be watchable within 15 to 60 minutes, depending on the speed of your Internet connection, the length of the

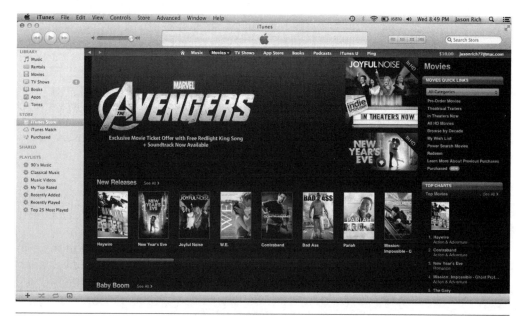

FIGURE 14-13   Shop for movies to purchase or rent from the iTunes Store.

movie itself, and whether you've purchased the standard definition or high definition version of the movie.

Once purchased, a movie becomes part of your digital collection and is available on the computer it's originally downloaded to, as well as any other devices you transfer it to from your iCloud account (such as your other Macs, PCs, iPhone, iPad, iPod touch, or Apple TV device). You're free to watch the movie as often as you'd like using the iTunes software.

Did You Know?

Renting Movies from iTunes

In addition to purchasing movies from iTunes, which costs about the same as the price of a DVD or Blu-ray version of the same movie, iTunes also offers movie rentals. For $3.99 (standard definition) or $4.99 (high definition), many movies available for sale from iTunes can also be rented.

When you rent a movie, it will be downloaded to the computer or iOS device that it's rented on, and will remain there for up to 30 days or until you begin playing the movie. After 30 days, the movie file will automatically be deleted. Once you begin playing the rented movie, you can watch it as often as you'd like for a 24-hour period, after which time the movie file will automatically be deleted from your computer.

(continued)

A movie that's rented from iTunes can only be stored on one computer or device at a time, but during the 30-day storage period or 24-hour viewing period, you can transfer it (not copy it), via iTunes, between your MacBook Air, iMac, PC, iOS mobile device, and/or Apple TV.

Once you select a movie to rent, within two or three minutes after the download process begins, you can typically begin watching the movie at the same time it gets downloaded to your computer. Otherwise, you can wait for the entire movie to download, and then watch it at your convenience, whether or not an Internet connection is available.

In addition to movies released by major studios, iTunes offers a vast selection of independent movies, including films released on iTunes either prior to or at the same time they're released in theaters. The pricing to purchase or rent these movies is typically higher than traditional movies. To discover some of the independent films available from iTunes, click on the In Theaters Now option that's displayed under the Quick Links menu on the right side of the screen.

To view a listing of popular movies available from iTunes, check out the Top Charts listings that are displayed on the right side of the main iTunes Store Movies screen. To see a more extensive list of popular movies, click on the See All option that's displayed to the right of a Top Charts list.

Based on your past music, TV show, or movie purchases, the iTunes Genius option uses artificial intelligence to offer you personalized recommendations for future purchases from the iTunes Store's content library. From the main Music, TV Shows, or Movies page in the iTunes Store, scroll down to view the listings under the Recommended For You heading.

Watching TV Show Episodes and Movies Using the iTunes Software

The iTunes software is also used to watch TV show episodes and movies that you've purchased from iTunes and that are stored on your MacBook Air, or that are accessible from your iCloud account.

Movies rented from the iTunes Store are also viewed using the iTunes software. To access rented movies stored on your MacBook Air, click on the Rentals option that's listed under the Library heading on the left side of the iTunes screen. Remember, once you begin watching a rented movie, the 24-hour window for watching it begins.

Movies
option

TV Shows
option

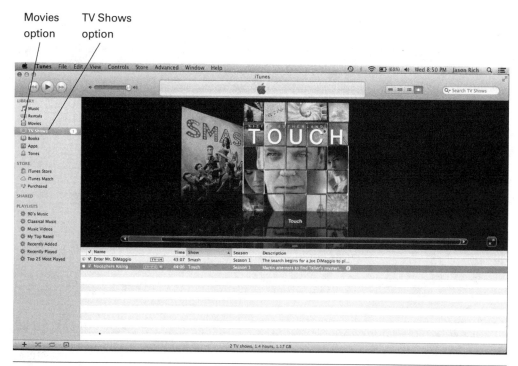

FIGURE 14-14   To watch a TV show episode, first click on a TV show, then click on one of the episodes you've already purchased and downloaded in order to begin watching it.

To watch TV show episodes or movies that are stored on your MacBook Air, launch the iTunes software and click on the TV Shows or Movies option that's displayed on the left side of the screen, under the Library heading (shown in Figure 14-14).

Depending on the viewing option that's selected using the icons displayed near the top-right corner of the screen, the available show episodes or TV series seasons will be displayed as text-based listings or graphic icons. Figure 14-15 shows a text-based listing, while Figure 14-16 shows a more graphic-oriented listing of the TV shows available on your MacBook Air.

As applicable, these listings can be sorted by name or genre. You also have the option to display only unwatched episodes or movies, for example. When you click on a specific TV show listing, the available episodes that you have purchased and that are stored on your MacBook Air are displayed. Click on a listing for an episode to begin watching it. If you want to watch a movie, click on the listing that displays the movie title or related icon.

 To enhance your TV episode or movie viewing experience, consider using your MacBook Air with noise-cancelling stereo headphones or connecting the computer to external speakers.

Viewing option icons

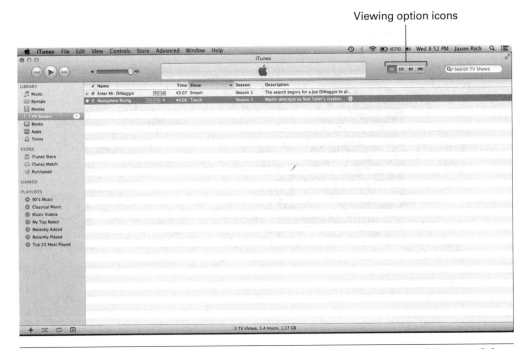

FIGURE 14-15 Click on the leftmost View icon to display a text-based listing of the TV shows you have stored on your computer.

FIGURE 14-16 Click on the View icon that's third from the left to display the icon viewing option.

Controlling Your Viewing Experience

At the top of the screen, the onscreen controls used to watch TV show episodes and movies are displayed. They are similar to the controls used for listening to music. However, once you click on a TV show episode or movie to begin playing it, VCR-like controls are displayed near the bottom-center of the screen as well.

 When watching purchased video content, you can switch to Full Screen mode by clicking on the Full Screen icon that's displayed near the top-right corner of the iTunes window, or on the extreme right of the onscreen control window.

 The onscreen controls automatically disappear after a few seconds. To make them reappear, move the cursor around in the video playback window. If the onscreen controls don't automatically disappear, move the cursor away from the window displaying the controls.

The video control window that appears near the bottom-center of the screen when purchased video content is playing consists of a handful of command buttons used to control the video playback.

When viewing the controls window that appears, to the left is the volume slider. Moving to the right, you'll see the Chapter Back icon, followed by the Rewind icon, Play/Pause icon, Fast Forward icon, Chapter Forward icon, captioning icon, and Full Screen icon. Below these icons is a timer slider. The left side of this slider displays how much of the video content you've already watched. Simultaneously, on the right side of the timer display you'll see how much of the video is remaining.

How to... **Block Your Kids from Purchasing or Viewing Unsuitable Content**

The music, television, and motion picture industry all have a rating system which can be used by parents to help determine what content is and is not suitable for their kids to experience. The iTunes software allows you to control what content your kids are able to download and/or experience on the MacBook Air, based on ratings.

To control the content that your kids can access on your MacBook Air, launch System Preferences, and select the Parental Controls option that's displayed under the System heading. You can then set up a new account on your computer that your kids can sign into when they're using the MacBook Air.

(continued)

Once this new account is set up, you can set limits as to how the computer is used, whether or not new content can be purchased and downloaded from the iTunes Store, and what type of content can be accessed. For example, if you allow movies to be purchased, rented, and viewed, you can opt to block rated-PG and/or rated-R movies from being acquired or viewed.

Separate controls can be set related to purchasing or downloading content from iTunes, listening to music, as well as watching other video-based content. It's also possible to set up Parental Controls related to what other apps (including games) can be used on the MacBook Air. Using Parental Controls, it's possible to disable the iTunes Store and App Store altogether, or limit the type of content that can be purchased and downloaded.

If you opt to allow your kids to make online purchases from the iTunes Store, but don't want to give them access to your iTunes account that's linked to your credit card, you can set up a monthly iTunes Allowance and "deposit" a predetermined amount of money to their unique Apple ID account, which can be used to make online purchases from the iTunes Store, App Store, iBookstore, Newsstand, and Apple's other online business ventures.

From the main iTunes Store screen, click on the Buy iTunes Gifts option that's displayed in the Quick Links menu on the right side of the screen, and then scroll down to the Allowances option and click on the Set Up An Allowance Now option.

Streaming Web Content Instead of Purchasing and Downloading It

Purchasing and then playing purchased music, TV show episodes, or movies via iTunes has some advantages. For example, once the digital file for the content is stored on your MacBook Air, an Internet connection is no longer required to experience that content. You can also watch or listen to the content as often as you'd like.

 Purchased TV show episodes can be viewed commercial free if they're acquired from the iTunes Store.

Instead of purchasing iTunes content, however, you have the option to stream music, TV show episodes, or movies from a wide range of sources. For example, for a flat fee of $7.99 per month, you can subscribe to Netflix (www.netflix.com) or Hulu Plus (www.hulu.com), and stream on an unlimited basis the service's collection of TV show episodes and movies, including current releases and thousands of classics.

Content streamed from Netflix or Hulu Plus is also commercial free. To stream TV show episodes, you can also use Safari and visit the websites of television networks to watch full episodes of popular shows. There is no cost to stream these shows, but they do contain commercials as if you're watching them on television.

If you're interested in streaming music from the Internet, there are thousands of Internet-based radio stations and music services, such as Pandora (www.pandora.com) and I Heart Radio (www.iheart.com), that allow you to listen to music for free via the Internet. Depending on the streaming music service you access, you may or may not hear commercials as part of the programming.

When you stream content from the Internet, it gets transferred from the web-based server to your computer and played using your Internet web browser (or specialized software). As a result, to stream content from the Web, a constant Internet connection is required. The iTunes software is not used to stream content from the Internet from non-iTunes sources.

15

Play Games on Your MacBook Air

HOW TO...

- Find, download, and play games on your MacBook Air
- Play online-based games on your MacBook Air
- Access Apple's Game Center online service

Sure, your MacBook Air is a powerful computer that allows you to handle a wide range of personal productivity and work-related tasks while on the go. However, when you want to kick back and have some fun, your MacBook Air can be there for you as well, serving as a feature-packed entertainment device.

In addition to playing music, watching TV shows and movies, and streaming content from the Internet, which was the focus of Chapter 14, you can experience fun, challenging, and often addicting games on your MacBook Air.

Many popular computer and video game developers have adapted their popular PC, Microsoft Xbox, Nintendo, and Sony PlayStation games to the Mac. These games can be purchased for a one-time fee, downloaded, stored on your computer's flash drive, and then later typically experienced on your MacBook Air whether or not an Internet connection is present.

Another option is to purchase, download, and experience multiplayer games that allow you to compete against other human opponents via the Internet. This allows you to challenge your friends and family members who are located a few feet away, across town, across the country, or just about anywhere in the world for that matter. You also have the option to compete against total strangers and showcase your computer gaming prowess. These games also often require a one-time purchase fee, but can then played on an unlimited basis. A continuous Internet connection is required.

 Some multiplayer games require all players to be situated around the same computer and are turn-based. However, others allow you to virtually link multiple computers together via the Internet or a wireless network in order to experience the same game simultaneously and compete against each other.

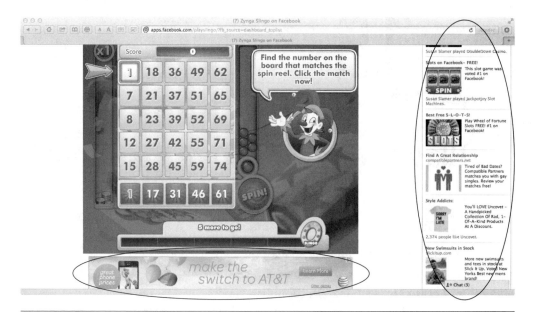

FIGURE 15-1 Many free online-based games are advertiser supported, meaning you'll need to view ads as you play.

There are also an ever-growing number of online-based games that require continuous access to the Internet to play. These typically require no special software to be downloaded. As you'll discover, many of these games are free of charge to play, but are advertiser supported. This means you can play them as often as you'd like, but you'll need to view advertisements while playing. An example of this is shown in Figure 15-1.

To play online-based games, you'll use a web browser, such as Safari, to access the game's website. Several of the popular online social networks, including Facebook, also serve as conduits for playing online-based multiplayer games, such as *FarmVille* (shown in Figure 15-2) and other games offered by companies such as Zynga (http://company.zynga.com).

 Some online-based games are initially free of charge to play but offer in-game purchases that are optional but greatly enhance the gameplay experience. As a result, over time, you could wind up spending a significant amount of money playing a game you ultimately get hooked on, and invest (or some would say squander) dozens or hundreds of hours playing.

FIGURE 15-2   *FarmVille* from Zynga is a popular online-based game that's free to play, but that has in-game purchase options available.

You Can Transport Yourself to a Galaxy Far, Far Away...

Just as a good book or movie allows your imagination to transport you to distant locations and potentially places you into exciting situations that aren't necessarily possible in real life, computer games also offer this type of immersive experience, but with an added interactive and often social element.

Games like *The Sims 3*, *Starcraft II*, *Diablo III*, *Star Trek Online*, *Star Wars Knights: Old Republic*, and *Civilization V: Campaign Edition*, for example, are just a few examples of single player and multiplayer games that allow you to take on the role of a human or non-human character and experience adventures that take place in another time, another place, and often in an imaginary environment that's filled with challenges.

Whether you enjoy sports simulations, action-based adventure games, first-person shooters, card games, traditional board games, casino simulations, recreations of classic arcade games, strategy or puzzle challenges, driving simulations, or science fiction or fantasy-based RPG (role playing game) adventures, hundreds of computer games are available to address your interests and gaming skill level.

(continued)

Some games are designed to immerse you in an interactive world for countless hours at a time. Others, like *Angry Birds* or *Words With Friends*, offer entertainment options that can be experienced in just five or ten minute intervals. These provide a quick escape from real life.

As you'll discover, many of today's computer games combine photo-realistic animated graphics, stereo sound effects, original soundtracks (just like movies), in-depth storylines, and the opportunity to communicate with and challenge other players in real time via the Web. All this can be done from your MacBook Air. However, because sound plays such an integral role in many of the latest games, consider connecting your computer to external speakers or stereo headphones to get the most out of the auditory experience.

While most games can be controlled using the computer's keyboard or the MacBook Air's trackpad, in some situations you may find it advantageous to connect an optional controller, game pad, or joystick to your computer via a USB cable or wireless Bluetooth connection. If you visit an online price comparison website such as Nextag (www.nextag.com/mac-joystick/stores-html), you'll find literally hundreds of optional game pads and joysticks available that are compatible with the MacBook Air and many popular games.

Finding the Best Games to Experience on Your MacBook Air

When it comes to discovering, purchasing, and downloading games for your MacBook Air, one of the first places to visit is the App Store. From your MacBook Air's Dock (or from the Launchpad), launch the App Store app.

Located near the top-center of the App Store window, click on the Top Charts or Categories tab (shown in Figure 15-3). To view a listing of the bestselling and most popular games for the Mac that you can purchase, download, and play, click on the Top Charts tab. Then, on the right side of the screen, look for the Top Charts Categories listing and click on the Games option.

Displayed on the screen will be a listing of Top Paid Games, Top Free Games, and Top Grossing Games. Each of these categories will display a dozen game listings, shown in their order of popularity.

To see a more expansive listing of games sorted by popularity, click on the See All option that's displayed to the immediate right of the Top Paid Games, Top Free Games, or Top Grossing Games heading. Game listings are then displayed in their order of popularity, as shown in Figure 15-4.

FIGURE 15-3 After launching the App Store, click on the Top Charts tab, followed by the Games option, to discover popular games.

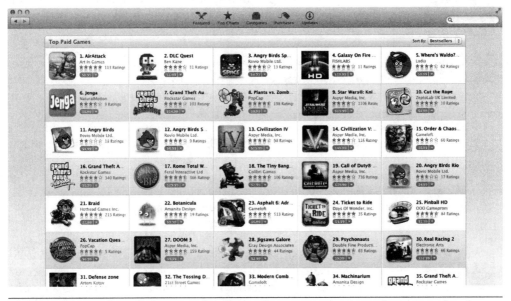

FIGURE 15-4 After clicking on the View All option, view game listings under the Top Paid, Top Free, or Top Grossing headings in their order of popularity.

From the App Store, you can browse through game offerings, but there are also many other entertainment-oriented apps available that can be found by choosing the Categories tab, and then clicking on the Entertainment or Lifestyle options, for example.

Discover Fun-Filled and Challenging Paid Games

The Top Paid Games listing includes games that can be purchased, downloaded, and played on your MacBook Air. These games require a one-time purchase fee to acquire the core game, which is then downloaded and stored on your computer. It can then be played at any time, as often as you wish.

Some paid games have optional in-game purchases that grant you access to additional gaming features, new levels, or special content.

You'll discover the initial purchase price of games for the MacBook Air varies from $0.99 to $49.99. You'll also discover that the price of a game is not a reflection of its quality or how much entertainment value it offers. Instead of just focusing on how much a game costs, also pay careful attention to a game's description and sample screenshots, as well as its ratings and reviews.

Many popular games have promotional websites created by the developer that offer animated trailers for the game (similar to movie trailers), as well as a free, downloadable trial version of the game.

While there are many original games available for the Mac, as you browse the App Store you'll discover games that are part of extremely popular game franchises or series that are available on a variety of gaming platforms. *Angry Birds*, *Grand Theft Auto*, *Star Wars Knights: Old Republic*, *Civilization V*, *Call of Duty*, *Quake 4*, *The Sims 3*, and *Doom 3* are just a few examples of game franchises that have been popular for years on other gaming platforms, and that have also been adapted to the Mac.

If there's a Windows-based PC game that you want to experience on your MacBook Air, but a Mac version has not yet been released, be sure to read Chapter 18, "Run Windows and Windows Software on Your MacBook Air."

Use the Top Paid Games chart as a way to discover what games are available for the Mac and are currently popular among other Mac users. The games listed in the Top Paid Games, Top Free Games, and Top Grossing Games charts change often as the popularity of each game on the list goes up or down.

Some Games Are Offered for Free from the App Store

After launching the App Store, by clicking on the Top Charts tab that's displayed near the top-center of the screen, and then choosing the Games category from the right side of the screen (located under the Top Charts Categories heading), you'll see a listing of popular games that can be downloaded and played on your MacBook Air for free.

In some cases, these are full-featured, stand-alone games that are made available as free downloads. Others are "quickie" games designed to be played for short periods of time. However, more often than not, the games listed in this section are scaled-down demo versions of popular paid games, or they're advertiser supported (meaning that you'll need to view ads as you're playing the game).

 Some free games start off free, but eventually require that you utilize in-game purchases to fully experience the game.

Top Grossing Games Often Offer Expandability

For a game to make it onto the Top Grossing chart, it needs to be popular and potentially have a high purchase price ($39.99 or $49.99), and/or require in-game purchases that are intricate to the gameplay experience. Depending on the game, in-game purchases may be optional or required, and will cost anywhere from $0.99 to $19.99 (or more) each.

 When a game is listed in the Top Grossing Games chart, it means that it's generated the most revenue based on initial purchases, as well as ongoing in-game purchases.

 As you're reading a game's description in the App Store, which can be done by clicking on a game listing's title or graphic icon, on the right side of the screen will be a box that's labeled Available In-App Purchases, if applicable (shown in Figure 15-5). The information in this box will tell you if optional purchases are available during gameplay and the cost of those in-game purchases.

If you take a look at the sample Top Grossing Games chart that's shown in Figure 15-6, you'll see that the second most popular game on this chart is *Civilization V: Campaign Edition*. It's priced at $49.99 and includes everything you need to fully experience the game. However, upon looking at the game's description screen and scrolling down (shown in Figure 15-7), you'll discover this game also offers in-app purchases priced at $2.99 each.

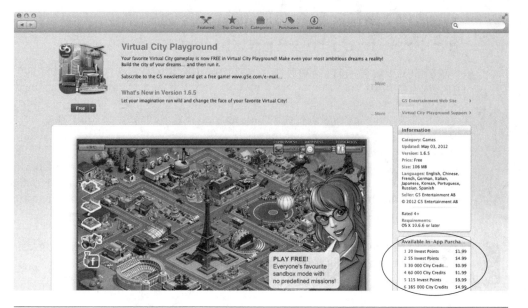

FIGURE 15-5 From a game's description screen in the App Store, you can determine if optional in-game purchases are available, and what they cost.

Also featured on the Top Grossing Games chart is a game called *Virtual City Playground*. This is a free game initially, but it offers a handful of in-game purchase options ranging in price from $0.99 to $49.99 each.

FIGURE 15-6 The Top Grossing Games chart from the App Store

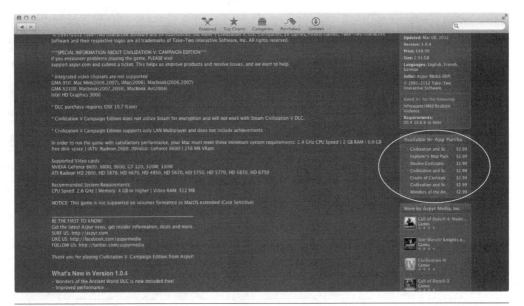

FIGURE 15-7 The In-App Purchases box in the *Civilization V: Campaign Edition* game description screen is shown here.

Browse the App Store to See All Games Offered

After launching the App Store app, instead of clicking on the Top Charts tab, if you want to browse through all of the games available, click on the Categories tab that's also displayed near the top-center of the screen. Then, from the Categories screen, click on the Games option.

Near the top of the main Games screen of the App Store (shown in Figure 15-8), you'll see a large animated banner that promotes games that Apple is currently showcasing. To the right of this large banner are three smaller graphic banners that also promote featured games.

Scroll down a bit on the screen to discover the New and Noteworthy, What's Hot, and Staff Favorites sections. Each of these sections displays a collection of game listings selected by Apple.

To browse through games based on a special interest category (created by Apple), such as "Gorgeous Games," "Retro Games," "Multiplayer Games," or "Adventure Games," look toward the right side of the screen and click on an option displayed under the Quick Links heading. Upon clicking on one of these options, a new screen that displays a collection of applicable game listings for that category will be displayed (as shown in Figure 15-9).

FIGURE 15-8 The main Games screen of the App Store

Displayed along the right margin of the main Games screen in the App Store are top 10 lists for the Top Paid, Top Free, and Top Grossing games. Below that is a More Games box (shown in Figure 15-10) that allows you to choose from 16 popular gaming categories: Action, Adventure, Arcade, Board, Card, Casino, Educational, Family, Kids, Puzzle, Racing, Role Playing, Simulation, Sports, Strategy, and Word. If you know the type of game you enjoy playing, click on one of these categories to browse through available free and paid game options.

FIGURE 15-9 The App Store creates an ever-changing selection of specialized game categories that you can browse through.

FIGURE 15-10   The More Games box allows you to choose a game category and browse through the App Store's game offerings that are specific to a category, like action or board games.

Access a Game Listing's Description

As you learned from Chapter 5, "Install New Software onto Your MacBook Air," the App Store showcases apps, in this case games, using a series of listings. Each listing represents one app or game that's available for download from the App Store.

A typical game listing (shown in Figure 15-11) includes a graphic representing the game, its title, the game's developer, its average star-based rating, the total number of ratings it's received, and a price icon.

To purchase and download the game immediately (or download a free game), click on its price icon. It will change from gray to green and say "Buy App." If you're acquiring a free game, the price icon will display the word Free initially, but when you click on it, it will turn green and say "Install App." When prompted, enter your Apple ID password. The game will download to your computer and be installed. It will then be available from your computer's Applications folder and potentially the Dock and Launchpad.

FIGURE 15-11   A game listing from the App Store

Once you purchase a game from the App Store, you can download that game to your MacBook Air as well as to your other Macs that are linked to the same iCloud account without having to repurchase it. How to do this is explained in Chapter 5.

However, before purchasing or downloading a game, you have the option to view the game's detailed description screen. Click on the game's graphic icon or title to do this. A detailed description screen for a game includes a:

- Large graphic banner at the top of the screen
- Price icon for purchasing the game
- Text-based description of the game
- Detailed listing of what's new in the latest version of the game
- Selection of sample screenshots from the game
- Customer ratings section
- Customer reviews section

Displayed along the right margin of a game's description screen is always a link to the game developer's website and/or a link to the game's own website, as well as an Information box that includes quick details about the game itself, including its category, when it was last updated, version number, price, the file size of the download, what languages the game is available in, and its seller. The game's rating will also be displayed.

Like movies, computer games have ratings that can help you determine if the content in the games is suitable for kids. For example, a Rated 12+ rating means that game is suitable for kids over the age of 12.

Near the bottom of the Information box, details about the game's system requirements are listed. If you have a relatively new MacBook Air (purchased within the last two years) and the computer is running OS X Mountain Lion, the majority of games available from the App Store will run on your computer with no problem.

If a game requires in-app purchases, a separate box that's labeled Available In-App Purchases will be displayed below the Information box along the right margin of a game's description screen.

As you're looking at a game's sample screenshots, try to determine if the screenshots depict actual game play or fancy computer-animated scenes that are seen at the beginning of a game or in between levels or stages. These animated scenes sometimes showcase much more elaborate or detailed graphics than what's featured during actual gameplay.

When reviewing a game's customer ratings (shown in Figure 15-12), refer to its average star-based rating, which can be between one and five stars. However, also pay attention to how many individual ratings the average is based upon. This rating system is more reliable when it's based on dozens, hundreds, or thousands of individual ratings offered by your fellow Mac users who have already experienced the game firsthand.

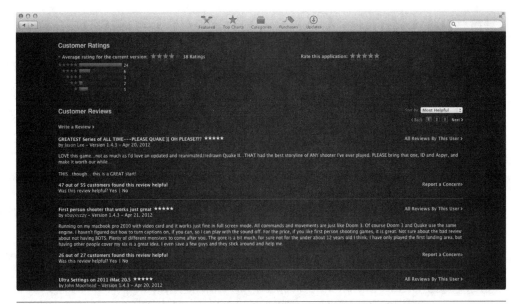

FIGURE 15-12 From a game's description screen, you can view its average star-based rating and see how many ratings the game has received.

From the Customer Ratings chart, you can quickly determine how many one-, two-, three-, four-, and five-star ratings a game has received. Obviously, a game with many five-star ratings and only a few one- or two-star ratings has been better received by your fellow Mac users than a game with lots of consistently low ratings and no four- or five-star ratings.

Below the Customer Ratings, the Customer Reviews section in a game's description screen allows you to read text-based reviews written by your fellow Mac users. These reviews often highlight the best and worst aspects of a game.

How to... # Find Games Beyond Searching the App Store

Beyond the App Store, you can learn about, purchase, and/or acquire games directly from a game developer's website, from a website that's dedicated to a specific game, or from a handful of gaming-specific websites that focus on Mac games.

Some game-related websites worth checking out include: the Mac Game Store (www.macgamestore.com), Inside Mac Games (www.insidemacgames .com), IGN (http://mac.ign.com), C/Net's Download.com (http:// download.cnet.com/mac/games/3150-2012_4-0.html), and GameSpot (www.gamespot.com/games.html?platform=42).

From these sites, you can learn about new games, read detailed game reviews, download free demo versions of some popular games, and/or purchase and download the full version of some games.

Online Games Offer Another Option for Entertaining Yourself

If you're active on Facebook, by clicking on the Apps And Games option, and then clicking on the Recommended Games tab, you can discover and experience a wide range of single player and multiplayer online-based games that are free of charge (although most offer in-game purchase options, plus advertising).

Some of the more popular games you'll discover that can be played directly from within Facebook (or directly from the game's own website) include *Angry Birds, Words With Friends, Bejeweled Blitz, Slingo, Tetris Battle, FarmVille, CityVille, CastleVille, The Sims Social, Scrabble,* and *Caesars Casino.* Many of these games are advertiser supported, and allow for single player or multiplayer experiences. Keep in mind, a constant Internet connection is required to play online-based games.

Pogo.com (www.pogo.com) is a stand-alone online gaming website that offers more than 100 free, online-based games you can access and play using Safari or another web browser. Computer versions of Scrabble, Bingo, Monopoly, and many different card games are available here. Another great source of free, online-based games is Yahoo! Games (http://games.yahoo.com). It too offers a massive collection of card games, board games, casino simulations, puzzle challenges, and arcade-style challenges.

Apple's Game Center Is Now Available to MacBook Air Users

For a while now, iPhone, iPad, and iPod touch users have had free access to Apple's own Game Center online service, which serves as a conduit for learning about new games, challenging others in multiplayer games, and posting your own high scores. In conjunction with the release of OS X Mountain Lion, Apple has made its Game Center service (shown in Figure 15-13) available to MacBook Air users as well.

Using Game Center, you can compete against other gamers using a Mac or an iOS mobile device. You can play against online friends whom you know or have the service safely link you with other players from around the world.

Obtaining a Game Center account is free and can be done in seconds using your existing Apple ID and password. Once you've signed up, not only can you begin playing a wide range of online-based games, you may also be able to use your iPhone, iPad, or iPod touch as a wireless controller as you experience certain compatible games on your Mac.

FIGURE 15-13   Game Center is a free online-gaming service operated by Apple. It's now compatible with the MacBook Air, as well as the iPhone, iPad, and iPod touch.

To launch Game Center on your MacBook Air, access the Applications folder and click on the Game Center icon, or launch the app from your Dock or the Launchpad. When prompted, sign in using your Apple ID and password. If you've already been using Game Center with your iOS mobile device, all of your account information, high scores, friends, and other content will be immediately accessible.

As you browse the App Store, look for the growing library of games that are Game Center compatible. One way to find these games quickly is to launch Game Center, click on the Games tab, and then scroll down to and click on the Find Game Center Games banner at the bottom of the screen. This will launch the App Store app and display a selection of Game Center-compatible games.

As you're experiencing games via Game Center, you can update your status by clicking on the Me tab that's displayed near the top of the screen, plus you can upload and display a photo of yourself. Depending on the game, it's possible to communicate in real time with other players via text messages and/or voice chat via the Web.

Just as the OS X operating system has evolved over time, so has Apple's Game Center. Now that it's Mac compatible, game developers are constantly working on new and innovative ways to allow MacBook Air users to better experience multiplayer games in a fun, safe, and highly social environment.

As a general rule, when playing online-based multiplayer games against strangers, refrain from using your complete first and last name, and don't provide any personal information about yourself to those you compete against.

PART V

Easily Handle All of Your Mobile Computing Needs

16

Travel with Your MacBook Air

HOW TO...

- Safely transport your MacBook Air
- Access the Internet while on the go
- Prepare to bring your MacBook Air overseas

With their 13-, 15-, or 17-inch screens, the Apple MacBook Pro notebook computers are designed to offer high-end computing power that can be taken with you. These notebook computers weigh between 4.5 and 6.6 pounds and can be cumbersome to lug around.

However, the MacBook Air computers are designed to offer enough computing power for the average user, and provide it in a lightweight, sleek, easy to carry, and convenient-to-use machine that weights less than three pounds.

 If you fly coach on a major airline, if the person sitting directly in front of you chooses to recline their seat even slightly, chances are you won't be able to place a MacBook Pro on your tray table, open it, and then use it comfortably...it's just too big (as are most notebook computers). This is not the case, however, with the MacBook Air.

While your MacBook Air can be used while sitting at a desk at work, it can also be used comfortably while sitting on a couch or your favorite chair at home; while lying in bed; as you travel on an airplane, bus, or train (even in the most confining space); in a hotel room; at a coffee shop; relaxing by a pool; or just about anywhere you want or need access to a computer.

In fact, one of the most attractive things about a MacBook Air is that is very easy to transport. But to keep the computer safe during transport, you'll definitely want to invest in a case or padded slipcover.

How to... **Keep Onlookers from Seeing What's on Your Computer Screen, Plus See Your Screen Better in Bright Sunlight**

By placing a privacy screen over your MacBook Air's screen, you can prevent strangers from looking over your shoulder or from the side and seeing what's on your screen as you use the computer in public.

3M offers a line of custom-fitted privacy filters for the various MacBook Air models. These privacy filters allow you to see the screen perfectly as you're using the computer, but if someone is sitting next to you—on an airplane, for example—all they'll see is a blank screen. The 3M screens are reversible and can also serve as antiglare filters.

Priced between $44 and $65 (depending on the screen size), the 3M privacy filter is ultra-thin and attaches to your MacBook Air in seconds, but is easily removable. To learn more, visit www.3M.com/PrivacyFilters.

Antiglare filters that fit over the MacBook Air's screen are slightly less expensive than the reversible 3M privacy filters, and they're designed to provide maximum visibility and clarity of the screen when the computer is being used outdoors in bright sunlight, for example. No privacy from prying eyes is offered.

Radtech (www.radtech.us/products/clearcal-displays.aspx) and Power Support (www.powersupportusa.com/accessories/macbook-air-13/anti-glare-film.html) are two companies that offer antiglare films custom-sized for an 11-inch or 13-inch MacBook Air, priced from $19.95.

Note A stand-alone case for your MacBook Air can be used to carry around your computer (and its related accessories, including the power adapter) safely. Most cases have a handle or are designed for use as a shoulder bag, messenger bag, backpack, or purse. A slipcover, however, is a padded pouch that your MacBook Air slides into. It can then be placed safely in your existing briefcase, messenger bag, backpack, or purse, for example, that doesn't have a built-in padded compartment suitable for a notebook computer.

Getting Your MacBook Air Ready to Transport

While you obviously don't want to drop your MacBook Air, expose it to extreme hot or cold temperatures, or allow any type of liquid near the computer at any time, as it's being transported you also want to protect its outer casing from nicks and scratches. To do this, you'll definitely want to use a padded case, hard shell casing, or slipcover.

Before transporting your computer, you can power it down altogether by accessing the Apple pull-down menu from the menu bar and selecting the Shut Down option. When the "Are you sure you want to shut down your computer now?" message appears, click on the Shut Down icon, or wait 60 seconds for the shutdown process to initiate automatically. When the MacBook Air's screen goes black, close the computer and slip it into a case.

If you know you'll be using your computer again soon, or you want it to continue running apps in the background, accepting new emails and generating alerts, alarms, and notifications, instead of powering off your MacBook Air, place it into Power Nap mode before transporting it.

At any time as you're using your computer, even if apps are currently running, simply close the MacBook Air to place it into Power Nap mode. As a precaution, you can save whatever you're working on first, but doing this is not mandatory. When you next open the computer, the apps will continue running just as they were before, and you can pick up exactly where you left off on your work. Once the computer is in Power Nap mode and closed, it's safe to transport.

Once the computer is powered off, remove any devices that are connected to your computer via the USB ports, Thunderbolt port, or memory card reader (if applicable). If you're placing your computer into Power Nap mode, be sure to manually eject each connected device first before removing it so you can transport the computer.

Avoid transporting your computer with a USB thumb drive, headphones, or other non-wireless devices still connected to it.

Choosing a Case for Your MacBook Air

Unless your briefcase, purse, backpack, shoulder bag, or messenger bag has a built-in padded compartment that snugly fits your MacBook Air, it should not be considered a case that's safe for carrying around your computer (unless you also use a slipcover that fits your MacBook Air model).

At any Apple Store, computer store, or online, you'll discover many computer cases that include a padded compartment designed for an 11-inch or 13-inch notebook computer, such as your MacBook Air. Some cases that you'll find will be sized to securely hold your computer, but nothing else. Others will also have room (or separate compartments or pockets) for computer accessories, like the power adapter and/or headphones, as well as papers, books, and whatever else you need to carry around.

When choosing a case with multiple compartments, make sure the one you'll be using to store your MacBook Air is sized to snugly fit the computer, is padded, and will protect the computer from drops, bumps, scratches, and liquids. The compartment your computer will be placed in should be separate from other compartments, so whatever else you're carrying can't damage your computer as the bag's contents get shuffled around during transit.

Stand-alone MacBook Air cases will typically be compact and have some type of handle. You'll also find specially designed briefcases, backpacks, messenger bags, camera bags, purses, and shoulder bags that have a built-in, padded compartment for a notebook computer that is suitable for your MacBook Air.

These cases come in leather, ballistic nylon, canvas, and a wide range of other durable materials, as well as in countless colors. A basic computer case might cost $30 to $50, but a case offered by a well-known designer might be priced in the hundreds (or higher).

Aside from meeting the criteria outlined earlier for protecting your MacBook Air during transport, consider a case that also has compartments for separately storing the computer's power adapter and other accessories, as well as other items you might want to carry around.

Choosing a Slipcover for Your MacBook Air

A slipcover for the MacBook Air should be custom-fitted to snugly hold your computer and offer protection on all sides. As you'll discover, slipcovers are made from a wide range of materials. Be sure to choose one, however, that offers ample protection for the computer. Since most people place the slipcover containing their computer within another bag (such as a messenger bag, shoulder bag, briefcase, or purse), the appearance of the slipcover is less important than the protection it offers.

Some slipcovers are ultra-thin and offer more scratch protection than protection against drops. Be sure to choose a design that's best suited for the conditions your MacBook Air will face as you're transporting it.

Add a Design and Scratch Protection to Your MacBook Air with a Skin

A skin is an ultra-thin vinyl film that can be placed over the top and bottom of your MacBook Air to provide an added layer of scratch protection, plus some extra protection against liquids (although applying a skin to your computer does *not* make it waterproof).

One advantage to adding a skin over your computer's outer shell is that many offer artistic designs or can be custom imprinted with your own digital photo or company logo, allowing you to more fully personalize the appearance of your MacBook Air.

Skins can be applied in minutes and removed in seconds, although they're designed to remain on the computer at all times. When choosing a skin, it's essential that you purchase one that's custom-sized for your specific MacBook Air model. They're typically priced under $30 each.

Instead of a Skin, You Can Add a Thin, Protective Casing to Your MacBook Air

Instead of a vinyl skin, it's possible to apply a removable thin shell casing to your MacBook Air. Doing this will provide added protection and a stylish look. Protective casings are available in a wide range of colors. They're typically made from form-fitting plastic, polyurethane, neoprene, or leather.

A wide range of skin designs are available from:

- Decal Girl (www.decalgirl.com)
- Gelaskins (www.gelaskins.com)
- Schtickers (www.schtickers.com)
- Skinit (www.skinit.com)
- Zagg (www.zagg.com)

 Even with a skin applied to your computer, for maximum protection you'll still want to use a padded case or slipcover when transporting it.

MacBook Air Case and Slipcover Manufacturers

Choosing the perfect computer case or slipcover for your MacBook Air is a matter of personal taste, needs, and budget. Check out the computer cases, slipcovers, and shells offered by the following companies as you begin your quest for a MacBook Air case:

- **Coach (www.coach.com)** This well-known leather company offers a selection of stylish and padded cases and covers that are universal, but work nicely with the various MacBook Air models. From the Coach website's home page, click on the Tech Accessories option that's displayed on the left side of the screen to see what's offered. These cases offer designer style combined with practical functionality. To save money, consider shopping for Coach products from a Coach Outlet store.
- **Incase (www.goincase.com)** In addition to offering a selection of cases and slipcovers for the MacBook Air computers, Incase offers specially made hard cover shells that fit over the top and bottom of the computer to offer added protection and a stylish and colorful look. As shown in Figure 16-1 and Figure 16-2, Incase's case offerings are made from leather, neoprene, plastic, or canvas, depending on the design. Prices range from $39.95 to $149.95.
- **Incipio (www.incipio.com/macbook-air-13in-cases-accessories/macbook-air-13in-cases-accessories.asp)** In addition to offering contemporary and stylish leather slipcovers (shown in Figure 16-3) specially sized for the MacBook Air models, Incipio offers form-fitting shells for the computers, as well as other padded case styles.

FIGURE 16-1   This particular case from Incase can be kept on the MacBook Air even when it's in use. When the computer is being transported, it zips shut.

- **Louis Vuitton (www.louisvuitton.com)**   Virtually all of the top handbag and luggage designers now offer either universal computer cases or cases with padded compartments that can nicely hold your MacBook Air. Louis Vuitton is no exception. The company's Petit Messenger bag, for example, has two inside compartments, one of which is ideal for your notebook computer. However, at $1,200, this particular Louis Vuitton bag is priced higher than the computer itself.

 The Apple Stores and Apple.com website also offer a selection of MacBook Air cases from third-party manufacturers. To view descriptions and photos of the cases offered, or to order a case from Apple.com, visit http://store.apple.com/us/browse/home/shop_mac/mac_accessories/notebook_cases.

- **Lusso Cartella (www.lussocartella.com/macbook-air.html)**   These handcrafted, fine leather cases and slipcovers are not only visually elegant, they also provide top-notch protection. Priced between $69.99 and $110.00, the company offers 16 different case and cover styles, some for the 11-inch, and others for the 13-inch MacBook Air models.

FIGURE 16-2   This is one example of a thin MacBook Air casing available from Incase.

FIGURE 16-3 This is what a typical MacBook Air slipcover looks like. This one, from Incipio, is made from leather.

- **Pad & Quill (www.padandquill.com/cases-for-macbook-air.html)** The Cartella Case for MacBook Air (available for the 11 or 13-inch models) offers bonded leather outside, but with a protective, hard case design that perfectly fits your MacBook Air. These cases are stylish, handcrafted in the U.S., and are priced starting at around $80.00.
- **Saddleback Leather Company (www.saddlebackleather.com)** This Texas-based company handcrafts a wide range of luxurious and extremely durable leather bags and briefcases that are highly fashionable and functional. Many of the company's briefcases, messenger bags, and other cases have separate compartments designed for a notebook computer or tablet. The company also offers a handmade, full grain leather slipcover case for the 11-inch or 13-inch MacBook Air ($68 to $88). The slipcovers come in several colors and will snugly hold and protect the MacBook Air during transport. The Saddleback Leather Company MacBook Air Slipcover combined with the large size satchel ($335), for example, make the perfect combination for transporting your computer, accessories, and other work-related items.
- **Speck (www.speckproducts.com/macbook-cases.html)** This company offers several hard plastic shells that snap onto the top and bottom of the MacBook Air to offer an added layer of protection in addition to a bright and colorful design. They're priced at $49.95 each. In addition to using one of these covers, you should transport your MacBook Air in a traditional case or slipcover (sold separately).
- **TimBuk2 (www.timbuk2.com)** These durable ballistic nylon cases come in a variety of styles, sizes, and color combinations. They can even be custom-designed from the company's website. For a small extra fee, a padded compartment suitable for the MacBook Air can be added to the inside of the messenger bags and shoulder bags. The TimBuk2 bags are manufactured in San Francisco, are water resistant, and extremely well-made. Prices start under $100 and go up from there based on the size and style of the bag, as well as the options you add to it.

FIGURE 16-4 Shown here is a padded, zippered case from Westfield Designs that holds the MacBook Air plus a handful of accessories.

- **Toffee (www.toffee.com.au/en/envelope/39-envelope-.html)** Priced at $91, this company's sleek leather case for the 11- or 13-inch MacBook Air looks like an envelope and offers a protective interior and a truly professional appearance. The Envelope is available in black or red leather.
- **Waterfield Designs (www.sfbags.com)** This company also offers a selection of padded cases (shown in Figure 16-4), bags, and slipcovers (shown in Figure 16-5) suitable for the MacBook Air. Some are available in leather, while others are made from ballistic nylon or other durable materials. From the home page of the company's website, click on the MacBook Air Cases option that's displayed along the left margin of the screen to view eight different case designs specifically for the MacBook Air models.

FIGURE 16-5 This padded slipcover from Westfield Designs has an outside pocket that can hold MacBook Air accessories.

When choosing a custom-designed case for the MacBook Air, be sure you select one that's created for your specific MacBook Air model in order to ensure a proper fit. If you're looking at generic computer cases with padded compartments, pay attention to the measurements of the compartments themselves, as well as the overall bag.

 To find other MacBook Air cases from other designers, use the search phrase "MacBook Air case" or "MacBook Air cover" when using your favorite Internet search engine such as Google, Yahoo!, or Bing.

Access the Internet While on the Go

You already know that your MacBook Air is capable of accessing the Internet using any Wi-Fi hotspot or wireless network. However, as you're traveling, you'll encounter many new Wi-Fi hotspots and networks—at airports, aboard airplanes, at hotels, in Internet cafes and coffee shops, in libraries, in schools, and in other public places.

Some Wi-Fi hotspots will be free and available to the public. When the Wi-Fi feature of your MacBook Air is turned on, the computer will seek out available networks and allow you to connect. To do this, click on the Wi-Fi icon that's displayed along the menu bar (near the top-right corner of the screen). First turn on the Wi-Fi feature, and then select the network you want to connect to.

 If you're at a hotel or visiting a business that offers a locked (or password protected) Wi-Fi hotspot, you can often acquire a password simply by asking for it.

As you travel around with your MacBook Air, you'll often find Wi-Fi hotspots that are fee-based and/or password protected. If the hotspot is fee-based, you'll need to purchase airtime by the hour or day, typically using a major credit card or debit card. When you attempt to connect to the network, you'll be informed it's a fee-based hotspot when you launch Safari or your favorite web browser.

In some situations, access to a Wi-Fi hotspot will be free, but you'll required to enter a special password to gain access to it, and then need to accept the terms of use for the network by clicking on an Agree or Continue button. When a listing of available networks is displayed, a small lock icon will appear next to the network's name if it's password protected. As soon as you click on that network listing to connect to it, you'll be prompted for a password.

 If there's no public Wi-Fi hotspot where you happen to be, chances are if you walk or drive around a bit, you'll find one. In the United States, most bookstores, coffee shops, libraries, hotel lobbies, airports, Internet cafés, and fast food restaurants (such as McDonald's) offer free Wi-Fi. Churches and other places of worship also sometimes offer public Wi-Fi hotspots.

Instead of relying on a Wi-Fi hotspot or wireless network to access the Internet wherever you happen to be, another option is to purchase a 3G or 4G wireless modem for your MacBook Air, which allows you to access the wireless data network offered by a wireless service provider, such as AT&T Wireless, Verizon Wireless, or T-Mobile.

Some wireless data plans require that you sign a one- or two-year service contract, but several wireless data service providers, including Virgin Mobile, offer prepaid wireless data options with no long-term contract. Similar options are available when traveling overseas; however, you'll need to purchase a wireless modem or mobile hotspot device.

Using a wireless data modem, you can connect your MacBook Air to the Internet wirelessly anywhere 3G or 4G wireless data service is offered by the provider you sign up with. Thus, you're not limited to the small signal radius of most Wi-Fi hotspots, or reliant on finding a Wi-Fi hotspot when you travel domestically or abroad.

 If you have a smartphone and a wireless data service plan that offers Internet tethering (the ability for the phone to create a private personal Wi-Fi hotspot), this too can be a way for your MacBook Air to access the Internet while you're out and about.

Preparing to Travel Overseas with Your MacBook Air

Your MacBook Air will work perfectly well anywhere in the world, but you'll need to keep its battery charged. When traveling overseas, in addition to packing the 45W MagSafe Power Adapter that came with the computer, you'll need to purchase an adapter or connector that's compatible with the electrical outlets where you'll be visiting.

The power adapter that came with your MacBook Air offers interchangeable connectors. So, when you travel overseas, you can slip off the existing power adapter connector (which plugs into a U.S. power outlet) and snap on a connector that's appropriate. From the Apple Store or Apple.com, be sure to purchase the optional Apple World Travel Adapter Kit ($39.99, http://store.apple.com/us/product/MB974ZM/B), which includes the Apple USB power adapter, a USB cable, and six interchangeable AC adapter plugs (each suitable for use in a different country or region).

 You also have the option of using any non-Apple power converter adapter with the MacBook Air's power adapter, based on where you're traveling.

 Once you have your MacBook Air powered by an electrical outlet wherever you happen to be, you can then connect your other mobile devices (such as your iPhone, iPad, iPod, or digital camera) to the computer via a USB cable to charge these other devices as well, without requiring extra power outlets.

17

Use FaceTime, Skype, or VoIP Software to Communicate and Video Conference

HOW TO...

- Use Apple's FaceTime app to video conference with other Mac, iPhone, iPad, and iPod touch users
- Use Skype to video conference or transform your MacBook Air into a full-featured telephone that works over the Internet with PC, Mac, and most smartphone users.
- Use other voice-over-IP (VoIP) software to make and receive calls on your MacBook Air

As long as your MacBook Air is connected to the Internet, there are many ways you can use it as a powerful communications tool. In previous chapters, you've learned how to send and receive emails using the Mail app, send and receive text messages and instant messages using the Messages app, and play games with other people using the Game Center app (in conjunction with compatible games).

Using Apple's FaceTime app in conjunction with an Internet connection and the MacBook Air's built-in video camera, microphone, and speakers (or headphone jack with headphones connected), you can transform your computer into a video conferencing tool, and participate in full-color video conferences from virtually anywhere there's a Wi-Fi Internet connection. This can be done for free on an unlimited basis.

The FaceTime app allows you to connect to Apple's own FaceTime video conferencing service. It's open to all Mac, iPhone, iPad, and iPod touch users. With FaceTime, you can experience a live, one-on-one video conference with someone else, enabling you to see and hear them, and for them to see and hear you.

An alternative to using FaceTime for video conferencing is to download and install the free Skype app and to use the Skype network. In addition to its video conferencing capabilities, Skype can serve as a feature-packed voice-over-IP service, which allows you to make and receive telephone calls via the Web. Skype has also partnered with Facebook, allowing you to use the service's video conferencing, screen sharing, and voice communication tools with your Facebook friends. Plus, like Apple's iMessage service, Skype has a free and unlimited instant messaging service built in.

 Screen sharing is a feature that allows two computers to link while a video conference or voice-over-IP conversation is being held, so one person can see exactly what's displayed on the other person's computer screen. This is great for collaborating on work or sharing information, such as a PowerPoint presentation, photos, or a Word document.

Video conferencing or using Skype's basic voice-over-IP features to communicate with other Skype users is always free. However, you can pay a bit extra to make and receive international calls to/from landlines and cell phones, and to participate in video conferences or voice calls with up to 10 people simultaneously. You can also obtain a unique phone number with voice mail, and utilize other calling features like call waiting and call forwarding.

 To use Skype as a free or paid service, you'll first need to choose a unique username which serves as your phone number or identifier. This is how people can make contact with you. However, if you upgrade your service, you can register for a unique phone number so people can call you (via your Skype account on your MacBook Air) from their landline or cell phone. A fee apples for the company's premium services.

Did You Know?

Video Conferencing and Voice-over-IP Are Ideal for International Calling

Whether you're in the United States and need to make calls overseas, or you're traveling abroad and want to call back to the United States, if you communicate with other FaceTime or Skype users, making or and receiving calls is always free, regardless of their duration.

However, if you're calling (or receiving calls) from a landline or someone's cell phone, using Skype (or a similar VoIP service) will cost just pennies per minute, compared to much higher rates if you initiate calls using a traditional phone line and long distance phone service.

If you're traveling overseas, making a call from your cell phone as you're roaming internationally will cost around $2 per minute with most service plans, and using a calling card from a pay phone or direct dialing from a hotel, for example, typically is not any cheaper.

As long as your MacBook Air has a stable and fast Internet connection, you'll experience crystal-clear calls using FaceTime, Skype, or similar services.

In addition to Skype, there are a handful of other voice-over-IP and video conferencing services you can subscribe to and utilize from your MacBook Air, as long as an Internet connection is available. Some of these services are free, but most are fee-based. Regardless of whether you use FaceTime, Skype, or another service, each greatly expands your ability to communicate with other people in real time using your voice, video, and in some cases with what's displayed on your computer's screen.

Keep in mind, while FaceTime, Skype, and other services offer similar functionality, none of these services are compatible with each other. FaceTime is used to communicate with other FaceTime users, while Skype video calls must be done with other Skype users. Thus, depending on whom you want to communicate with and how, you'll want to choose the service that offers the functionality that's needed.

Using FaceTime for Video Conferencing

FaceTime is a one-on-one, real-time video conferencing app that allows you to communicate for free with other Mac, iPhone, iPad, and iPod touch users. Before you can begin utilizing the service, you'll need to set up a free account. This involves signing into the FaceTime service using the FaceTime app and then entering your Apple ID and password.

By default, your Apple ID becomes your unique username for FaceTime, which works just like a phone number as an identifier, allowing others to find and initiate contact with you through the FaceTime service. However, as you set up your free account, you can utilize an alternate email address as your unique identifier.

As you'll discover, actually using the FaceTime app is a very straightforward process. The only confusing part is finding your friends online, and making that initial contact with them, because you'll need to know their unique FaceTime username (the email address they used when setting up their account). Keep in mind, when people use FaceTime with their iPhone, their iPhone phone number becomes their default FaceTime identifier.

 The Contacts app works seamlessly with FaceTime. So when creating individual entries in your Contacts database, it's important to differentiate between someone's mobile number and iPhone phone number. This is done by tapping on the phone number's label when creating or editing an entry. FaceTime and the Messages app, for example, automatically seek out iPhone-labeled phone numbers.

Launch the FaceTime app just as you would any other app. You can double-click on the app icon or app name in the Applications folder, click on the app icon that appears on the Dock, or click on the app icon from the Launchpad.

Setting Up Your Free FaceTime Account

As soon as you launch the app, the FaceTime app window will turn on your MacBook Air's built-in camera, and on the left side of the window, you'll initially see yourself.

What you see in this window is what other people will see once you initiate a video conference with them. To center yourself in the window, you can tilt the MacBook Air's screen forward or backward slightly, or prop up the computer on some type of stand. You can also move your head and body so it's better framed by MacBook Air's camera.

To enhance your clarity, remove any bright light sources that are behind you, and try to position a primary light source (such as a lamp) directly in front of you. Also, refrain from moving too much while video conferencing, especially if your Internet connection is being sluggish.

As you're actually participating in a video conference, center the video window portion of FaceTime's app window on your MacBook Air's desktop so it's just below the built-in camera. This way, when you look at the app window, it will appear as if you're looking into the camera (and by default, looking at the person you're video conferencing with). Ideally, you'll want to position the FaceTime window title that's displayed along the top-center of the app window below and one inch to the right of the camera. This way, the video window will be centered with the built-in camera.

Initially, when you launch the FaceTime app, on the right side of the window (shown in Figure 17-1) will be a Preferences option. Displayed near the upper-right corner of the window is a virtual on/off switch that's allows you to turn on or off FaceTime functionality on your computer. When you're ready to begin participating in video conferences, make sure the switch is set to the On position. Your MacBook Air will then automatically connect to the FaceTime service. Later, you can turn on and off the FaceTime service by accessing the FaceTime pull-down menu and choosing the Preferences option.

The FaceTime app must be running on your computer in order to make or receive calls. It can be running in the background, however, as you use other apps.

Next, on the right side of the FaceTime app window will be the log-in screen (shown in Figure 17-2). You'll be prompted to enter your Apple ID and password. If you want to use your existing Apple ID as your FaceTime username (your identifier), enter your Apple ID and password as prompted, and click on the Sign In button.

However, if you want to set up a FaceTime account using another preexisting email address, click on the Create New Account button. Upon doing this, follow the onscreen prompts for creating a new account. You'll be asked to enter your first name, last name, and email address, and then create and enter a password for the account. The password must be at least eight characters long and include at least one number, one uppercase letter, and one lowercase letter. Furthermore, you cannot use spaces in your password or the same number or letter more than three times in a row.

FIGURE 17-1 When you launch FaceTime for the first time, you'll need to turn on the service.

FIGURE 17-2 FaceTime's log-in screen appears on the right side of the app's window.

Near the bottom of the New Account setup screen (shown in Figure 17-3), you'll be prompted to select and answer a security question, which will be used if you forget your FaceTime password. Below that as you scroll down, you'll be asked to enter the month and day of your birthday, as well as the country or region in which you reside. Click on each field to access a pull-down menu to fill in the appropriate information.

After filling in all of the New Account setup fields, click on the Next button that's displayed near the upper-right corner of the FaceTime app's window. FaceTime will set up your account. Within a few seconds, a message that says, "People will call you using your email address... What email address would you like to use?" will be displayed. In this field will be the email address you used to set up the account.

To keep this email address as your FaceTime username, click on the Next button. Otherwise, in the Address field, enter the email address you'd like to use as your FaceTime username. If you opt to use an alternate email address instead of your Apple ID, Apple will then send you a verification email. Look for it in your email

FIGURE 17-3   Select a security question and enter your answer, then enter the month and day of your birthday.

account's inbox. When you receive the email, click on the link that's embedded in it to verify the address. This must be done before you can begin using FaceTime to participate in video conferences.

 If you use your existing Apple ID to set up a FaceTime account, no verification is required.

Participating in FaceTime Video Conferences

Once you sign into FaceTime from the FaceTime app using your Apple ID (or the verified email address you used to register for FaceTime), you'll see three buttons displayed near the bottom-right corner of the app window (shown in Figure 17-4). They're labeled Favorites, Recents, and Contacts.

Populating Your FaceTime Favorites List

The Favorites button allows you to create a customized list of the people you'll video conference with most often. Once someone is added to the list, you can initiate a video conference with them simply by clicking on their listing.

When you first launch the FaceTime app, the Favorites list will be empty (shown in Figure 17-5). However, you can populate it by picking and choosing specific contracts entries from your Contacts database, one at a time. To do this, click on the plus sign icon that's displayed near the upper-right corner of the app window.

After clicking on the plus sign icon, the All Contacts listing will be displayed. This is an alphabetical list of all entries in your Contacts database. Scroll through the list and click on the people you'd like to add to your Favorites list.

When that person's contact information is displayed, click on the email address or iPhone phone number that person uses as their FaceTime username. Now, when you're automatically returned to your Favorites listing, the person's name you just added will be displayed. Repeat this process to add additional contacts to your Favorites list.

 Once a contact entry has been added to your FaceTime Favorites list, simply click on it to initiate a FaceTime video conference call with that person. The other party will need to have FaceTime currently running on their computer or iOS mobile device and be willing to accept your incoming call for the connection to be established.

FIGURE 17-4   Initiate a FaceTime call from the Favorites, Recents, or Contacts list. Click on the command button of your choice and select a contact listing.

FIGURE 17-5   Populate your Favorites list with the people you plan to FaceTime video conference call with most often. You can then initiate a call with a single click.

   To edit your Favorites list, change listings, or remove listings from it, as you're viewing the Favorites list, click on the Edit button that's displayed to the immediate left of the Favorites heading near the top of the window.

Accessing Your FaceTime Recents List

The FaceTime app automatically keeps track of all your incoming and outgoing FaceTime calls. A detailed listing of them appears in your Recents list. One quick way to reconnect with someone you've video conferenced with before is to access the Recents list and click on the listing for a past call.

Displayed near the top-center of the Recents list are two command tabs labeled All and Missed. The All tab displays individual listings for all incoming, outgoing, and missed FaceTime calls. By clicking on the Missed tab, a listing of your missed calls (incoming calls you did not accept) will be displayed.

Finding People to Video Conference with from Your Contacts Database

By clicking on the Contacts button that's displayed near the bottom-right corner of the FaceTime app window, the All Contacts listing will appear. This is an alphabetical listing of all contact entries in your Contacts database. Scroll down to and click on the contact listing you want to initiate a FaceTime call with. When their complete listing details appear, click on their FaceTime username, which may be their email address or iPhone phone number. Upon doing this, FaceTime will initiate a call.

Receiving an Incoming FaceTime Call

As long at the FaceTime app is running on your MacBook Air and the computer is connected to the Internet, any Mac, iPhone, iPad, or iPod touch user who knows your FaceTime username can initiate a call with you.

When you receive an incoming call, you'll hear a ringing sound emanating from your MacBook Air. In the FaceTime app window will be a message that says "[Name] would like to FaceTime..." Near the bottom-center of the app window will be two command buttons, labeled Decline and Accept (shown in Figure 17-6).

To initiate a video conference with the caller, click on the green Accept button. To reject the call, click on the red Decline button. A listing for the incoming call attempt will show up on your Recents list as a missed call if you decline it.

Participating in a FaceTime Call

Whether you initiate a FaceTime call with someone else by first clicking on the Favorites, Recents, or Contacts button and then choosing a Contacts entry, or you accept an incoming call, once the FaceTime video conference has been initiated, the main area of the FaceTime app window will be replaced by the other person's live video feed.

Your video feed will shrink and be displayed as a thumbnail near the lower-left corner of the FaceTime window. You can drag this thumbnail image of yourself anywhere in the window.

During a video conference, you will be able to see and hear the person you're communicating with, just as they will be able to see and hear you. Near the bottom of the FaceTime window (shown in Figure 17-7), you'll see a command button and two command icons that appear during a video conference. To the left is the Mute icon.

FIGURE 17-6   Upon receiving an incoming FaceTime call, you can decline or accept it.

FIGURE 17-7   Use the Mute, End, or Full Screen mode button to control your video conference.

When you click on the Mute icon, the person you're conversing with will be able to see you, but the microphone on your MacBook Air will be deactivated, so they will not be able to hear you.

To end a video conference call, click on the End button. The call will instantly be terminated. FaceTime's Favorites, Recents, and Contacts buttons will reappear, and you'll be free to connect with someone else via FaceTime or exit out of the app altogether.

Displayed to the immediate right of the End button, as well as near the upper-right corner of the app window, is a Full Screen mode icon. Click on either of them to enter into Full Screen mode during a video conference. Press the ESC key to exit out of Full Screen mode.

 As you participate in a FaceTime video conference, the connection with the other person will remain active until either you or the other party click on the End button. If you launch another app, for example, and the FaceTime app window gets covered by other app windows, you will continue to be broadcasting and the MacBook Air's camera and microphone will remain on. You can tell when the MacBook Air's built-in camera is active because a tiny green light will appear to the right of the camera. Whenever this light is on, assume someone is watching you.

 You can participate in a FaceTime video conference and run other apps simultaneously. When you do this, the person you are communicating with will not be able to see what you're typing or what app(s) you're using. However, that person will be able to see and hear you as you're using those apps. FaceTime does not currently have a screen-sharing feature like the Skype service.

Using Skype for Video Conferencing or Voice-over-IP Calls

Now owned by Google, Skype is a powerful communications tool that allows for video conferencing, voice-over-IP calls, instant messaging, and screen sharing. Many of the calling features offered by Skype are free. However, the service offers a handful of premium (paid) services as well.

By establishing a free Skype account, you can video conference or participate in voice calls with other Skype users, regardless of whether they're using the Skype app on a Mac, PC, or any type of Internet-enabled mobile device. You can also use Skype's screen-sharing feature for free. Plus, Skype works seamlessly with Facebook, so you can communicate with your Facebook friends who also have a Skype account.

Skype-to-Skype calls are always free and unlimited. You can make and receive as many calls as you'd like, and they can be any length. There are no per-minute charges or limitations.

For a low monthly fee, you can obtain a unique phone number that allows you to receive calls from any landline or cell phone. Even if the caller does not have a Skype account or computer, they can call you using your Skype-specific phone number. A paid Skype phone number includes a voice mail account.

In addition, for a fee, you can make calls from your MacBook Air (that's connected to the Internet) to any phone number anywhere in the world, including landlines and cell phones. A very low per-minute fee applies, or you can sign up for unlimited calling domestically or internationally for a flat monthly fee.

Another premium service offered by Skype is the ability to participate in video or voice-based conference calls with up to 10 people simultaneously. To begin using Skype, you must first download and install the free Skype app onto your MacBook Air. To do this, launch Safari (or any web browser) and visit www.skype.com.

The free Skype app is not currently available from the App Store. You must visit www.skype.com to download the app and set up a Skype account.

From the home page of the Skype website (shown in Figure 17-8), click on the Get Skype menu option that's displayed near the top-center of the screen. Then select

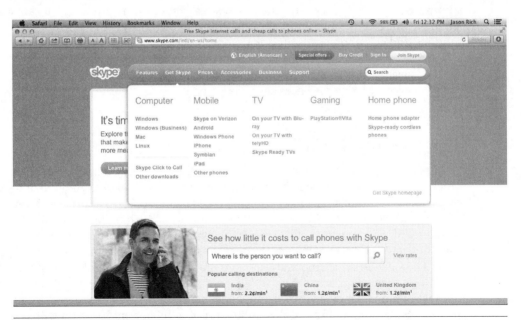

FIGURE 17-8   From the Skype website, you can download the Skype app, learn about the various paid service plans and features, plus sign up for a free account.

the Mac version of the software, which is listed under the Computer heading. Next, choose either the free Skype app or the Skype Premium app (which has a $4.99 monthly fee associated with it).

Tip
To improve call clarity and enhance privacy, consider connecting headphones to your computer when participating in calls. You can also use a Bluetooth wireless headset or USB headset. To learn about optional Skype accessories, visit http://shop.skype.com.

Choosing the Skype vs. Skype Premium App

The Skype free app allows you to make and receive unlimited Skype-to-Skype video and voice calls, use the Skype instant messaging service on an unlimited basis (which works very much like Apple's iMessage service), plus you can connect with your Facebook friends.

The Skype Premium app allows you to make unlimited calls within your home country, as well as unlimited calls to the countries of your choice. You can also initiate and participate in group calls with up to 10 people simultaneously, and use the screen-sharing feature as you communicate.

Even if you subscribe to the Skype Premium service, you will need to upgrade the service (for an additional fee) to receive your own unique phone number, as well as to initiate calls and receive calls to/from landlines and cell phones. A separate fee may apply for making calls, either domestically or internationally. However, the per-minute rates are less expensive than almost any other calling option. You can sign up to pay for calls on a per-minute basis, or be able to make and receive unlimited landline and cell phone calls for a flat monthly fee.

Tip
To learn more about the various price plans for using Skype's premium and fee-based services, click on the Prices menu option on the Skype website's home page.

Registering for a Free Skype Account

Either before or after you download and install the Skype app onto your MacBook Air, you'll need to set up a free Skype account. To do this, visit www.skype.com and click on the Join Skype button, which is displayed near the upper-right corner of the screen.

From the Create An Account Or Sign In screen (shown in Figure 17-9), you can register with Skype using your existing Facebook account information by clicking on the Connect With Facebook icon. Upon doing this, you'll be prompted to enter your existing Facebook username and password, and then approve the Facebook activation.

Alternatively, you can set up a Skype account from scratch by entering your first name, last name, email address, birthday, gender, country, city, native language, and mobile phone number. Any of this optional profile-related information will be visible to anyone who accesses your public Skype profile. Thus, you can opt to leave some or all of the profile-related fields blank.

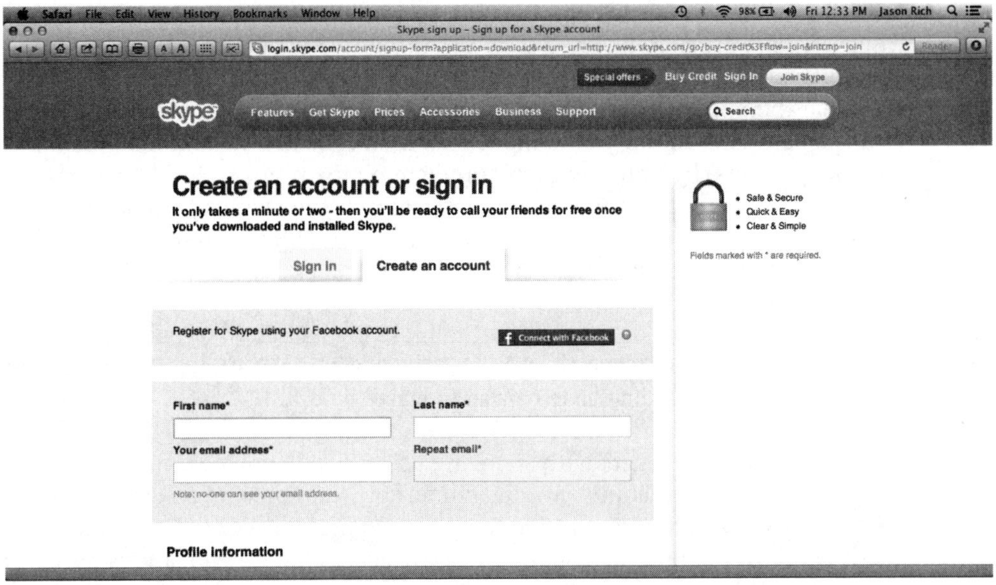

FIGURE 17-9   Creating a Skype account takes less than two minutes from the Skype.com website.

Scrolling down on the Create An Account Or Sign In screen, two mandatory fields you'll need to fill in are the Skype Name and Password fields. Part of the account creation process includes creating a unique Skype username which serves as your identifier so people can find you and initiate calls with you using the service.

Tip   When creating a password for your Skype account, it can be between 6 and 20 characters long and include numbers and/or letters. You'll be asked to enter your password twice during the account setup process.

When you're done filling in the account activation fields, click on the green I Agree – Continue icon to finalize your account setup. Once your Skype username and password are active, launch the Skype app and enter this information once as part of the app setup process. The information will then be saved, so you can launch and use the Skype app quickly from your MacBook Air in the future.

Using the Skype Free App

Once the Skype free app is installed on your MacBook Air, you can launch it just as you would any other app. For this app to function, your computer must be connected to the Internet.

Like FaceTime, the functionality of the Skype app is very intuitive. From the main Skype screen, you can view all of your contacts, your online contacts (fellow Skype users who are your friends and who are currently signed in to the Skype service), your Skype contacts (who are online and offline), and your Facebook contacts. Click on any contact listing to initiate a voice or video call with that person.

Near the upper-right corner of the Skype app window, a telephone dial pad icon is displayed. This allows you to make fee-based calls to any landline or cell phone (to non-Skype users) by entering their complete phone number, including area code.

Upon clicking on the telephone dial pad icon, the Dial Pad window will appear (shown in Figure 17-10). It looks like a telephone dial pad and includes the digits zero through 9, as well as the * and # buttons.

 If you're making an international call, use the pull-down menu on the dial pad to select the country you are calling. The app will automatically insert the appropriate international dialing code needed to make the call.

As you initiate contact with someone using Skype, you can make a voice call (using Voice-over-IP), launch a video conference call, or send an SMS text message using the Skype instant messaging network. Once a voice or video connection is made, to activate the screen-sharing feature, access the Conversations pull-down menu from the menu bar and select the Share Screen option.

 When engaged in a voice call, you have the option to place the call on hold or mute the computer's microphone by clicking on the appropriate command button. During a video conference call, you can also mute your microphone or turn off the camera and still maintain the connection.

When you begin using the Skype free or Skype Premium app, invest a few minutes to customize the app by accessing the Skype pull-down menu from the menu bar and selecting the Preferences option. At the top of the Preferences window, you'll see seven command buttons. One at a time, click on each command button, starting with General, and customize each of the submenu options that are displayed in that window (shown in Figure 17-11).

FIGURE 17-10   The dial pad that's built into the Skype app is used to manually dial landline and cell phone numbers.

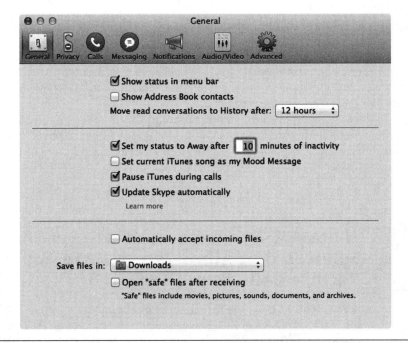

FIGURE 17-11   Customize the app from the Skype Preferences window.

Adjusting or personalizing the Skype Preferences allows you to better control the functionality of the app itself, plus adjust the privacy settings associated with the app. You can also determine who can initiate calls to you, how calls get answered, and whether or not you want your name displayed and searchable in the Skype user directory.

Later, as you begin participating in voice or video conference calls, you'll discover that the Skype app works very much like a cell phone when you're engaged in a voice call. To end the call, for example, click on the End button.

When you're engaged in a video conference, the app works in much the same way as FaceTime, in that you can mute your microphone or end the call by clicking on the appropriate command button. The person you're video conferencing with will be displayed in the main area of the app window, but what the other person is seeing (you) will be displayed in a smaller thumbnail, which you can position anywhere on the screen or hide.

Especially if you take advantage of some or all of Skype's premium and fee-based services, this service offers more features and functions than FaceTime. Plus, you can participate in Skype voice or video conversations with Mac, PC, or Linux computer users, iOS, Android or most other smartphone users, as well as people who use Skype-enabled TVs, home telephones, or gaming systems.

Alternatives to FaceTime and Skype

There are many services that offer similar functionality to FaceTime and Skype when it comes to video conferencing, instant messaging, and screen sharing. Two fee-based services that are popular among business users are WebEx (www.webex.com) and GoToMeeting (www.gotomeeting.com).

Other free and fee-based video conferencing services that are MacBook Air compatible include Paltalk (www.paltalk.com), ooVoo (www.oovoo.com), Google + Hangouts (www.google.com/+), and Cisco's TelePresence (www.cisco.com/web/telepresence).

There Are Hundreds of Voice-over-IP Services that Allow You to Make and Receive Calls from Your MacBook Air

A VoIP service allows you to make and receive voice calls from your MacBook Air. You can call other VoIP phone numbers, landlines, or cell phones. Your computer's built-in microphone and speakers (or headset jack) serve as the telephone. Most of these services offer a vast selection of calling features such as caller ID, call waiting, call forwarding, hold, conference calling, and voice mail. Some allow you to receive your voice mail messages via email. When you subscribe to a particular VoIP service, you're given a unique phone number.

As for Voice-over-IP options, you also have an ever-growing selection, some of which are free, while others are fee-based. Some of these options include Vonage (www.vonage.com), RingCentral (www.ringcentral.com), AT&T CallVantage (www.att.com), Voip.com (www.voip.com), and Callcentric (www.callcentric.com).

The majority of these services have their own apps that you'll need to download, and have flat-rate monthly or annual plans for making and receiving unlimited domestic and international calls directly from your MacBook Air. Depending on the app, you may be able to use a wireless Bluetooth headset when participating in calls. This gives you an added level of freedom and privacy.

One benefit to using a VoIP service is that you can receive calls to your phone number anytime your computer is turned on and connected to the Internet, no matter where you are. This is ideal for someone who travels often because it's much more cost effective than a cell phone, especially when traveling overseas.

18

Run Microsoft Windows and Windows Software on Your MacBook Air

HOW TO...

- Run Microsoft Windows on your MacBook Air using Boot Camp
- Run Microsoft Windows on your MacBook Air using the optional Parallels Desktop 7 for Mac software
- Use remote desktop applications to control Windows-based PCs or Macs from your MacBook Air

Apple has done an incredible job developing OS X and transforming it over time into a reliable, feature-packed, easy-to-use, and well-supported operating system. Between the apps that come bundled with OS X Mountain Lion, Apple's optional Mac software that's available from the App Store, and the tremendous level of third-party support from software developers that Apple now receives, most popular Windows-based software applications are also now available for the Mac. Software that offers similar (and compatible) functionality to Windows-based software is also readily available.

 Note Proprietary software designed for your business to run on PCs, some vertical market software, and popular Windows-based games are the types of software that might not yet run on a Mac using the OS X operating system.

If you currently use your Windows-based PC to run software that is not available for the Mac, you have the option of installing Microsoft Windows onto your MacBook Air and then running your computer with Microsoft Windows or OS X Mountain Lion. This gives you the best of both worlds. You can run your favorite PC software when necessary, but then switch to OS X to enjoy using popular Mac software.

If you opt to install both OS X Mountain Lion and Microsoft Windows on your MacBook Air, as well as Windows-based software and Mac software, this is going to require a significant amount of storage space on your MacBook Air's internal hard drive (at least 16GB of storage for just the Windows operating system), so plan accordingly when selecting which MacBook Air system configuration to purchase. A faster processor, 4GB of RAM, and a larger capacity hard drive are all beneficial for this purpose, although you can run Microsoft Windows and Windows-based software on any MacBook Air model.

If you use Apple's Boot Camp option to run Microsoft Windows on your MacBook Air, it will be necessary to reboot your computer each time you want to switch between operating systems. Boot Camp comes free with OS X Mountain Lion. You simply need to acquire a copy of Microsoft Windows 7 or 8, plus whatever Windows-based software you want to install and run on the MacBook Air.

Using the optional Parallels Desktop 7 for Mac software to run Microsoft Windows and Windows-based software, however, allows you to quickly switch between operating systems without having to reboot your computer each time. Both operating systems can be run simultaneously, and you can freely switch between them as easily as you switch between running several Mac apps at the same time on your MacBook Air.

Regardless of which method you use to run Windows on your MacBook Air, the initial installation and setup process will take between 30 and 60 minutes.

Using Boot Camp to Run Microsoft Windows and Windows-Based Software

Boot Camp comes bundled with all Macs and is set up using the Book Camp Assistant utility, which is accessible by launching System Preferences, opening the Utilities folder in the Applications folder, and then double-clicking on the Boot Camp Assistant utility (shown in Figure 18-1).

Once you launch Boot Camp Assistant, it will walk you through the process of initially installing the necessary software (including the Microsoft Windows operating system) onto your MacBook Air. It will also create a partition on your MacBook Air's hard drive for storing and running Windows and Windows-based software. You must install Microsoft Windows onto the internal hard drive of your MacBook Air. It cannot be run from an external drive.

It's a good idea to print out the 14-page Installation & Setup Guide for Boot Camp before you get started. To do this, click on the Print Installation & Setup Guide button that's displayed in the lower-left corner of the Boot Camp Assistant window as soon as you launch the app (shown in Figure 18-2). When you're ready to begin the Microsoft Windows installation and setup process, click on the Continue button that's displayed in the lower-right corner of the Boot Camp Assistant window.

FIGURE 18-1   Launch Boot Camp Assistant from the Utilities folder in your MacBook Air's Applications folder.

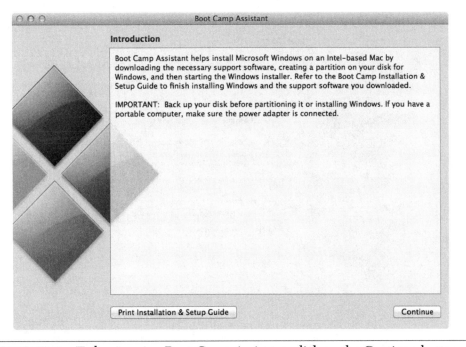

FIGURE 18-2   To begin using Boot Camp Assistant, click on the Continue button, but first print out the Installation & Setup Guide.

Before using Boot Camp Assistant, use Time Machine to back up your entire MacBook Air. Then, as you run Book Camp Assistant, make sure your computer is plugged into an external power source.

Using Boot Camp Assistant, you will be able to run either Microsoft Windows (and Windows-based software) or OS X (and Mac-based software) on your MacBook Air, but you will not be able to use both simultaneously, like you can when using the Parallels Desktop 7 solution.

Before you get started, you'll need to obtain or create a Microsoft Windows installation disk that's stored on a USB flash drive (with at least 4GB capacity). You'll need to begin the process with a full installation Microsoft Windows 7 Home Premium, Professional, or Ultimate disk (or a full installation disk for Windows XP or Windows 8). You cannot use a Windows upgrade disk.

Alternatively, you can insert the Windows installation disk into an iMac or MacBook Pro, for example, and then share that other Mac's SuperDrive with your MacBook Air, or you can connect the optional MacBook Air SuperDrive to your computer.

Running Boot Camp Assistant for the First Time

After launching Boot Camp Assistant and printing out the Installation & Setup Guide, click on the Continue button to proceed. You'll discover that Boot Camp Assistant (shown in Figure 8-3) breaks up the process of installing Windows into a multistep

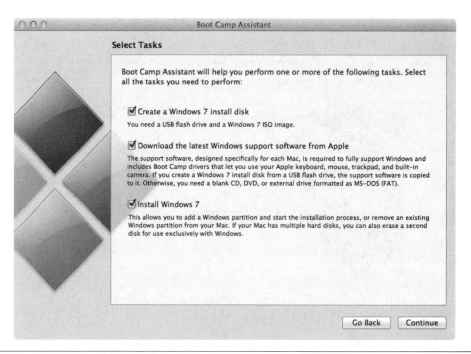

FIGURE 18-3 Make sure all three steps are selected from the Select Tasks screen in Boot Camp Assistant, and then click on the Continue button.

process, starting with the creation of a Windows 7 install disk. Step two involves downloading the latest Windows support software from Apple. During step three, you'll actually install Windows onto your MacBook Air.

Follow the onscreen prompts and the directions in the Installation & Setup Guide to get Microsoft Windows running on your MacBook Air using the Boot Camp Assistant. Once Windows is running, you can then install your favorite Windows-based software, just as you normally would when running a Windows-based computer.

During the setup process, when asked by the computer where you want to set up and install Windows, be sure to choose the partition that's labeled BOOTCAMP. Choosing any other option could result in the loss of important data and files on your MacBook Air.

 Once Microsoft Windows is installed on your MacBook Air, don't forget to download and install the necessary Windows Support software. You will automatically be prompted to begin this process.

Once Windows is operational on your MacBook Air, it may be necessary to manually adjust the computer's screen resolution in order for some Windows-based applications to display properly on your MacBook Air's screen. This can be done from Windows using the Display option found in the Control Panel.

Choosing Between OS X or Windows When Turning on Your MacBook Air

After Microsoft Windows is installed on your MacBook Air (along with the required support software), each time you turn on and boot up your computer (or reboot it), it's necessary to choose which operating system you want to load. To do this, when you turn on or reboot your computer, hold down the OPTION key until the disk icons appear on the screen. Then make your operating system selection. Otherwise your default operating system will automatically load.

From within System Preferences, you can set either OS X or Microsoft Windows to be your computer's default operating system. This is the operating system that will load automatically when your computer is turned on or rebooted if you don't hold down the OPTION key during the boot up or reboot process. To set the default operating system for your computer, launch System Preferences and select the Startup Disk option when running OS X. Or while running Windows, access the Startup Disk option from the Boot Camp Control Panel.

While running Windows and Windows software using Boot Camp, the fastest way to switch back to the OS X operating system is to click on the Boot Camp icon that's displayed in the System Tray, and then select the Restart In OS X option.

 If you encounter problems using Boot Camp, visit www.apple.com/support/ bootcamp, or contact AppleCare. Keep in mind Apple's technical support (including Apple Geniuses in the Apple Stores or Apple's toll-free AppleCare phone number) does not support Macs running Microsoft Windows. For help using Windows, visit http://windows.microsoft.com.

How to... **Remove Microsoft Windows from Your MacBook Air**

If you later choose to remove the Windows operating system from your MacBook Air (along with Windows-based software you've installed), you will need to delete the Windows partition and restore your MacBook Air's hard drive to a single-partition OS X Mountain Lion volume.

To accomplish this, launch OS X Mountain Lion on your MacBook Air. Quit all applications running on the computer and then launch Boot Camp Assistant. Choose the Remove Windows option and then click on the Continue button. When prompted, click on the Restore button.

Taking Advantage of the Parallels Desktop 7 Alternative

An alternative to using Apple's Boot Camp on your MacBook Air in order to run Microsoft Windows and Windows-based software is to use the optional Parallels Desktop 7 for Mac software ($79.99, www.parallels.com). The benefit to using this software as a solution for running Microsoft Windows is that you can instantly switch between the two operating systems without rebooting your computer.

Note Parallels Desktop 7 is a Mac application that allows you to run Microsoft Windows in a virtual machine. In addition to this optional software, VMware Fusion 4 ($49.99, www.vmware.com) offers similar functionality and is yet another alternative for running Microsoft Windows on your MacBook Air.

As a result, you could run one or more Windows-based applications, plus one or more Mac software apps simultaneously, and then switch back and forth in seconds. Plus, you can cut and paste content (or drag and drop objects) between apps, regardless of which operating system they're running under. The latest version of Parallels Desktop 7 supports OS X Mountain Lion and Microsoft Windows 8 (as well as some earlier versions of both operating systems).

If you'll be needing to run Microsoft Windows applications on your MacBook Air frequently, using the Parallels Desktop 7 solution is definitely the most efficient option. Plus, the initial setup and installation process is much more straightforward and automated compared to using Boot Camp Assistant.

Tip If you already use your Windows-based PC to run software that maintains a database of your personal data, you can continue running the PC version of those applications on your MacBook Air, and never have to worry about transferring or importing/exporting your data between operating systems and dealing with potential data or file incompatibility issues.

Once Parallels is running on your MacBook Air, you can use the Parallels Mobile app on your iPhone or iPad to run Mac OS X or Windows-based software on your computer, but control it remotely from your iOS mobile device.

To test out the Parallels Desktop 7 for Mac application, download and install it on your Mac. A free trial version is available from the company's website. When you launch it, you'll be given multiple options (shown in Figure 18-4). After selecting your source for the Microsoft Windows operating system software, you'll need to decide if you want Microsoft Windows to work "Like a Mac" or "Like a PC." This is shown in Figure 18-5.

If you don't yet have a version of Microsoft Windows that can be installed on your MacBook Air, you can purchase one directly through the Parallels Desktop 7 software during the setup process, and then download it to your computer. If you opt to purchase and download Windows 8, for example, just the download process (shown in Figure 18-6) will take approximately 30 minutes, depending on the speed of your Internet connection.

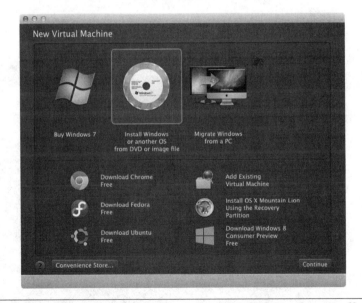

FIGURE 18-4   When launched for the first time, Parallels Desktop 7 offers multiple options for acquiring Microsoft Windows or using a version of Windows you already possess.

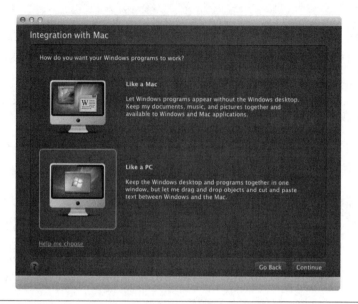

FIGURE 18-5 Before the Windows installation process begins, choose how Windows will be set up on your MacBook Air.

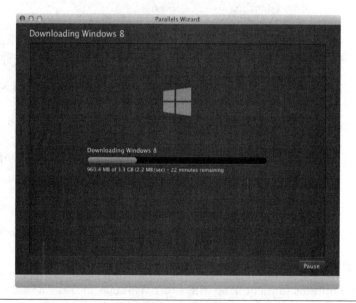

FIGURE 18-6 Just downloading Windows 7 or Windows 8 onto your MacBook Air will take approximately 30 minutes. You then need to go through the setup and installation process using Parallels Desktop 7.

If you choose the "Like a Mac" option, you will be able to run Windows programs, but you won't see the familiar Windows desktop on your computer screen. In addition, for your Mac and PC apps, your documents, music, and pictures will be stored in their same respective folders. Thus, all of your documents, for example, will be kept in one place, whether they're created using Windows or OS X software.

By selecting the "Like a PC" option, your MacBook Air will truly look and act like a Windows-based PC. You will see the familiar Windows desktop, and separate directories will be created to store your documents, music, pictures, and other data that's created using Windows applications. You will, however, retain the ability to cut and paste text or drag and drop objects between apps.

If you opt to purchase, download, and install Microsoft Windows 7 or 8 from within the Parallels Desktop 7 software (which is recommended to keep the process simple), once you get the process started, the operating system install process will begin automatically after the operating system has been downloaded directly to your MacBook Air (shown in Figure 18-7).

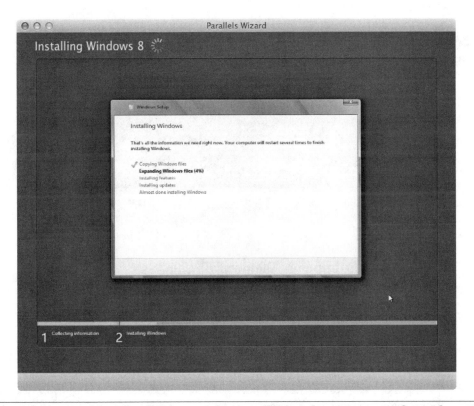

FIGURE 18-7   If downloaded from within Parallels Desktop 7, Microsoft Windows 7 or 8 will auto-install on your MacBook Air, a process that will take up to 15 minutes.

Click on the Full Screen icon that's displayed in the upper-right corner of the Microsoft Windows program window to display Microsoft Windows (or any Windows software you're running) in Full Screen mode. To exit out of Full Screen mode, instead of pressing the ESC key, you'll need to move the cursor to the top of the screen to make the Parallels menu bar appear, and then select the Exit Full Screen option from the View pull-down menu.

Unless you're in Full Screen mode, when running Windows on your MacBook Air via Parallels Desktop 7, Windows will run in its own program window and within that, your Windows-based apps will run. In Figure 18-8, the Microsoft Internet Explorer web browser is running under Windows 8.

As you can see from Figures 18-9, 18-10, and 18-11, the new look and interface of Windows 8 can be fully utilized on a MacBook Air. Once Windows is running, you can then install Windows-based software onto your MacBook Air.

To simulate a right mouse click on your MacBook Air, press the COMMAND (⌘) key on the keyboard at the same time you click on the MacBook Air's trackpad.

For free online help using Parallels Desktop 7 for Mac to run Microsoft Windows and Windows software, visit www.parallels.com/support/desktop-virtualization/desktop.

FIGURE 18-8 Microsoft Internet Explorer is just one of many Windows programs you can run on your MacBook Air once Microsoft Windows is installed and running.

FIGURE 18-9 Windows 8 can take on a whole new look. Click on the Desktop graphic displayed toward the right side of the screen to view the familiar Windows desktop.

FIGURE 18-10 The new layout of Windows 8 is easy to navigate when it's running on your MacBook Air.

FIGURE 18-11 The Windows 8 Desktop with a customized wallpaper selected

Once Windows is running on your Mac, you can use Parallels Desktop 7 for Mac to transfer your data, files, photos, and other content from a Windows-based PC to your MacBook Air. This can be done using a direct USB cable connection between two computers, by using an external storage device, or you can transfer information wirelessly over a network. While running Windows, run the Parallels Transporter Agent software (which comes with the Parallel Desktop 7 for Mac software). You can also download this Windows-based software from www.parallels.com/download/desktop.

While running Windows on your MacBook Air using Parallels Desktop 7 for Mac, after Windows is also installed, you can launch a Windows application from the Windows Applications folder that's displayed on the Dock, from the Windows Start menu, from within OS X Finder, from the OS X Dock, using the Spotlight Search feature of OS X, or using Launchpad (in OS X).

Free Windows PC Software Is Available Online

In addition to the many thousands of Windows-based programs you can purchase and run on your MacBook Air, you'll also discover a vast selection of free, shareware, and open source software available that can be downloaded and installed directly onto your MacBook Air that's running Microsoft Windows. For example, you'll find a nice collection of downloadable software on CNET Download service (http://download.cnet.com/windows).

Taking Advantage of Remote Desktop Solutions for Controlling Windows Software from Your MacBook Air

Instead of installing Microsoft Windows and Windows-based software on your MacBook Air, another option is to use a remote desktop application, which allows you to use your MacBook Air to take control over another Mac or PC via the Internet or a wireless network, and then run software from that other computer so it can be controlled and seen from your MacBook Air.

The drawbacks to this option is that you may experience a lag time when controlling software remotely that's running on another computer, plus the other computer must be turned on and connected to the Internet or wireless network in order for your MacBook Air to gain access to it.

 The benefit to using this solution is that whatever you would see on the other computer's screen (whether it's a Mac or PC application) can be seen and controlled remotely from your MacBook Air. None of your MacBook Air's internal hard drive space is needed to store Windows or Windows-based software files.

Depending on the remote desktop solution you select, you may need to purchase software from the App Store (or a developer's website) that will run on both your MacBook Air and the computer(s) you'll be accessing remotely. An example of this is Splashtop Desktop Remote ($6.99), which is available from the App Store. Using this software, you can securely access a Mac or PC from your MacBook Air, as long as both computers are connected to the Internet or the same wireless network.

There are also subscription-based services, like GoToMyPC (www.gotomypc.com), that offer free software, but that require a monthly fee, starting at $9.95, to be able to access your computer(s) from anywhere using your MacBook Air.

A

What to Do if Something Goes Wrong

Some of the reasons why so many people are making the switch from Windows-based PCs to the Apple Macs are because the Macs are easier and more intuitive to use, they are not susceptible to computer viruses, and they make it easy to synchronize and back up data automatically. However, like any other computer or electronic device, things can go wrong with your MacBook Air.

If you take basic precautions, you can reduce the chances of something going wrong, be prepared if something does happen so that you don't lose any important data or files, and be able to get yourself up and running again quickly with the least amount of stress and frustration.

Take Precautions with Your MacBook Air

Regardless of what you use your MacBook Air for, taking the following precautions will help prevent things from going wrong, plus make it much easier to recover from problems:

- When your MacBook Air is not in use, keep it in a padded case, especially when it's being transported.
- Keep your MacBook Air away from any liquids and extreme hot or cold temperatures.
- Maintain a backup of your MacBook Air's contents using the Time Machine app that comes preinstalled on your computer. You'll need an optional external hard drive with a capacity that's larger than your MacBook Air's internal flash storage for this purpose.

 The importance of maintaining a backup of your computer cannot be emphasized strongly enough. Using the Time Machine app with an external hard drive is the easiest and most automated way to accomplish this on an ongoing basis.

- Set up iCloud to automatically synchronize and back up your contacts, calendar, notes, reminders, documents, data, and Safari bookmarks. This way, even if something goes wrong with your MacBook Air while you're on the go, you can always access your data from any computer or mobile device with Internet access by visiting www.iCloud.com. Plus, your most recent data is stored online automatically (and is accessible from the other Macs and iOS mobile devices linked to your iCloud account).

- Set up the Find My Mac feature of iCloud. If your computer gets lost or stolen, you will easily be able to find it using any Internet-enabled device by visiting www.iCloud.com/#find.

- Purchase Apple's optional AppleCare support for your MacBook Air ($249). This covers your computer and provides unlimited technical support for two years. For more information, visit http://store.apple.com/us/product/MD014LL/A.

- Keep your OS X Mountain Lion operating system and all of your apps up to date, so you're always using the most current versions available. This is done from the App Store app by clicking on the Updates tab at the top of the screen.

- If you'll be working with your MacBook Air using a Wi-Fi hotspot from a public location, such as an airport, coffee shop, or hotel, be sure to configure the Security & Privacy settings on your MacBook Air. These settings are accessible from System Preferences. For example, you can turn on the password protection feature to prevent unauthorized people from accessing your computer. From the Sharing option within System Preferences, you can adjust the File Sharing and Remote Login options to prevent strangers from accessing your data wirelessly.

 If you choose to use your MacBook Air at an airport, coffee shop, hotel lobby, or any other public place, never leave your computer unattended, even for a minute. It only takes a few seconds for an unattended computer to be stolen, and this is a more common occurrence than you might think.

What to Do if Something Goes Wrong

Even if you operate your MacBook Air exactly how it's supposed to be used, there is always a risk that something could go wrong. More often than not, however, there's usually a quick fix to whatever problem you experience.

Restarting an App that Crashes

If an app crashes (but the rest of the computer continues to function properly), click on the Apple icon that's displayed on the left side of the menu bar, and then choose the Force Quit option. A listing of all apps currently running will be displayed. Click on the app that crashed to highlight it. It will typically have a "Not Responding" message associated with it. Next, click on the Force Quit button. You can then relaunch the app. If a problem still persists, power off your MacBook Air, wait one minute, and then turn it back on.

Tip Another way to Force Quit a frozen application is to use the COMMAND (⌘)-OPTION-SHIFT-ESC keyboard shortcut.

What to Do if Your MacBook Air Won't Turn On

It's possible that the MacBook Air's battery is dead. In this case, plug in the computer, wait a minute or two, and then press the power button. Allow the battery to recharge before attempting to operate it on battery power again.

Note As long as it's plugged in, you can continue using your MacBook Air while the battery is recharging. The charging process will take a bit longer, however.

If the computer freezes when you attempt to turn it on, it displays a flashing question mark, or all you see is a black screen after pressing the power button, try pressing and holding down the power button for about 10 seconds. The computer should reboot and run normally. If not, try pressing the power button and the OPTION key simultaneously for about 10 seconds. When the startup screen appears, choose the MacBook Air's internal flash storage icon and then click on the right arrow to continue.

Tip If your computer fails to turn on and boot up properly, try pressing and releasing the power button, and then hold down the COMMAND (⌘), OPTION, P, and R keys simultaneously while it's booting up until you hear the Startup sound twice in a row. Release the keys and allow OS X Mountain Lion to launch.

If you continue to have a problem turning on your MacBook Air, contact AppleCare or visit any Apple Store.

Note To determine if your MacBook Air is experiencing some type of hardware problem (for example, a USB port stops working), disconnect all devices from your computer except for the power adapter. Next, restart the computer while holding down the D key. Choose a language when the Apple Hardware Test screen appears, and then press the RETURN key. Follow the onscreen instructions to determine if something within your computer is not functioning properly. If your computer is experiencing a hardware problem, a visit to an Apple Store or authorized Apple reseller may be necessary.

The MacBook Air Won't Connect to the Internet

First, make sure that the Wi-Fi feature of your MacBook Air is turned on. Next, make sure you're within the signal radius of a Wi-Fi hotspot or wireless network. If the hotspot is password protected, be sure to enter the appropriate password in order to gain access to the Internet.

If the problem persists, from the Apple pull-down menu on the menu bar, select System Preferences. Next, choose the Network option. Near the bottom of the Network window, click on the Assist Me icon, and then follow the onscreen prompts.

How to Get Help from Apple

If you have access to the Internet, you can access Apple's online-based technical support forums by visiting www.apple.com/support. When you purchase a new MacBook Air, it includes 90 days of unlimited, free telephone and in-person support. This extends to two years if you purchase the optional AppleCare coverage.

To reach Apple by phone, call (800) 275-2273. You can also visit any Apple Store to receive in-person help from an Apple Genius. An appointment, which can be made online, is required.

 To make an appointment with an Apple Genius at any Apple Store within the U.S., visit www.apple.com/retail/storelist, and then click on the link for the closest Apple Store location. Next, click on the Make Reservation option for the Genius Bar at that location.

 Also available from the Apple website are online support message boards and "communities" that allow MacBook Air users to communicate with each other to discuss solutions to common problems. To access this area of Apple's website, visit https://discussions.apple.com/community/notebooks/macbook_air.

Keep Your MacBook Air's Serial Number Handy

When requesting technical support from AppleCare or an Apple Store, you will be asked for your MacBook Air's serial number. This unique number is printed on the bottom of your MacBook Air in very small type. You can also access it by clicking on the Apple icon from the menu bar and then choosing the About This Mac option. When the About This Mac window appears, click on the More Info button. Details about your computer, including its serial number, will be displayed on the screen.

Index